THE ADVANCING WRITER

THE ADVANCING WRITER

BOOK 1

SENTENCES AND PARAGRAPHS

Karen L. Greenberg

Hunter College
The City University of New York

Peter Rondinone

LaGuardia Community College
The City University of New York

Harvey S. Wiener, Series Editor
Adelphi University

HarperCollinsCollegePublishers

Senior Editor: Jane Kinney
Development Editor: Leslie Taggart
Project Editor: Katharine H. Glynn
Art Director/Design Supervisor: Jill Yutkowitz
Text Design: Circa 86 Inc.
Cover Design: Jill Yutkowitz
Cover Photo: Superstock Inc.
Photo Researcher: Sandy Schneider
Production Administrator: Valerie A. Sawyer
Compositor: Ruttle, Shaw & Wetherill
Printer and Binder: R. R. Donnelley & Sons Company
Cover Printer: The Lehigh Press, Inc.

94 95 96 97 9 8 7 6 5 4 3 2 1

CONTENTS IN BRIEF

CONTENTS IN DETAIL

FROM THE SERIES EDITOR

The Advancing Writer series addresses the needs of college students who require a course or a series of courses in basic writing skills. Focusing on sentence, paragraph, and essay building as well as essential grammar and usage skills for successful revising and editing, *The Advancing Writer* provides a flexible yet comprehensive program for the beginning student writer in college. Each book in the series is self-contained, student oriented, and course specific; yet the three books together represent an integrated program in written language development. Philosophy, pedagogy, and design features unify the series.

Through this series beginning college writers will learn the power of language in confronting existence and the riches in transforming their private pasts into sensory language. In celebrating personal autobiography as a major force in the basic writing program, *The Advancing Writer* series recognizes that critical thinking begins with examining the self, acknowledging individual history, and thinking about language that connects one's personal reality to the larger worlds of school, work, and society. Yet, even though the writers addressed by these texts may not have fully explored their own linguistic power, they are ripe for challenge to their intellect and creativity. Unlike other basic writing texts, *The Advancing Writer* does not exclude intellectual and creative matters for reflection and analysis by taking a "remedial" approach; instead, it provides rigorous college-level tasks while showing students how to analyze the decisions they confront as they think and compose.

In each book, students start by examining their own attitudes toward writing and then move on to consider a variety of strategies for prewriting, drafting, revising, and editing. Although drafts of both student and professional writing are provided for discussion of content and analysis of form, students work mainly on their own writing, revisiting earlier drafts as they assimilate new strategies for revising and editing. Students learn to consider the audience for their writing through collaborative reading, writing, and revising activities that give student writers immediate feedback as they think and compose. The series emphasizes that reading and writing are both processes to create meaning, thus promoting a holistic approach to literacy and enabling students to see how writing can help them learn about and understand their academic readings. The practice of syntax, grammar, and usage is merged with genuine rhetorical goals; activities rooted in connected discourse make clear the relation between content and form.

Students and instructors who use the three-tiered program will benefit from the regular reinforcement strategies presented throughout. The books are recursive—building on concepts introduced earlier, or anticipatory—looking ahead to skills to be developed later on, or both. Each text can be used alone; but taken as a whole, *The Advancing Writer* series is a set of interlocking tools for improving students' writing at the beginning level.

Harvey S. Wiener

PREFACE

RATIONALE

The Advancing Writer series presents writing as an active process of constructing meaning from personal experience. Building on related theoretical, pedagogical, and design elements, this series provides instructors and students with a systematic and comprehensive approach to writing. The books introduce varied strategies for developing, revising, and editing academic discourse. The instructional material and activities in each book build on each other in a recursive instructional format.

This book is the first in the series. It is aimed at helping advancing writers express their ideas clearly and correctly by improving their abilities to develop, revise, and edit academic sentences and paragraphs. The text accomplishes this goal by explaining and illustrating the ways in which writers' purposes and strategies and readers' concerns and expectations influence details, syntax, and grammar. Students are encouraged to try a variety of forms and strategies, to examine the relations between their choices and their intentions, and to cast their sentences in correct academic English syntax and grammar. The book uses a step-by-step approach to identifying and correcting errors. Each chapter includes numerous graphic elements and charts to help visual learners and to reinforce key concepts and terms.

Many basic writing textbooks address students as ''beginners''—as students who have little experience with writing and who need ''remediation.'' These books condescend to students by oversimplifying the writing process as a ''nuts-and-bolts'' activity that they can learn by following a fixed set of rules and steps. *The Advancing Writer,* on the other hand, assumes that these students are creative and intelligent writers who simply have not had enough experience writing in a variety of roles and registers for a diverse group of concerned readers. Moreover, this book reflects the influence of current philosophies of writing and rhetoric, including social constructivist theory, reader-response theory, and critical thinking pedagogy. All of the activities require students to reflect on their writing processes and to use this self-reflection to improve their writing.

Hundreds of basic writing students have tested the writing activities and assignments in this book. Their responses indicate that these activities helped them examine, expand, and improve their writing processes and paragraphs. This book also affirms students' voices and multilingual heritages. The sample paragraphs and essays reflect the diverse experiences of students who value their own personal and cultural identities. These samples also help students see the connections among reading, writing, and critical thinking.

UNIQUE FEATURES OF THIS TEXT

Clearly the most unique feature of this book is that it is part of an integrated program in written language development. The emphasis throughout the series is on fluency, then clarity, then correctness. Eight other features distinguish this book:

1. *Every chapter emphasizes the importance of writing for personal, academic, and professional development.* The content and organization of the book reflect the belief that writing matters for self-expression, for personal and intellectual reflection and analysis, and for achievement of career goals.
2. *The book illustrates the full complexity of writing as a process that leads to a product.* It explores the entire continuum of the composing process, giving students practice in all stages of it. Detailed help with prewriting, drafting, revising, and editing appears throughout the text. In every chapter, instruction emphasizes that good writing is determined by students' critical analysis of their purpose and their readers' expectations. Moreover, each chapter provides students with opportunities to practice revising their writing for the most important qualities of good writing: focus, development, unity, coherence, and correctness.
3. *Collaborative learning activities help students think and act like writers and demonstrate differences in students' writing processes.* Students work together to read critically, to generate ideas, to respond to drafts, and to edit final revisions. ''Group Work'' activities enable students to see writing as a social activity—to see the effects of their rhetorical and linguistic decisions on their readers. The many collaborative activities in the book help students build confidence in their skills as writers and editors in nonthreatening contexts.
4. *The content of the readings, the writing activities, and the exercises comes from the ''real'' world—from the workplace, the physical and social sciences, and the humanities.* The book acknowledges that experiential description and narration are essential for advancing writers and help students use their personal experiences to illuminate their academic discourse. The text provides intellectual challenges while simultaneously encouraging students to learn about writing from their own efforts to compose and revise.
5. *The text includes a variety of student and professional readings written by people from diverse ethnic and cultural backgrounds.* These readings serve as springboards for writing activities, as models of different stages

in the writing process, and as realistic examples of the skills students can attain. The readings also address problems that concern today's college students and ask them to articulate views on issues that will define their futures.

6. *Every exercise is composed of connected discourse.* The sentences in the exercises are logically and rhetorically related, enabling students to practice skills within the connected discourse of paragraphs rather than in isolated sentences. Writing instructors know how common it is for students to complete textbook exercises correctly, only to produce paragraphs full of the very errors that they had just seemed to master in the exercises. Part of the reason for this lack of transfer of knowledge is that the learning context of disconnected sentences eliminates the relation between content and form. In the exercises in this text, the practice of skills is merged with genuine rhetorical goals. Students are encouraged to perceive correct grammar and mechanics as tools for expressing their ideas clearly and precisely.
7. *Reading and writing are integrated.* Each chapter includes reading and writing assignments relevant to the chapter's thematic content and rhetorical strategy. These readings illustrate the various stages of the writing process and serve as models for paragraph and essay development. In addition, the readings are preceded by introductions that guide students through the text, and they are followed by ''Discussion Questions'' that send students back to the text for a variety of analytic purposes. These questions also ask students to bring their own experiences and understanding to bear on their interpretations of the readings. Thus, this book presents reading as an integral part of students' writing processes.
8. *Multiple checklists and visual learning aids help students examine and improve their writing.* Students can use the guidelines and questions in the checklists to analyze and evaluate their own writing and to help their peers improve their writing. The boxes, charts, and illustrations appearing throughout the book also appeal to visual learners. Also included in every chapter are ''Reminders''—summaries of the major points in each section. In addition, the end-of-chapter ''Points to Remember'' highlight important concepts and skills discussed in the chapter.

OVERVIEW OF THE TEXT

Advancing writers need to begin from the ''top down''—from large elements, such as the elaboration of ideas and details—and move to smaller elements, such as features of syntax, grammar, and mechanics. Thus, this book asks students to write drafts of whole paragraphs in the very first chapter. It is pointless to begin the semester examining the parts of speech if students have not yet done any writing that requires them to use coherent sentences to communicate their ideas in writing.

Part 1 Principles of Effective Writing

The first chapter of the text helps advancing writers understand the complexity of the writing process. Its presentation of various prewriting strategies is aimed at discouraging students from doing the premature revising and editing that research indicates causes so many of the rhetorical and syntactic breakdowns in their writing. Chapter 2 shows students how to focus and develop a topic sentence and how to plan and write strong paragraphs based on focus, purpose, and audience. Chapter 3 explains the most important qualities of good writing and helps students revise and edit their drafts for clarity and correctness.

Part 2 The Writer's Handbook

These eleven chapters review principles of sentence structure, grammar, usage, vocabulary, spelling, capitalization, and punctuation. Also included is a chapter on sentence variety and style (including sentence-combining activities). The Writer's Handbook presents syntax and grammar as a set of choices that depend on the writer's topic and purpose and on the reader's expectations. Punctuation is discussed in terms of its functions (rather than as a series of rules). The aim of the Writer's Handbook is to engage students in using their linguistic resources to expand their ability to write well in a variety of academic contexts. Rather than merely summarizing rules or conventions, the chapters in this section ask students to experiment with sentences and explore the stylistic implications of grammar.

Each of the Writer's Handbook chapters ends in an ''Exploring Further'' section which presents traditional strategies or patterns that student writers can use to develop their ideas and details: description, narration, analysis of processes, comparison and contrast, division and classification, definition, analysis of causes and effects, and argumentation. The strategies are not presented as categories or forms of writing that students must select before they decide how to develop your ideas. Rather, these are the patterns of thinking that we all use to sort out the events and experiences of our daily lives. The samples in the ''Exploring Further'' sections show students how rhetorical patterns overlap and help them move from one to another as they try to communicate their ideas in writing. In addition, these sections offer examples of strategies for writing in different content areas and provide students with opportunities to practice writing across the curriculum.

ACKNOWLEDGMENTS

We want to thank our friend, colleague, and muse—Harvey S. Wiener—who developed the idea for this series and who made it a reality. He read several drafts of each chapter of this book with incredible care and attention. We are also grateful to Jane Kinney and Mark Paluch of HarperCollins for believing in the *The Advancing Writer* series and for their vision in overseeing the developmental of all three books. Our development editor, Leslie Taggart, deserves praise and credit for her meticulous attention to every word and detail in this book and for her enthusiastic support of the series. Our thanks also go to the other key members of our HarperCollins editorial team: Laurie Likoff, Ann Stypuloski, and Katharine H. Glynn.

In addition, we also want to thank the following reviewers, whose thoughtful comments and suggestions helped us improve each draft:

Mary S. Benedetti, University of Cincinnati
George Brannon, Valdosta State College
Laurie Warshal Cohen, Seattle Central Community College
Donna Estill, Gavilan Community College
Elaine Foster, Hudson County Community College
Eddye Gallagher, Tarrant County Junior College
Carin Halper, California State University-Fresno
Jan Hausmann, Southwest State University
Lee Brewer Jones, DeKalb College
Mary S. Lauberg, St. Louis Community College
Jim Link, Prince George's Community College
Amanda S. McBride, Durham Technical Community College
Joseph A. Scherer, Community College of Allegheny County
Charles Smires, Jacksonville Community College
Patrick Sullivan, Manchester Community College
Beatrice Tignor, Prince George's Community College
Betty Jeane Wallace, Sinclair Community College

We are indebted to all the CUNY students whom we have taught—and who have taught us so much. We hope this book lives up to their expectations and achievements.

Karen L. Greenberg

A Visual Guide To

THE ADVANCING WRITER SERIES

Editor: **Harvey Wiener** Adelphi University

BOOK 1	BOOK 2	BOOK 3
SENTENCES AND PARAGRAPHS	**PARAGRAPHS AND ESSAYS**	**READING AND WRITING ESSAYS**
ISBN: 0-06-500301-2	ISBN: 0-06-500302-0	ISBN: 0-06-500303-9
Karen L. Greenberg Hunter College, City University of New York	**Karen L. Greenberg** Hunter College, City University of New York	**Judith R. Lambert** Richland College
Peter Rondinone La Guardia College, City University of New York		

Informed by current theory and research on developmental writing, this exciting new series actively engages students in each stage of the writing process. These comprehensive texts cover all the basics of writing from sentence-level skills to composing the essay while incorporating contemporary teaching strategies, peer collaboration exercises, and grammar in the context of writing. Multicultural readings and student writing are included as bridges from personal to academic writing.

These books were developed as a series right from the start. Instructors can use the one that suits their course level, or all three for consistency across their basic writing program.

Finally, imagine a totally different audience: business people who were considering opening a bookstore in your town or city. What examples should you discuss if you were trying to convince these business people to open their store in your town?

How do the details that you listed to support this topic sentence *differ* for the three different audiences ______________________

Here are some questions to consider as you develop ideas and details to support your topic sentence.

QUESTIONS TO ASK YOURSELF ABOUT YOUR PURPOSE AND AUDIENCE

Who exactly am I writing for? Who would be interested in reading this paragraph?

- What are these readers like?
- How similar are they to me? Would they react as I do?
- Do I want to share my thoughts and feelings with them?
- Do I want to explain something to them?
- Do I want to persuade my readers to think or to feel or to do something? What? Why?
- How much do my readers already know about my topic?
- What else do they need to know about this topic?

REMINDER:

Good writing may have several purposes. When you w you may also be expressing your feelings and/or trying to ers to do or to feel or to think something.

from Book 1

from Book 2

Take notes as the person responds. Repeat this activity with several different readers. Then reconsider the focus, purpose, and audience for the draft and decide which of your readers' suggestions you should include in your revision. Revise the paragraph as many times as you need to in order to accomplish your purpose in writing it.

A Revision Springboard: Branching. If you decide that your draft needs additional supporting details, you can try freewriting, brainstorming, and clustering to develop new insights, ideas and details. In addition, you might try doing a form of clustering called branching to evaluate your details and to generate new ideas for your revision. *Branching* is a form of critical thinking that enables writers to analyze the relations among their ideas and details.

BRANCHING A DRAFT TO SEE PROBLEMS IN ITS DEVELOPMENT

Analyze the ideas and details in your paragraphs by doing the following:

- Write the topic sentence in a circle in the middle of a sheet of paper.
- Write each of your supporting points in its *own* circle and connect it to the main circle.
- Draw branches out from each supporting point and write in the specific experiences, examples, and reasons you used to develop each supporting point.
- Evaluate each supporting point by asking yourself whether it is clearly related to the topic sentence and is explained in enough specific detail.
- Cross out irrelevant details.
- Develop new details for the circles that do not have enough branches (enough supporting details).

Branching lets you see exactly where you do not have enough supporting details. Here is an example of a student's use of branching to determine whether a draft was developed effectively. The final version of this draft (which appeared on pages – and – in Chapter 2) is printed after the branched analysis.

1st Draft: My First College Registration

My first registration for courses at Valley Central College was a nightmare. I didn't have all the forms I needed. I was very nervous about registering. When I went to registration, the woman behind the desk told

Writing Process Emphasis

This series explores the full **writing process.** Maintaining a focus on the final product, these texts give students detailed help with prewriting, drafting, revising, and editing strategies. Book 1 emphasizes grammar and sentence-level writing. Book 2 concentrates on writing paragraphs.

Book 3 is a rhetorical reader featuring student and professional essays.

from Book 3

Responding by Writing

1. Acts of courage come in all sizes. Since the quality of courage is one we all admire, tell a story of personal courage. It may be your own or one you witnessed. It may be physical, mental, or emotional courage. Write for your classmates so they can experience the event as you did, not as disinterested spectators.
2. Tell the story of the bus incident that led to Rosa Parks' arrest from the viewpoint of the bus driver, the white man who didn't have a seat, or another black passenger. How might the event have looked from their eyes? What would they have felt and thought?
3. Create an imaginary dialogue between you and Parks or between Parks and the courageous person you described in question 1. Remember to begin a new paragraph each time the speaker changes and to use quotation marks around each speaker's words.
4. In reporting the story of her research, Ragghianti creates a portrait of her heroine Rosa Parks. Is this an effective portrait of courage? Why or why not? Remember to evaluate the article, not Rosa Parks herself. You might talk about the author's interviews with several people, her selection of Parks' past and present activities, her use of dialogue, the physical description of Parks, her use of historical facts, or anything else that makes this effective or not effective as a portrait of courage.

Momma, the Dentist, and Me

by Maya Angelou

Maya Angelou is best known for her book *I Know Why the Caged Bird Sings,* which is one of four books that make up her autobiography. Her life is the story of joyful triumph over hardship. In this excerpt from *I Know Why the Caged Bird Sings,* Angelou narrates two versions of the same incident with Momma, who is her grandmother.

Thinking Before You Read

Have you ever been treated badly by someone whose service you needed — perhaps a car salesman, personnel in a doctor's office or clinic, a teacher or other personnel in a school, a policeman or other person of authority? Write
1 about that incident in your Idea Bank. Tell what happened a

Expanding Your Vocabulary from Reading

excruciating (1) intensely painful
penance (1) payment for a sin, act performed to show sorr

from Book 3

eer Collaboration

eer collaboration discussions ısk students to work together to jenerate ideas, respond to drafts, ınd to help edit final revisions.

help you at the current stage of drafting. Your feedback will be only as good as the questions you ask of your readers.

Your questions and concerns about your draft can help a reader look for new possibilities in a draft. First, check your understanding of the assignment (or writing situation, if you are writing for work or personal reasons). Then decide what questions and concerns you have about your draft and inform the reader about them. You should also let your reader know where you are in the writing process. Are you just getting started? Do you know some things you want to write about but can't find a focus or main point? Does the reader see your main point or thesis? Here are some questions whose answers are usually helpful to writers. They are based on the five qualities of good writing and a priority of concerns. Don't overwhelm your reader with too many questions. Choose several whose answers would help you take your draft to the next stage.

Asking for Helpful Feedback

1. Am I on the right track? Am I addressing the assignment?
2. What do you think is my thesis (main point)?
3. Have I written appropriately for my intended audience?
4. What are the strengths of this draft?
5. Is every part well developed? Are there enough details and examples?
6. Are there any confusing or missing parts?
7. Do all of the parts have a clear connection to the thesis?
8. Is the essay well organized? Is the organization obvious to the reader?
9. What are two or three things I could do to take this draft to the next stage?

Writers are rarely helped by yes and no or right and wrong answers to these questions. If you are giving feedback, write two or three sentences to answer them. Notice that some of them can be answered by paraphrasing parts of the draft or by asking questions or by making suggestions. Even a question seems to call for a yes or no answer, such as "Am I addressing the assignment?" expand on your answer. A description of what you see the writer doing or saying is more helpful than a one-word answer to a question. For example, you have been assigned to write about a lesson you learned as a child and to use examples to explain your thesis. After reading your draft, a reader might write, "You wrote about learning to hide your Hispanic origins because of discrimination. I counted four examples." You could tell from this comment if what is coming through to your reader is what you meant. If it is not, you would know that you need to revise.

from Book 1

In Chapters 1 and 2, you learned how to plan and write discovery drafts of paragraphs. This chapter will show you how to evaluate, revise, and edit your drafts for the most important qualities of good writing. These qualities are described in the chart that follows.

FIVE IMPORTANT QUALITIES OF GOOD WRITING

1. Good writing has a ***focus:*** Each paragraph has a clear main point or topic sentence.
2. Good writing has adequate ***development:*** Each paragraph supports the main point with enough specific details.
3. Good writing has ***unity:*** Each paragraph sticks to its main point.
4. Good writing has ***coherence:*** Each paragraph is organized logically and flows smoothly.
5. Good writing is ***correct:*** Each paragraph has complete sentences that are relatively error-free.

Begin revising by looking for strengths in your writing—for sentences and words that you really like. Try to figure what you did to achieve these effective parts so that you can improve the weak parts. Here are additional strategies for revising:

- Ask a friend, relative, or classmate to respond to your paper.
- Reread your details: Did you provide enough relevant, specific details to support your main point?
- Add new ideas, details, and descriptive words.
- Cross out ideas, sentences, and words that do not sound logical or interesting or that are not clearly related to your main point.
- Cross out sentences or words that are repetitious.
- Use circles and arrows to indicate how sentences or words should be reorganized.
- Use scissors and tape to cut out sentences or ideas and move them to different places in the draft.

The first strategy—asking for feedback from readers—is the most important one. If you want to see how professional writers use this strategy, get a copy of the film *All the President's Men* (about the Water brought down the Nixon administration). This film profile sional writers work. In one scene, one writer (played by Du ishes a draft of a newspaper story and puts it in a bin for pu writer (played by Robert Redford) walks by the bin, picks it, and begins making changes in the story. When the Hoffm

Five Qualities of Good Writing

An emphasis on **Five Qualities of Good Writing** in every book helps students remember the important features of good writing: **"Focus," "Development," "Unity," "Coherence,"** and **"Correctness."** Student written samples are included to illustrate effective and ineffective writing.

Writer's Portfolio

Books 1,2 and 3 include a **Writer's Portfolio** that covers the rhetorical modes, always with a consideration of the writing situation, audience, and purpose.

from Book 3

For a business course in personal finance, you might be asked to keep a list of your expenditures and create categories for a budget. Division and classification is a way of organizing and simplifying diverse behaviors, information, or ideas.

ORGANIZING DIVISION AND CLASSIFICATION ESSAYS

There are many ways to divide and classify any collection of facts, ideas, items, behaviors, or expenditures. However, the categories should be consistent and exclusive. Consistency means that you decide on one system, or determining principle, for dividing and classifying and stick with it. To classify kinds of desserts, you could use the categories pies, cakes, cookies, but not pies, cakes, and chocolate because "chocolate" is a flavor and the others are not. Exclusivity means categories should not overlap. Each category should be distinct from other categories. To classify kinds of tippers in a restaurant, you could use the categories men and women, but not men, women, and business men because the category "business men" overlaps with the category "men" and excludes business women.

When using categories to make a point, writers usually announce their thinking and organizing pattern with a sentence, such as "Oppressed people deal with their oppression in three characteristic ways." Words such as ways, kinds, types, levels, categories, and groups are signals of classification and division. Writers may announce, for example, that there are "several ways to face oppression," "three kinds of discipline," "several levels of friendship," or "two groups of drivers."

Transitions. Good writers also follow an announcement of the division and classification pattern with clear transition words and phrases as they name and discuss each category. Here are some of the transition words and phrases writers use:

one way	the most	there is
the second way	the next	then there is
the third way	the last	last there is
the fourth way		

Writers may organize their categories from least to most important, from most to least effective, or from largest to smallest. However they order the categories, they help the reader stay on track by using transition phrases and by repeating key words or phrases. Here are sentences from an essay by Martin Luther King, Jr. , about the ways of dealing with oppression. Several paragraphs with discussion and examples follow each of the categories in King's essay. The transition phrase if underlined; the repeated key words are in boldface.

Integrated Reading and Writing Approach

In all three books, an integrated reading and writing approach as evidenced in the **Exploring Further** sections encourages students to respond to each other's writing and to the sample readings. In Book 3, critical reading coverage carries this approach one step further.

from Book 3

REMINDER

There are many ways to end an essay. A conclusion often echoes something in the introduction–the thesis, a key word, an image, or an incident.

POINTS TO REMEMBER FOR WRITING AN ESSAY

- Use your Idea Bank or other discovery strategies to find main point to write about.
- Write a trial thesis and test it.
- Describe your intended audience and purpose.
- Write a discovery draft.

Although you should give your best effort at each step of the writing process, don't overinvest in your discovery draft. Trying to "get it perfect" may create writer's block. Charge through with a draft and be ready for revising.

■ EXPLORING FURTHER

1. Reread "Don't Press Your Luck" on pages 0-0 and the writing you did about peer pressure for Exploring Further in Chapter 1.
2. *Group Work.* Talk about the ideas that emerged in your freewriting or group discussions about peer pressure. What struck each of you as the most important idea about each situation? Take notes about your own and your classmates' ideas.
3. *Writing Activity.* Write a trial thesis for an essay about peer pressure. Usc the strategies for writing a trial thesis described in this chapter.
4. *Group Work.* Think about who needs to know what you have written. What audience would benefit and use what you have to say? Parents? Elementary school children? Young teens? College students? Voters? Teachers? Consumers? What do you want them to do or believe?

   Tell your group what your trial thesis is (the main point of your essay), and describe your intended audience and purpose. Help each other test and clarify an appropriate audience and purpose. Write down your group's comments and suggestions about your trial thesis.
5. *Writing Activity.* Write a description of the audience and purpose for your essay on peer pressure.
   Writing Activity. Write a discovery draft of an essay about peer pressure in which you discuss the reasons for peer pressure and give examples. Draw on the ideas and examples of peer pressure you have read, written, and talked about. Name the person or writer whose examples you use.

CHAPTER 4

READING FOR COMPREHENSION

from Book 3

In Chapters 1 through 3 you have been reading about writing. In Chapters 5 through 13 you will be reading selections from newspapers, magazines, and books. Although this is a writing course, reading, thinking, speaking, and listening are inseparable from writing. Because the communication skills reading, writing, speaking, and listening are interrelated, you can use your stronger ones to help improve your others. For instance, your stronger communication skill may be talking to others. You can use this strength to improve your writing by talking to others as you look for ideas to write about, as you try to find a focus for your writing, and as you revise. Because communications skills are interrelated, good readers are usually good writers and the reverse. Use what you know about writing to help you read better, and use what you know about reading to help you write better.

Reading and writing, as well as the other communication activities, are skills that you can learn and improve by practice, just as you might practice juggling or skateboarding, Like juggling or skateboarding, these communication activities are part mental, part physical, and part emotional. For instance, freewriting is a physical activity that stimulates the mental activity of thinking. Reading is a mental activity that creates physical changes such as in respiration, eye movements, pulse rate, and brain activity. All of these complex activities are affected by your emotional state-how you feel and what you are about.

Earlier you read that negative self-talk creates writer's block for many people, and you looked briefly at your own. You also read how two writers use positive self-talk to create positive feelings that allow them to think and write, and you considered how you can help yourself write. Reading, too, is affected by your feelings, attitudes, and self-talk. Since reading essays is a way of learning to write, let's look at some negative messages that make it harder to read.

Contextualized Grammar Issues

Grammar concepts are discussed in relation to how they affect students' writing. Sentence-level issues are covered both in the writing and grammar chapters.

from Book 2

In Chapter 6, you practiced writing in the "first-person" point of view (*I, we*) and the "third-person" point of view (*he, she, it, they*). Most process analyses are written in a form of the "second-person" (*you*) point of view called the *imperative* ("command"). The subject of an imperative sentence is always you, but the pronoun *you* does not appear; it is "understood." For example, when Group Work activities direct you to "Form a group with two or three other students," you understand that the subject of this command is you (*"You form a group with two or three other students"*).

If all the sentences in your process analysis are imperatives, then your paragraphs or essays will sound like monotonous orders. To avoid this, try varying your sentence beginnings so that they don't all start with the verb. Here is an example:

ALL IMPERATIVES:

> To cure insomnia, go to bed at the same time every night, including weekends. Wake up around the same time every morning. Develop a bedtime ritual and use it every night. Drink a glass of mild before retiring, but don't ever drink alcohol, because it disturbs sleep patterns. Finally, stop worrying about your insomnia; that will only make the problem worse. You'll fall asleep way before you die from lack of it.

VARIED SENTENCE BEGINNINGS:

> Here are some tricks for curing insomnia. First, try going to bed at the same time every night and waking up around the same time every morning, including weekends. Since bedtime rituals prepare the mind to relax, develop a bedtime ritual and remember to use it every night. You might drink a glass of milk before retiring, but don't drink any alcohol because it disturbs sleep patterns. Finally, you should try to stop worrying about your insomnia; that will only make the problem worse. You'll fall asleep way before you die from lack of it.

The second version of this paragraph sounds less abrupt and more friendly and interesting than the first one. (For more information on sentence variety, see pages 122-124).

WRITING ACTIVITY 10

Write a "how-to" paragraph about one of the topics below:

- Choose a college (or a university)

from Book 2

There are two ways to correct missing-verb fragments:

1. Attach the fragment to the sentence that precedes
   (You may have to cross out the subject of the frag
   subject of the sentence to which it is being connec
2. Add a verb to the fragment.

Here are two fragments, followed by each type of correction:

Viruses as deadly as bacteria. Are responsible for many human diseases.

1. *Attach the fragments to form a sentence:*

   Viruses as deadly as bacteria are responsible for many human diseases.

2. *Add a verb to each fragment:*

   Viruses are as deadly as bacteria. They are responsible for many human diseases.

Cowpox, a virus that can have painful effects on milk cows. Does not have serious effects on humans.

1. Cowpox, a virus that can cause painful effects on milk cows, does not have serious effects on humans.
2. Cowpox is a virus that can have painful effects on milk cows. It does not have serious effects on humans.

WRITING ACTIVITY 3

Underline the fragment in each set of word groups below. Then use one of the two methods noted above to correct each fragment. The first one has been done both ways as an example.

1. The videotape is a fairly recent invention. *Only about seventy years old.*
2. The idea of storing information on a magnetic tape first occurred to Valdemar Poulson. A famous Danish scientist.
3. The videotape that Poulson created. It was a band of stretched plastic.
4. The plastic covered by a film of magnetic iron oxide.
5. The iron oxide has tiny particles in it. Particles with the ability to carry an electric current.
6. A magnetic recording head emits electric signals. These signals, which change the currents in the iron oxide particles.

Grammar Exercises

All exercises are composed of **connected discourse**: sentences (or paragraphs) that are thematically related. This puts grammar skills in the context of rhetorically sound writing. Exercise topics reflect multicultural sensitivity and span the curriculum.

WRITING AND EDITING LOG

Each time your instructor returns a piece of your writing — in your writing course and in every other course—make notes about the piece in this log. You will be able to chart progress and to identify areas that need further improvement.

Date ______________ Course ______________________________

Title of Paper ______________________________________

Strengths:

Problems and Errors:

Writing Process Log and Teacher Conference Log

These logs provide an easy format for recording the progress of students' writing.

from Book 2

Writing Activity 9

Brainstorm for five minutes about your favorite place. Write everything down that comes to your mind. If you get stuck, ask yourself the questions on page xx.

Group Work 4

Form a brainstorming group and — together — choose a problem concerning your school (for example, the registration process, placement tests, class size, or student fees). Choose one person to be the group recorder. Then take turns calling out ideas about the problem and solutions for it. Jot down a brief note about every solution that you and your classmates call out. If the group gets stuck, the recorder should read aloud the questions on page xx. When the group finishes, each person should discuss the solution he or she thinks would best solve the problem.

Writing Activity 10

Write a paragraph or two about the problem that your group discussed in the preceding activity. What is this problem? Why does it cause you (or other students) so much aggravation or trouble? What could the school's administrators, teachers, or students do to solve this problem?

from Book 1

Writing Activities, Writing Assignments, Group Work

These **writing exercises** help students develop and practice their skills and promote peer collaboration. Many are based on the readings and writing samples authored by students and professional writers of different ethnic backgrounds.

that explains the advantages of learning the process. Make sure that you tell readers what materials they will need to accomplish the process; also define any terms that they might not understand. Finally, explain each step of the process in detail and arrange these steps in the order readers must perform them.

✔ POINTS TO REMEMBER ABOUT PROCESS ANALYSIS

1. Make sure that your process is narrow enough to explain in a paragraph or an essay.
2. Keep your purpose and your readers in mind as you brainstorm the details for you process analysis. What exactly do you want them to know? What else might they want or need to know?
3. Make your introduction interesting and briefly explain the importance or advantages of the process.
4. Describe any materials or equipment that readers will need to perform the process.
5. Define any terms that readers may not understand.
6. Explain each step in the process clearly and in detail. Also, anticipate readers' confusion or mistakes, and explain what they should *not* do.
7. Use concrete descriptive words and vivid images.
8. Make sure that your details are logically organized— in the order in which they are to be performed—and that you have included transitional words and phrases.
9. Experiment with different conclusions for your narration. Choose the ending that suits your purpose better.
10. Vary your sentence structure so that your process analysis is not a curt set of imperative commands.

from Book 2

Learning Aids

All three books in the series feature learning aids such as **"Points to Remember," "Reminders," checklists, charts,** and **boxes** that reinforce key concepts.

PART 1

Principles of Effective Writing

CHAPTER

THE WRITING PROCESS

Writing is like dancing. If you want to learn how to dance, you can't just sit home and read about it. Sooner or later you have to get up and do it. Similarly, you can't learn to write just by reading about writing. At some point, you have to pick up a pen or a pencil and do it. As often as possible!

Successful dancers spend several hours a day practicing steps. They watch themselves in mirrors, noting where they may have missed or forgotten steps. To be a successful writer, you must develop the ability to examine your work as if in a mirror—to see where you have forgotten some steps or made errors. Think of your readers as dance partners whom you want to please. Writing a paragraph that is confusing or filled with errors is as embarrassing as stepping on your partner's feet when you're dancing.

So get up and dance. And when you dance with a partner—or write for a reader—think of that person's needs and expectations. In doing so, you will have taken your first steps as an advancing writer.

GETTING STARTED

Dancers dance and writers write. Let's look at writers. How do they get started? Some writers spend hours thinking about a topic before they write a word. Others rewrite a sentence or a paragraph three or four times until they are satisfied with it. Some writers need to talk about their ideas and get reactions from friends and relatives. How do you get started writing?

One way to make writing easier is to think of it as a series of overlapping activities:

- Thinking and reading about the topic
- Talking to others about your ideas
- Jotting down ideas and notes
- Using prewriting strategies (described in this chapter)
- Discovering what you know and think about the topic by writing about it
- Rethinking and rewriting your draft several times
- Proofreading and editing the final version

You already have the skills needed to accomplish these activities. Here are some suggestions for improving these skills.

Think and Behave like a Writer. Good writers are always looking for interesting sights, behaviors, and problems and recording their reactions to these things. In addition, good writers are always writing, especially to themselves. They set aside time every day to write in a journal or an *Idea Bank.*

Idea Banks are similar to diaries. Perhaps when you were younger, you poured your secrets into a private notebook. An Idea Bank is also a place to store your deepest thoughts. Only, rather than confine their work to secrets, many writers also use their Idea Banks to store observations, notes, and ideas that interest them or that may serve for future paragraphs and essays. Some writers organize their Idea Banks into categories. For example, some people divide their Idea Banks into ''personal,'' ''social,'' ''school,'' and ''political'' sections. If these people were assigned an essay on a political topic, they might discover in their Idea Banks interesting observations and notes that they had jotted down in the past.

Perhaps the following categories could help you to start your own Idea Bank. Feel free to ignore them or to add categories that interest you.

SUGGESTIONS FOR YOUR IDEA BANK

1. Vivid or important events that occur during your day and your reactions to these events
2. Emotions (fear, anger, pleasure, or surprise)
3. Unusual sights and conversations
4. Memories of a place (or a person) and what it (or he or she) means to you
5. Descriptions of a picture in a magazine or a newspaper and your reaction to the picture
6. Reactions to a movie, story, or poem
7. Political problems or issucs
8. School topics
9. Hopes, dreams, or goals
10. Your feelings about writing or about this class

REMINDER

A journal or an Idea Bank is a notebook in which writers record their observations, thoughts, and feelings.

Here is a sample entry from a student's Idea Bank in which the student wrote down something she had overheard. Notice that the writer did not correct her grammar or sentence structure errors.

Sitting in Streets Diner on Waverly Rd, I overheard a waiter complaining "I don't believe anyone who wants to be president should make more money than the people they represent. The president should make the money that I make, I work very hard on my feet 10 hours a day. That's the only way that the president would know what people in this country are feeling." I thought about it and I think that the waiter was right. How can rich presidents or candidates understand the needs of working men and women?

If this writer were asked to write a report about the presidential election, she might use the waiter's quote as the opening paragraph to introduce a main idea about the qualifications of presidential candidates. Here is an entry from another writer's Idea Bank.

My worst boss was Artie, on the farm. I was only a 14 year old kid, I didn't know anything. Artie used to watch me like a hawk, come to think of it, he looked like a hawk or a bald eagle. His job was to make sure I picked enough peaches from the trees on the farm. I remember several days he wouldn't pay me because he said I damaged too many peaches. But he was pocketing my money! I hated Artie.

Perhaps this writer might one day be asked to write about work. He could use this story to illustrate his feelings about an unpleasant boss.

Like the writers of the preceding entries, you should think of your Idea Bank as a journal in which you should write every day. Get into the habit of writing regularly, so that the physical act of getting words onto paper (or a computer screen) becomes normal and routine for you. Use your Idea Bank to loosen up your hand and mind and to understand that it is okay to write down your thoughts and feelings without knowing exactly what it is you are writing about. Your best ideas will probably occur to you *as you write.*

WRITING ACTIVITY 1

Start thinking and acting like a writer today: Begin an Idea Bank. Carry around a small notebook for recording your ideas whenever they occur to you. Write at least three entries in your Idea Bank today.

WRITING ACTIVITY 2

Look through a magazine or a newspaper to find one or two photographs that strike your eye. Describe them in your Idea Bank. Describe your reactions to them.

WRITING ACTIVITY 3

In your Idea Bank, describe a person who surprised or angered you. What happened? Why were you surprised or angered? How else did you feel? Why do you think you reacted this way?

REMINDER

Spend some time each day writing in your Idea Bank. Later, look back through your entries to find ideas for writing.

Think of Writing as a Process. Like dancing, writing involves a combination of steps. However, many advancing writers don't know this. They think that good writing flows magically from the pens of successful writers. Some students think that good writers can sit down and write until they have exhausted their thoughts. But this is not how experienced writers work or how they think about writing. Good writers know that writing is a process.

THE WRITING PROCESS

Here are some of the steps that many writers follow.

Step 1: Think about a topic.
Step 2: Talk to others about your ideas.
Step 3: Use prewriting strategies (described in this chapter) to develop your ideas.
Step 4: Narrow your focus and develop a topic sentence.
Step 5: Write a discovery draft.
Step 6: Rethink and revise your draft.
Step 7: Edit and proofread the final version.

The remainder of this chapter explains the first three steps in the writing process. Chapter 2 describes Steps 4 and 5 (developing a topic sentence and writing a discovery draft). Chapter 3 discusses Steps 6 and 7 (revising and editing drafts).

STEP 1: THINK ABOUT A TOPIC

What do writers write about? What topics should you write about? In school, you will find yourself confronted with three types of topics. First are topics that you select. For example, a teacher might say, "Write about something that interests you." Second are general topics that your teachers present, such as ''Write a paragraph about high school.'' Third are teacher topics that are very specific: ''Write a composition explaining at least two similarities and two differences between the high school you attended and the college you are currently attending.''

When you are given directions such as ''Write about what interests you,'' select a topic you can develop fully. Although no rules exist to guide you in selecting topics of your choice, two pointers may help you choose an idea that you can write about in detail: (1) Choose a topic related to an event that occurred recently, so that the details are still fresh in your mind. (2) Choose a topic with great emotional meaning for you. Chances are that your most wonderful or most awful experience will be more vivid than something ordinary.

When your teacher assigns a general topic, you need to find some aspect of the topic that interests you. One way to do this is to discuss the topic with others.

STEP 2: TALK TO OTHERS ABOUT YOUR IDEAS

Talking is an important strategy for narrowing down a topic and finding out what you know about it or what interests you about the topic. For a long time, many teachers tried to keep students from talking to each other in class. However, research confirms what good teachers have always known: Talking is learning. For example, NASA (National Aeronautics and Space Administration) scientists often work in teams in order to find solutions to problems that might plague a space mission. Together, the team writes down different ideas and discusses the advantages and the weaknesses of each potential solution. In addition, most companies rely on the team approach to generate ideas, solve problems, and develop new sales strategies. Finally, you have probably had the experience of discussing a problem with a friend and discovering that by talking about your difficulties, you can work out solutions.

Talking with others will help you to explore and narrow your topics. Below are some guidelines for talking in groups.

GUIDELINES FOR TALKING IN GROUPS

1. Choose the first *talker* to speak about a topic that the teacher has assigned or that the group has selected.
2. The other members are the *listeners;* they take notes on interesting points and ideas that the talker reveals.
3. Once the talker has finished, the listeners review what the talker has said. Together the listeners and the talker find issues

or ideas the talker has focused on. For example, if the general topic is "My Ideal Vacation," and the talker has mentioned her trip to Puerto Rico several times, the group may advise her to discuss that trip or to elaborate on one aspect of the trip.

4. The listeners then help the talker qualify his or her points and explain them in specific detail. For instance, if the talker said she liked swimming in Puerto Rico but never elaborated on this activity, the listeners should ask why swimming in Puerto Rico was so ideal.
5. The group goal is to help the talker select the aspect of the topic that he or she has the most ideas about. To do this, the group should write one sentence that they feel reflects the aspect of the topic which the talker seemed most interested in.
6. Everyone in the group should get the opportunity to be the talker.

GROUP WORK 1

Form a group with two or three classmates. Think about the topic "My Ideal Vacation." Then use "Guidelines for Talking in Groups" to talk about your ideal vacation with your group. After you have finished talking, take notes about the listeners' responses to what you have said. At the end of the talking session, write a sentence reflecting the one idea that each other group member seemed most able to talk about in detail.

GROUP WORK 2

Form a group with two or three classmates. Spend three minutes silently thinking about the word *friendship.* Then follow "Guidelines for Talking in Groups" to talk about friendship with your group. After you have finished talking, remember to take notes about the listeners' responses to what you have said.

WRITING ACTIVITY 4

Examine the sentence and the notes that you wrote for Group Work 2. Circle the words and phrases that seem most important, and draw lines between circles that seem related in some way. Then look at these circles and select any two or three that interest you. Use the material in these circles to write a paragraph about friendship.

STEP 3: USE PREWRITING STRATEGIES TO DEVELOP YOUR IDEAS

Have you ever found yourself staring at a blank page (or a blank screen) thinking that you don't know what to write? Or that you have some ideas but you don't know how to phrase them? This is the time for prewriting.

Sharpening pencils, drinking coffee, and raiding the refrigerator are *not* prewriting strategies. Prewriting strategies are activities that writers use to generate ideas about a topic before they write a draft about it. These strategies include the following.

- Freewriting
- Brainstorming
- Outlining
- Clustering
- Asking yourself the five W questions
- Asking yourself what-if questions

Freewriting. *Freewriting* is writing continuously about anything that comes to mind. This kind of limbering-up activity is a wonderful technique for discovering what you are thinking and for exploring your ideas about an assigned topic. All you have to do is write for five or ten minutes without stopping. Your pen or pencil should not leave the page. If you get stuck, you can write ''I can't think of anything to write'' over and over again until new ideas start to flow from your mind to your page. The writing teacher who developed this technique, Peter Elbow, noted the following about freewriting:

> Freewriting is the easiest way to get words on paper and the best all-around practice in writing that I know. To do a freewriting exercise, simply force yourself to write without stopping for ten minutes. Sometimes you will produce good writing, but that's not the goal. Sometimes you will produce garbage, but that's not the goal either. You may stay on one topic, you may flip repeatedly from one to another: it doesn't matter. Sometimes you will produce a good record of your stream of consciousness, but often you can't keep up. Speed is not the goal, though sometimes the process revs you up. If you can't think of anything to write, write about how that feels or repeat over and over ''I have nothing to write'' or ''Nonsense'' or ''No.'' If you get stuck in the middle of a sentence or thought, just repeat the last word or phrase till something comes along. The only point is to keep writing.

Here is sample of a student's freewriting about his high school. As you read this example, think about which ideas you would focus on if you were this writer.

It's crazy, thinking about DeWitt Clinton High School, the front steps were always crowded with kids of every color and background, this was the 1970s and most kids were in gangs. The white kids were in the White Angels, the Black and Hispanic kids were in the Turbans. Sometimes they would fight. What else? what else? what else? I avoided fights, I was always avoiding all the mess. I think I was a good kid, I tried to be one. I liked English, I wanted to be in a band but I didn't have a band. Uh, I can't remember, now I have to think, where was I? WHAT was I? Well, I started to go off—I didn't use drugs right away but after a year I tried pot. But then I decided I wanted to write, I wanted to be smart and I didn't care what my friends thought. They probably thought I was crazy. In high school, I started deciding that I wanted to be a teacher. I did okay and Thank God, I got out of high school. What else? I'm going to succeed, I'm going to make something of myself, I'm going to be the person I started becoming while I was in high school. Help????

These notes represent the writer's private thoughts. He could read and make sense of them, just as you will be able to read your freewriting. The important thing to notice is that this writer didn't stop writing to worry about grammar. He simply let his thoughts flow onto the paper.

Let's practice this prewriting technique. Imagine for a moment that your teacher has asked you to write about a school you used to attend. Close your eyes for a few minutes and try to recall an elementary, an intermediate, or a high school that you attended. Picture the front steps, the doors, the classrooms, and the teachers. Hear the bell ring and listen to the noise of students' feet. See the lunchroom and smell the food. Stand in the hallways and smell the air.

Now open your eyes, take out a piece of paper, and begin writing about your school. Write down everything that you saw, heard, smelled, and felt while your eyes were closed. Just write without stopping. Do not worry about spelling, correctness, or neatness.

REMINDER

When you are freewriting, do not lift your pen or pencil from the page. Use interruptions like "Uh" or "What else?" or "Help" or "????" to keep your thoughts flowing and to fill in the gaps between your ideas.

WRITING ACTIVITY 5

Write in your Idea Bank for at least five minutes about your future. Write everything that comes to your mind when you think about your future. Do *not* reject any of your thoughts. Do not worry about your sentence structure, spelling, or grammar. Time yourself: Keep writing for at least five minutes.

WRITING ACTIVITY 6

Freewrite for five minutes about the topic "Music." Write continuously about everything that comes to your mind when you think of the word *music*. If you run out of things to say, write how you feel about running out of things to say. Your goal is to fill a page with words, impressions, thoughts, ideas—anything that comes to mind.

You can use your freewriting notes to find out how you feel about your topic and to discover a purpose for writing about it. Look for a dominant or main idea in your freewriting—an idea that seems to be more on your mind than other ideas. A good way to do this is to review the free flow and to look for words or phrases that stand out or that are repeated. Circle these words and phrases. Do they all seem to refer to one person, place, object, or idea? If so, write a sentence about this focus. If not, do more freewriting, and then look for your focus.

For example, reread the student freewriting on page 11. What word does the writer repeat most frequently? What other words does this writer repeat? In this freewriting, the writer keeps returning to the kind of person he felt he was in high school. He uses the word "I" twenty-nine times. Clearly he wants to focus on his sense of himself. The other word he repeats is ''high school.'' If a teacher asked this writer to write a paragraph about high school, he could use the ideas in this freewriting to develop a composition about beginning to discover his identity in high school.

GROUP WORK 3

Form a group with two or three classmates. Spend five minutes silently freewriting everything you can think of about the high school you went to. Write your ideas in a list. When time is up, group members should take turns reading a word or sentence from their lists. Your classmates' ideas will probably stimulate you to think of totally new ideas about high school. Add these new ideas to your list.

WRITING ACTIVITY 7

Examine the notes that you wrote for Group Work 3. Circle the words or phrases that seem most important, and draw lines between circles that seem related in some way. Then look at these circles and select one or two that interest you. Use the notes in these circles to write a paragraph about the high school you attended.

WRITING ACTIVITY 8

Spend five minutes freewriting about one of the topics below.

- My favorite childhood memory
- Why I like (or dislike) birthdays
- My favorite movie
- Life on other planets
- Meeting new people
- If I were the President of the United States

After you finish, circle the repeated words and phrases or underline the main idea. Write a sentence about these words or phrases or about this main idea.

Brainstorming. *Brainstorming* is another prewriting strategy for discovering and developing ideas. Brainstorming is best done in groups. You begin by thinking about the problem or the topic that is your focus. Then each person calls out an idea (and writes it down), and no one is allowed to criticize any of the ideas. The goal is to get down on paper as many ideas as possible, no matter how unreasonable or silly they might seem. If you are brainstorming alone, begin by writing the topic that you have chosen, or have been assigned, to write about. Then list everything that comes to mind about it. If you get stuck, ask yourself the questions given in ''Questions to Help You Brainstorm.''

QUESTIONS TO HELP YOU BRAINSTORM

Ask yourself the following questions, and write down your answers.

- What do I know about this topic?
- How does this topic make me feel? Why?
- What are the effects of this topic on me or my friends?
- What interests me about this topic?
- What is my point of view about this topic?
- What might my readers want to know about this topic?

Here is an example of brainstorming based on a student's jottings about the ideal vacation.

- Windham, the best vacation in the world
- Located in the Catskill Mountains
- Big ski area
- Lots of deer and pine trees
- Soaring eagles and gulls
- Magnificent dawns and breathtaking sunsets
- A small cabin in the woods
- A porch overlooking the valley
- Went bird watching
- Followed a raccoon family
- Watched robin eggs hatch in a nest under the porch
- Swimming in the lake
- Brought home some newts
- Chased a muskrat into the lake
- Didn't find the town library

As you can see from this example, brainstorming is like freewriting with a very specific focus, and it generates much information. Each phrase in this list represents a well of ideas. The next step in brainstorming is to choose one or two of the items on the list that seem most interesting (to the writer and for potential readers).

Can you find the focus of the preceding brainstorming list? Review the list, and then write a sentence that reflects this idea.

____

____

____

Did your sentence focus on the writer's interest in the wildlife at this ideal vacation spot? If so, you have rightly noted that quite a few jottings seem to allude to animals.

WRITING ACTIVITY 9

Brainstorm for five minutes about your favorite place. Write down everything that comes to your mind. If you get stuck, use "Questions to Help You Brainstorm."

GROUP WORK 4

Form a brainstorming group, and—together—choose a problem concerning your school (for example, the registration process, placement tests, class size, or student fees). Choose one person to be the group recorder. Then take turns calling out ideas about the problem and solutions for it. Jot down a brief note about every solution that you and your classmates call out. If the group gets stuck, the recorder should read aloud from "Questions to Help You Brainstorm." When the group finishes, each person should discuss the solution he or she thinks would best solve the problem.

WRITING ACTIVITY 10

Write a paragaph or two about the problem that your group discussed in Group Work 4. What is this problem? Why does it cause you (or other students) so much annoyance or trouble? What could the school's administrators, teachers, or students do to solve this problem?

Outlining. Another technique for creating and organizing ideas is *outlining*—listing ideas by headings and indented subheadings. Making an informal, or "scratch," outline of your freewriting or brainstorming can help you select and organize your ideas and make sense out of your seemingly chaotic notes.

However, remember that it may be pointless to outline your ideas if you have not generated enough of them. Also, outlining gets some writers in trouble because they feel that once they have prepared an outline, they must stick to it and ignore any new ideas that occur to them as they begin to write a draft. If you are one of these writers, stop outlining and use clustering instead.

Clustering. *Clustering* is a visual technique that helps you record ideas as they occur to you and relate these ideas to one another in a logical way. Begin clustering by writing your topic in one word or phrase in the middle of a piece of paper and drawing a circle around it. Then follow these guidelines.

HOW TO USE CLUSTERING TO GENERATE IDEAS

Clustering is a visual form of brainstorming. Write your topic in a circle in the middle of a blank piece of paper. Then do the following.

1. Think about this circled word or phrase. What related ideas does it bring to mind?
2. Write down a word or phrase to summarize each related idea.
3. Draw a circle around each word or phrase, and then draw a line connecting this circle back to the circle that inspired it.

Like freewriting and brainstorming, clustering allows you to see the range of ideas you may have on any given topic, so that you can narrow the topic to one main idea that you want to write about. Let's say you were given this assignment.

> Write 350 words on what you like or dislike about your college.

You can't write everything you think about college in 350 words. Try clustering to find a focus. Here is an example.

Note that the writer of this cluster starred the circles that seemed most interesting to her. These contain the ideas that she might want to develop in a paragraph or an essay.

Clustering is a powerful tool for generating and developing details; it shows you where you need to add examples and illustrations. When you get stuck, you can return to the original circled word—or to any of the clusters—and begin a new cluster. Because clustering relies on visual prompts—circles and lines as well as words—it can help you see the interrelations between your ideas and details.

The cluster about college (above) helped the writer narrow down her topic and find an aspect of it that was interesting to her. Clustering also helped this writer identify where she needed to think of additional details to illustrate her ideas. For example, when the writer examined the cluster labeled "Teachers," she realized that it had fewer details than the other clusters. She decided to add several more details to this cluster.

WRITING ACTIVITY 11

Create a cluster around one of the topics below, and select one or two circles to focus on for a paragraph.

- Money
- Qualities of a good friend
- Career choices
- Marriage

Write your topic in a circle in the middle of your paper. As ideas occur to you, write them down, circle them, and connect them to the ideas that inspired them. When you finish, put a star next to the most interesting circles in the cluster. Then write a paragraph about the circle (or circles) that you have selected.

WRITING ACTIVITY 12

Do some clustering about the word *health.* When you finish, star or check the circle (or circles) that interest you most. Suppose you were going to write a paragraph based on this cluster. Number the circles in the order in which you might discuss them. Then examine the circle (or circles) to see what additional details are needed.

REMINDER

Effective writing begins with careful observation and listening. It also requires a willingness to discover what you have to say through writing in an Idea Bank and experimenting with different prewriting strategies.

Asking Yourself the Five W Questions. Another prewriting strategy that may be familiar to you is asking the five W questions—Who? What? Where? When? Why?—and How? These are the questions that journalists and reporters ask to find out important information, and you can use these questions to interview yourself. For example, imagine that you have an assignment asking for a response to the following question.

> Based on your experiences and observations, what is your attitude toward working?

You could begin generating ideas about this topic by interviewing yourself with the five W questions.

Who is you current employer? How do you feel about him or her?
Who is (or was) your favorite boss?
What do you do in your current job (or *what* did you do in a past job)?
What job did you like best?
What have you liked the most about working?
What job would you like to have now or in the future?
Where do you work now?
Where was your first job?
Where would you like to work?
When did you start working at your first job?
When did you do the work you liked or disliked most?
Why are you working (or *why* aren't you working) now?
Why did you want (or not want) to do the work that you are currently doing?
Why do you like some jobs and dislike others?
Why did you leave a job?
Why is working important?

Now you take over: Add to the preceding questions. Keep in mind that these questions don't have to be in any special order. The goal of all prewriting activities, including this one, is to help you explore your ideas by allowing you to get them down on paper so you can then pick and choose from your scattered thoughts. First, you want to see what is going on inside your head. Oncc you think you have written all the questions possible (or all that come to mind), begin writing answers to your questions. Then, examine your answers, and circle the ideas which seem most interesting or important to you.

Here is an example of how a student used this strategy to focus ideas for an essay.

WHO?

My current boss is a man from India. He manages the food and beverage section at the supermarket where I work. He is unlike my first boss, Artie, who was the foreman of the farm in Wisconsin where I used to work. Artie made sure that I didn't slack off in the orchards, miles from the farmer's view. He made sure that I picked at least 10 baskets of peaches an hour. He was rotten. He was my worst boss. Whenever he saw that I was not completing the 10-basket load, he would yell at me.

WHAT?

In my new job, I don't have to worry about picking a certain load. I just need to make sure I stock the shelves by midnight. I don't think that I like working. But I do know that what I dislike most about it is having a boss. I once had a job without a boss. I mean, I had a boss, but he wasn't there to supervise me. I used to sell key chains for a man downtown who would come to collect his money only once a month.

WHERE?

I now work in Nyack, New York. It's a pretty suburb filled with Victorian homes and antique shops. My very first job was in Wisconsin in a place that was once dairy farm country.

WHEN?

I got my new job a month ago. I first started working when I was 14 on that farm with Artie. I had to get farm papers. I was a kid, too young for a boss with a mean streak.

WHY?

I got my supermarket job to help pay for my college tuition. I need the money and I need to know that I earned it myself. I don't like having to work. I find that having a boss looking over my shoulder is very irritating. I am sure when I graduate from school, I'm going to start my own business. I will be my own boss. No one will tell me what to do. In fact, this is why I quit every job I have ever had.

What idea seems to dominate this writer's answers? It seems to be the following.

> Based on my job experiences, I find working very unpleasant when an employer oversees my activities.

WRITING ACTIVITY 13

What was the most rewarding or pleasant experience of your life? What experience made you feel most proud or pleased? Think about this experience. Then ask yourself the five W questions: Who was involved? What occurred? When? Where? How? Why was this experience important? How did it make you feel? Why? How do you feel about it now? Write answers to these questions. Write a paragraph about this experience based on your answers.

Asking Yourself What-if Questions. One additional strategy for generating ideas is asking yourself what-if questions: What if I were the teacher of this class instead of a student? What if we could read each other's minds? What if the computer had never been invented? What if every person in the United States could have free health care? Asking and answering what-if questions develops your imagination and creativity. As you answer these questions, new ideas may pop into your mind. Jot these ideas down in your Idea Bank as possible topics for future pieces of writing.

GROUP WORK 5

Work with a partner or two classmates on this exercise. Together, write at least five what-if questions for each of the following topics: (1) guns, (2) sports, and (3) television shows. Here is an example of a what-if question about guns.

> What if all the guns in our country suddenly disappeared?

When you finish writing your questions, share them. Then discuss possible answers to these questions.

COPING WITH WRITING ANXIETY

All of us have some anxieties about writing, especially when we are writing under the pressure of a deadline or when we know that our writing will be evaluated or judged. Confront these anxieties by making writing a part of your daily experience. Write every day, wherever you are—on the bus, in the bath, in a subway, in the back seat of a car, in a doctor's waiting room.

Remember that in the real world, few people write in complete isolation and calm. Most people have to write with interruptions from colleagues, family, employers, and clients. Worse, many people have to do their writing at a desk in an open space where other workers are passing by or chatting about last night's television movie or the lunch special. Get used to writing inside *and* outside the classroom.

WRITING ACTIVITY 14

Go to your school cafeteria or local restaurant—at the height of lunch hour if possible—and take notes for a description of the place. What does it look like? What kinds of people do you see? What do you overhear people saying? As you sit in this crowded space, describe the kinds of distractions that occur while you are writing. Do not leave until you have finished writing a paragraph about the place.

Another way to reduce writing anxiety is to plan ahead. Never leave your writing for the last minute! If you don't give yourself enough time to think and talk about your ideas and to plan what you want to write, you are undermining your efforts.

EXPLORING FURTHER

Here is an opportunity to practice what you have learned. Think about the word *love.* What comes to your mind? Plan a composition about what *love* means to you by following the three steps of the writing process that you practiced in this chapter.

1. Think about love. What images come to your mind? Family love? First love? Love of God? Love for your country? Passion? Happiness? Simple joy?
2. Talk about your ideas about love with friends, family, and classmates. Write down their reactions and responses. Get feedback from as many people as you can.
3. Explore the topic of love by freewriting, brainstorming, clustering, asking yourself the five W questions, and asking yourself what-if questions.

Here are some pictures to help you start thinking about this topic. These pictures won a photography contest in which people were asked to submit a photo showing what love meant to them.

Doris Hutchins, 68, and her husband, Edwin, 67, have been best friends for 44 years. Photo by their granddaughter, Suzanne Hutchins of Beverly, Mass.

Richard Wille and his daughter, Amanda, 3. Photo by Robin Kinsely of Williamsburg, Va.

We're friends: Marguerite Paul and Joseph Pamphile. Photo by Stephan Kenn of New York, N.Y.

WRITING ASSIGNMENT

Write a draft of an essay describing or explaining what love means to you. Imagine that your readers are classmates who do not know you well. Your purpose is to help them understand exactly what you mean by *love.*

POINTS TO REMEMBER ABOUT THE WRITING PROCESS

1. Think and behave like a writer: Observe what goes on around you, read newspapers and magazines, and listen to other people's ideas.
2. Every day, use your Idea Bank to record interesting or puzzling things that you have seen, read, or heard *and* to describe your reactions to these things.
3. Talk about your ideas to friends, family, and classmates. Write down their reactions and responses. Get feedback from as many people as you can.
4. Use prewriting strategies to develop your ideas. Experiment with free-writing, brainstorming, clustering, asking yourself the five W questions, and asking yourself what-if questions.
5. Remember that good writing results from a series of overlapping activities, including thinking, planning, note-taking, drafting, and rewriting. Be willing to devote time and effort to each part of the process.
6. Don't criticize your ideas, notes, and drafts. Instead, concentrate on what is particuarly good about your ideas and your writing.

CHAPTER 2

PLANNING AND WRITING STRONG PARAGRAPHS

In Chapter 1, you practiced using the first three steps of the writing process to select and narrow a topic. You learned how to think about a topic (Step 1), how to talk about a topic (Step 2), and how to use prewriting strategies to develop your ideas (Step 3). This chapter provides you with opportunities to practice Step 4—narrowing your focus and developing a topic sentence—and Step 5—writing a discovery draft.

Regardless of its length or purpose, a paragraph is a group of sentences that develop one main point. An effective paragraph often begins with this main point, called the *topic sentence.* The rest of the paragraph gives illustrations of or evidence for this topic sentence.

STEP 4: NARROW YOUR FOCUS AND DEVELOP A TOPIC SENTENCE

How do you figure out the main point you want to make in a paragraph? Sometimes your teacher will tell you the focus of your writing assignments. Other times, you will have to choose a topic to write about. Use the prewriting strategies that you practiced in Chapter 1 to narrow your focus and decide what interests you most about the topic.

An appropriate main point for a paragraph can be a feeling or an experience that you want to describe to your readers.

My current job is my favorite one so far.

This past semester has been the best one in my academic career.

It can also be an idea that you want to explain or to prove:

If students worked together on class projects, they probably would learn more and get better grades.

The drinking age should be lowered to eighteen.

Like a title, a topic sentence lets readers know what the paragraph is about. However, a paragraph's title and its topic sentence are different. A title (or a topic) is usually a fragment or a part of a sentence. A topic sentence is always a complete sentence. A fragment—as in ''My Favorite Job'' or ''The Best Teacher I Ever Had''—might be an effective title, but it is not a topic sentence. A topic sentence is a complete thought that limits the paragraph to a single point. Here are examples.

My favorite job was being a lifeguard at the public beach.

My English 100 instructor is the best teacher I ever had.

WRITING ACTIVITY 1

This activity will help you identify the differences between titles (or topics) and topic sentences. In the space next to each set of words below, write *T* if the words would make an effective *title* or write *TS* if they would make an effective *topic sentence* for a paragraph.

1. ______ Ways to overcome writing anxiety.
2. ______ An essay about my mother.
3. ______ The worst job I ever had.
4. ______ The complexity of college registration procedures.
5. ______ A wonderful role model.
6. ______ The ideal place to vacation.
7. ______ My favorite holiday.
8. ______ The need for everyone to have health care.

After you finish labeling the ideas above, rewrite each one that you labeled *T* (a title or a topic) to turn it into a topic sentence for a paragraph. Here is an example.

1. ___T___ Ways to overcome writing anxiety.

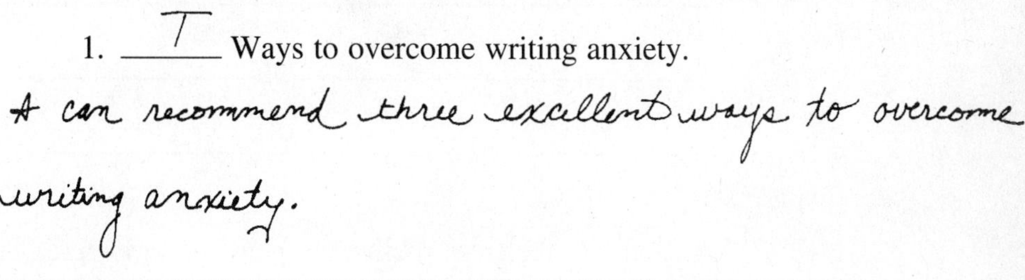

I can recommend three excellent ways to overcome writing anxiety.

A topic sentence can come in the middle or at the end of the paragraph; some paragraphs don't even have a topic sentence. However, beginning a paragraph with a topic sentence will keep you focused on your main point and will let readers know immediately what the paragraph is about.

An effective topic sentence has two parts: (1) a topic and (2) key words that limit the topic and express the opinion or point you want to make about this topic. Here are examples.

A. My best friend Alexis is one of the most fascinating people I know.

B. Chita Rìvera and Andy Garcia, Puerto Rican actors, are wonderful role models for all children.

The topic of sentence *A* is "My best friend Alexis," and the key words that limit the topic are "one of the most fascinating people." Given this topic sentence, both the writer and readers know what to expect from the paragraph that will follow it: details showing how and why Alexis is so fascinating. Thus, the key words *limit* what the writer can say about the topic. They focus the writer (and readers) on only one aspect of the topic. In developing this topic sentence, the writer cannot describe Alexis's looks or personality. The writer must focus only on the woman's fascinating qualities.

Reread sentence *B* above. What is the topic of this sentence?

____

What are the key words in sentence *B* that limit this topic?

____

What kinds of details would you expect to read in a paragraph about topic sentence *B*?

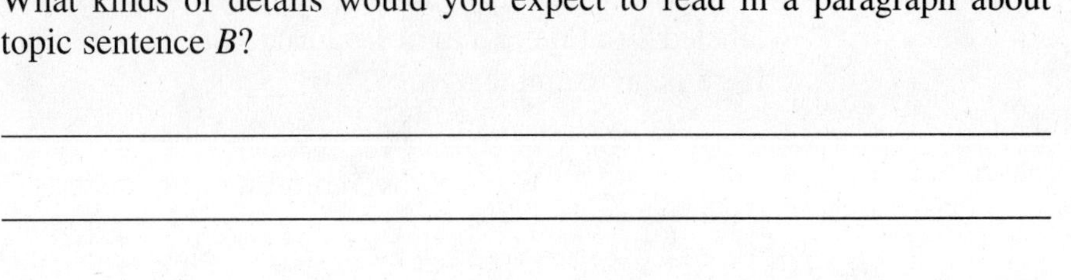

As you can see from these examples, the key words in a topic sentence have two important purposes:

1. They remind the writer what the paragraph is about and what it is *not* about.
2. They provide a focus for the writer to develop in the remainder of the paragraph.

> **REMINDER**
> Some writers do not write a topic sentence for a paragraph until *after* they have thought up details for it.

WRITING ACTIVITY 2

Here are a student's prewriting notes. Read them carefully. Then, in the space that follows these notes, write three different topic sentences that the writer might develop from these notes.

My current boss is a man from India. He manages the food and beverage section at the supermarket where I work. He is unlike my first boss, Artie, who was the foreman of the farm in Wisconsin, where I used to work. Artie made sure that I didn't slack off in the orchards, miles from the farmer's view. He made sure that I picked at least 10 baskets of peaches an hour. He was rotten. He was my worst boss. Whenever he saw that I was not completing the 10-basket load, he would yell at me. I was only 14 years old.

Write possible topic sentences for these notes in the space below.

1. ____

____

2. ____

____

3. ____

____

REMINDER

A topic sentence includes a topic and key words. The key words limit the topic and convey the point that the writer wants to make about the topic or the writer's opinion of the topic. When you write a topic sentence for a paragraph, choose precise key words to express your idea or opinion about the topic. Avoid vague all-purpose words such as *good, nice, great,* and *bad.*

The student who wrote the notes in Writing Activity 2 felt that he needed to do additional freewriting to narrow his focus and develop a clear topic sentence. Here is his next freewriting on the same topic.

Artie was the foreman at Pochuck Valley Farms. He was my first boss when I was 14 years old. I was a city kid. I didn't know a thing about peach picking. The only thing I ever picked from a tree was a leaf and that was from the tree in front of my apartment building. Anyway, I got this summer job on the farm and Artie told me that I would only get paid for every basket of peaches I picked. This being my first job I didn't even ask how much money I was going to earn—I felt funny asking because I was already staying in the farmer's house for the summer. My job was part of a city program to get street kids out into the fresh air.

I later learned that Artie lied about the money per basket. He pocketed some of my profits. When I found out about this, I was furious. It made me feel like I never wanted to work for a boss again (although I know that's not realistic, still it's how I feel). I want to decide the rules of how I work.

Artie was responsible for teaching me my job. And while you would think this was my first job and I was very young, so he would be sensitive. But he wasn't. From day one he watched my every move and yelled at me when he thought I was doing something wrong. If I leaned the ladder into the peach tree too quickly, he would say I was knocking good fruit to the ground. He would say I was destroying the farmer's profits. I hated working for him.

Notice how these notes helped this writer narrow down his topic to one main idea.

> Working is very unpleasant when a mean employer oversees your activities closely.

WRITING ACTIVITY 3

Reread the prewriting notes for one of the topics you explored in Chapter 1. Circle the main idea of these notes. Now freewrite for five more minutes about this main idea. When you finish, compose a sentence that sums up this main idea. Make sure that the sentence states the topic and includes key words that reveal your attitude toward this topic.

At this stage, writers often turn to their journal or Idea Bank to see if at some time in the past they may have reflected on the topic that they are currently exploring. For example, here is the Idea Bank entry of the student who wrote about "Artie" (on pages 5 and 6 in Chapter 1).

My worst boss was Artie, on the farm. I was only a 14 year old kid, I didn't know anything. Artie used to watch me like a hawk, come to think of it, he looked like a hawk or a bald eagle. His job was to make sure I picked enough peaches from the trees on the farm. I remember several days he wouldn't pay me because he said I damaged too many peaches. But he was pocketing my money! I hated Artie.

This entry is a gem, a writer's dream. This writer can now add this thought—especially the point about losing pay to Artie—to his notes. This will help the writer focus his ideas and generate supporting details.

WRITING ACTIVITY 4

Reread a topic you explored for Chapter 1. Then reread your Idea Bank to see if anything you have written can help you narrow this topic and develop a topic sentence. Copy this material from your journal onto a separate sheet of paper, and write a topic sentence.

One of your first challenges as an advancing writer is to learn how to develop a topic sentence that is neither too general nor too narrow for your paragraph. For example, examine the following statements, *none* of which is an effective topic sentence for a paragraph.

A. A career is important. (This is too general. It would take an entire essay—or book—to explain the importance of careers.)

B. Students can learn the steps necessary to succeed in their profession. (This is also too general. These steps would take much more than one paragraph to develop in detail.)

C. The classrooms at Central State Community College are painted grey. (This is too narrow. It is a statement of fact that needs no development.)

Here are revisions of these statements. Each includes key words (in *italics*) that limit the topic and that express the writer's attitude toward the topic.

A. A career is important because *it provides people with self-esteem.*

B. Students can learn the steps necessary to study for *a test in mathematics.*

C. The grey classrooms at Central State Community College make the place *seem like a prison.*

GROUP WORK 1

Form a group with two or three classmates. Choose one person to write the group's responses on a separate piece of paper. Following are several statements. Decide if each one would make a good topic sentence for a paragraph. If not, explain why not and revise the statement to make it into an effective topic sentence. The first one has been done as an example.

1. My family is very important to me. Too broad. Without my family's help, I never could have gone to college.
2. The field of psychology offers many career possibilities.
3. A pediatrician takes care of sick infants and children.
4. Neighborhood friends are important.
5. My favorite way to travel is by bus.
6. Going to school in the day and working at night is exhausting.
7. Summer is usually hotter than spring.
8. People drop out of college for many reasons.

WRITING ACTIVITY 5

In the space given, write a topic sentence for a paragraph about each of these topics. Do not write a paragraph; just write an appropriate topic sentence. Make sure that each topic sentence is a complete sentence.

1. A holiday

____

____

2. A sport

____

____

3. Your favorite place

____

____

4. An important person in your life

____

____

GROUP WORK 2

Form a group with two other students. Take turns reading aloud one of the topic sentences that you wrote for Writing Activity 5. Write down each classmate's topic sentence. Next, list the ideas and details that you would expect to find in a paragraph about the topic sentence. If you have difficulty listing any supporting details for a group member's topic sentence, tell your classmate. Help your classmates improve their topic sentences.

Know Your Purpose and Audience. After you write a topic sentence, reread your prewriting notes and begin developing details for a paragraph that will explain or illustrate your point. In order to do this, you must think about your purpose (why you are writing) and your audience (your intended readers). Many writers feel that their only purpose in writing is to please their teacher. They don't realize that they should develop their own purpose for writing a particular paragraph or essay. Strong writing achieves a clear purpose. Here are three common purposes.

- To *express* something important to ourselves or to others.
- To *explain* something or share information with readers.
- To *persuade* readers to think or feel or do something.

Your purpose governs the length of each paragraph that you write, and it influences the details you select to develop the topic sentence. For example, suppose a writer wants to develop a paragraph about the following topic sentence.

Growing up in a small town has given me much satisfaction.

If the writer's purpose is to express her feelings, she can tell a story that depicts her happiness as a youth in a small town. If she wants to explain why growing up in a small town is a good experience for children, she might present examples that illustrate her point. Or if the writer wants to convince readers to raise their children in a small town, she can provide facts and reasons to support her assertion.

Successful writers also think about their audience—the readers for whom they are writing. This helps writers figure out how much their readers already know about the topic and what their attitudes are toward it. Writers can then select appropriate details to develop the topic sentence—details that the reader will understand and that will not offend the reader.

For instance, suppose you decided to develop a paragraph about the following topic sentence.

The town (or city) where my college is located is a terrific place for college students.

Imagine that your purpose is to convince readers of this assertion.

What examples or reasons would you need to provide if your intended audience were people who go to your college?

____

____

____

____

____

Now imagine that your readers are high school students.

What examples would you provide if you were writing for high school students who were trying to decide where to go to college?

____

____

____

____

____

Finally, imagine a totally different audience: business people who were considering opening a bookstore in your town or city.

What examples should you discuss if you were trying to convince these business people to open their store in your town?

____

____

____

____

____

The details that you listed to support this topic sentence may be different for the three different audiences.

How do the details *differ* for the three audiences?

____

____

____

____

____

Here are some questions to consider as you develop ideas and details to support your topic sentence.

QUESTIONS TO ASK YOURSELF ABOUT YOUR PURPOSE AND AUDIENCE

- Who exactly am I writing for? Who would be interested in reading this paragraph?
- What are these readers like?
- How similar are they to me? Would they react as I do?
- Do I want to share my thoughts and feelings with them?
- Do I want to explain something to them?
- Do I want to persuade my readers to think or to feel or to do something? What? Why?
- How much do my readers already know about my topic?
- What else do they need to know about this topic?

REMINDER

Good writing may have several purposes. When you write to inform, you may also be expressing your feelings, or trying to convince readers to do or to feel or to think something, or both.

WRITING ACTIVITY 6

Do some clustering about the topic of television. Then choose the most interesting idea in your cluster and write a topic sentence about it. Next, write notes about the details you might use to develop a paragraph about this topic sentence if you were writing for your classmates. Also decide on your purpose in writing about your topic sentence: Do you want to be expressive, informative, or persuasive? (If clustering does not help you generate enough details to achieve your purpose, try freewriting or asking yourself the five W questions.)

GROUP WORK 3

Work with two classmates on this activity. Share your notes from Writing Activity 6 with your group. Ask them if they think that your purpose and your details would interest them. Also, ask them to suggest additional ideas and details to illustrate or support your topic sentences.

Keep in mind that most of the time you are writing for readers other than yourself. Thus, you should think of the impact you want your words to make on your readers. For example, imagine planning a paragraph about teenage alcoholism for a group of junior high school students. You would need to use different details and vocabulary for them than if you were writing to their parents. Here is a possible topic sentence for a paragraph intended for teenagers.

Drinking alcohol causes many serious health problems.

And here is a possible topic sentence for a paragraph for their parents. Note the difference in the ideas and the language.

Frequent absences from school and declining grades may be early warning signs of teenage alcoholism.

WRITING ACTIVITY 7

In the spaces given, write a topic sentence for a paragraph about each topic. Remember the specified *purpose* and the *audience.* Do not write a paragraph; just write an appropriate topic sentence. Make sure that each topic sentence is a complete sentence.

1. Purpose: to convince readers to exercise
   Audience: overweight teenagers

   ____

   ____

   ____

2. Purpose: to convince readers to exercise
   Audience: elderly men and women

   ____

   ____

   ____

3. Purpose: to convince readers that plagiarism is a form of cheating
   Audience: classmates

   ____

   ____

   ____

STEP 5: WRITE A DISCOVERY DRAFT

A *discovery draft* is a writer's first attempt to develop a topic in paragraph form. You have already written discovery drafts for some of the writing activities in Chapter 1 and in this chapter. As its name implies, a discovery draft is a rough copy in which writers discover what they know about a topic and what they want to say about it *as* they write about it. A discovery draft usually is disorganized and messy because it is merely a first draft.

Before you write a discovery draft, use one or more of the prewriting strategies—freewriting, brainstorming, clustering, asking yourself the five W questions, and asking yourself what-if questions. Next, compose a topic sentence about the most important or interesting point in your notes or clusters. Decide on a purpose and an audience for your writing, and write these at the top of your paper. (You may also find it helpful to use ''Questions to Ask Yourself About Your Purpose and Audience'' earlier in this chapter. Write your answers down before you develop your draft.)

Select the prewriting notes or clusters that seem to illustrate or support your main point. Rewrite these notes in complete sentences. As you do this, you will probably think of new ideas and sentences to add to your notes. Don't be afraid to cross out sentences and write in new ones. Add details in the margins and connect them to sentences with lines, loops, or arrows. Just make sure that you can read your own writing!

If you get stuck, read what you have written (from the beginning). Use the five W questions to figure out what you still need to say about your topic. Do some additional freewriting or clustering on the last idea that you wrote about in your draft. Or stop writing and talk about your ideas with a thoughtful person whom you trust. As you have already learned, talking about your ideas can help you express them more clearly in writing. Here are some questions to help you compose your drafts.

QUESTIONS TO CONSIDER AS YOU COMPOSE A DISCOVERY DRAFT

You might find it useful to ask yourself the questions below. Jot down your answers. Use the answers to help you continue drafting.

1. What do I want my readers to know about this topic?
2. What point (or points) do I want to make about it?
3. Whom am I writing for?
4. What do these readers already know about this topic?
5. What might they need or want to know about it?
6. What do I want to make my readers think or feel or do about this topic?

Remember that a discovery draft can be messy and filled with mistakes. Just concentrate on getting your ideas onto the page in a way that makes sense. Don't worry about a particular sentence or word or about your grammar, spelling, or punctuation.

WRITING ACTIVITY 8

Choose one of the entries in your Idea Bank. Write a discovery draft of a paragraph about that topic. If you can't make any progress, do some freewriting. Then ask yourself questions from "Questions to Consider As You Compose a Discovery Draft."

WRITING ACTIVITY 9

What is your writing process like? Is writing a discovery draft like shaping a lump of clay? Is it like cooking a meal from raw ingredients? Baking a cake? Practicing a new sport? Write a paragraph that begins with this opening: "For me, writing a draft is like . . ."

Good paragraphs are built from supporting details—examples, facts, stories, and reasons that enable readers to understand the writer's point. How do experienced writers decide how many details are enough to support a topic sentence? They make this decision by reconsidering their purpose and audience. Here are some questions they consider.

QUESTIONS TO ASK YOURSELF ABOUT PARAGRAPH DEVELOPMENT

- How familiar is my reader with me and with my topic?
- What might my reader want to know about my topic?
- What kinds of details should I include in the paragraph to develop or to prove my main point to this reader?
- How specific should these details be to help my reader understand exactly what I mean?

WRITING ACTIVITY 10

Choose one of the following topics, and do five minutes of brainstorming or clustering about it. Examine your notes and develop a main point that you want to make about this topic. Think about a purpose for writing and an audience, and compose a topic sentence about your main point. Then do five minutes of brainstorming or clustering about your main idea, your purpose, and your audience. Use your notes to write a discovery draft of a paragraph that develops or supports your topic sentence. (See ''Questions to Consider As You Compose a Discovery Draft'' on page 39 of this chapter.)

- A friend
- A pet
- A favorite place
- A problem in school
- A film or video that you loved or hated
- A problem in your neighborhood

USING SPECIFIC LANGUAGE

All words have meanings that you can find in a dictionary, but people often add their own shades of meanings to these words. For example, what do you mean when you talk or write about a ''good'' friend? A ''fun'' night? A ''bad'' movie? A ''lot'' of money? Your answers to these questions will differ from those of other people. Thus, you must spell out exactly what you mean so that your readers will understand your ideas.

You need to think about what your readers already know about your topic and what they know about you. For example, suppose you wrote the following sentence. How do you determine whether it is specific enough?

The school that I went to was *awful.*

If this sentence were part of a letter to your family or close friends, its vague language (''the school,'' ''awful'') would be acceptable. Family and friends would know exactly what you were referring to. However, if the sentence were part of a college essay, readers would find it very vague: What school? When did you go there? What do you mean by ''awful''? What was so bad about this school?

School is a vague word. A more specific term for school might be *elementary school* or *high school.* ''Hilton Falls Elementary School'' is even more specific. Use the most specific words you can think of. (Also, see pages 318–323 about using a thesaurus to find precise synonyms for vague words.)

WRITING ACTIVITY 11

In the space given, rewrite each group of words in order from most general to most specific. The first one has been done as an example.

1. cat, Siamese, animal, pet

   animal, cat, pet, Siamese

2. goalie, athlete, hockey player, person

   ____

3. orange, citrus fruit, tree, plant

   ____

4. school, University of Texas, building, college

   ____

5. soda, liquid, Diet Pepsi, cola

   ____

Strong paragraphs have details that are *concrete* and *sensory.* A concrete word or phrase refers to a thing that is touchable, a thing that can be seen or heard or touched. For example, *desk* is a concrete word, but *peace* is not. *Peace* is an abstract term—it refers to a concept that we cannot see or touch.

A sensory word refers to a quality that we know through one of our five senses (sight, hearing, smell, taste, and touch). The phrase *brand-new steel computer desk gleaming like a silvery mirror* creates a sensory image that helps a reader see the object from the writer's perspective. Concrete and sensory words communicate ideas more clearly than do abstract words. They enable readers to understand exactly what the writer means.

For example, here are some details from a story by a reporter for the Louisville, Kentucky, *Courier Journal.*

> Gaunt, glassy-eyed and passionless, they crouch in the heat amid thousands of others, hungry and diseased. They stoop over small, dry plots of rock-hard soil. And they wait. They wait in tight lines for hours to get today's ration of food from international relief agencies: a bowl of rice, gruel, two bananas, a bucket of brown drinking water. But what kind of sanctuary is it? For many it's a rectangle of bare, hard ground the size of a desktop. It's a plastic sheet for cover, so low overhead that it rubs the noses of some who sleep. It's this searing odor of sweat, defecation and death. It's the ceaseless buzzing of a million flies and the hack of 10,000 coughs. Death and destruction. Seven million Cambodians have been caught between the two since 1975.

Notice the sensory details the reporter uses: sights, sounds, smells, and feelings. How did these details add to your experience as a reader? For instance, the writer recorded the buzzing of flies. Did you hear them too? Without concrete, sensory details, writing is dry and boring.

> There are approximately one million Cambodians living in overcrowded refugee camps because of the invading Khmer Rouge and Vietnamese.

WRITING ACTIVITY 12

Rewrite each vague sentence in the space given. Add concrete, sensory words to create distinct images that a reader can imagine, or make up specific details to include in each sentence. The first one has been done as an example.

1. The fire was really scary.

The purple tongues of flame from the fire terrified me.

2. I felt great about doing well on my math test.

3. The breakfast I ate this morning was terrible.

4. The rotting garbage smelled gross.

5. The child is gorgeous.

6. The music video was awesome.

Here are guidelines for making your writing more specific.

HOW TO MAKE YOUR DETAILS MORE SPECIFIC

Here are some strategies for making the details in your paragraphs more effective.

- Refer to people or objects by their exact names. (For example, rather than writing *a famous Native American writer,* use the person's name: *N. Scott Momaday.*)
- Use specific words rather than general ones. (For instance, instead of writing *The woman has a cool car,* use specific words: *Diane Feng, the vice president of Feng Computer Systems, has a gleaming new black BMW.*)
- Use sensory words that illustrate sights, sounds, smells, tastes, textures, and feelings. (Rather than describing a pie as *a cherry pie,* use words that enable readers to see and taste it: *an oozing pink cherry pie tasting so sweet it made my teeth ache.*)
- Use precise verbs to express emotions and actions. (For example, instead of writing that someone *walked* across a room, use an expressive verb, such as *rambled, strutted, strolled,* or *sauntered.*)

Here is an example of a student paragraph that includes specific details to support the writer's main idea.

Oranges are good for your health. Doctors and medical researchers have observed that people who eat oranges daily have more resistance to illness than do people who don't eat oranges. They don't catch colds often, and when they do get sick, they recover in only two or three days. This resistance may be due to all the Vitamin C that an orange has. Moreover, some scientists have noted that taking Vitamin C, particularly the kind in citrus fruits like oranges, can lessen the risk of cancer. Finally, the sugar in oranges gives people added energy, particularly if they eat this delicious fruit at the end of the day. Tangy, tart, and sweet—oranges are a wonderful way to stay healthy.

WRITING ACTIVITY 13

Plan and write a paragraph describing your favorite food. Include details that appeal to all five senses to make the reader experience this food as you have.

GROUP WORK 4

Exchange the description that you wrote for Writing Activity 13 with a classmate. Read your partner's description. Then write answers to the following questions, and give your answers to your partner.

1. What is the topic sentence of this paragraph (if it has one)? What are the key words that express the writer's opinion?
2. Which supporting details were most effective in conveying the writer's impression of his or her favorite food?
3. Which words helped you see, hear, smell, taste, and feel this food?
4. Where does the writer need to add more specific sensory words and images?
5. Are any details or sentences unrelated to the topic sentence? If so, which ones?
6. What suggestions do you have for improving this paragraph?

Have you ever been asked to describe someone? This kind of assignment requires specific details, but where do you begin? How can you describe a person in a paragraph or an essay? Here are some guidelines.

DEVELOPING A TOPIC SENTENCE AND SUPPORTING DETAILS FOR A DESCRIPTION OF A PERSON

Write down answers to the following questions.

1. Exactly who is this person? What is your relationship to him or her?
2. What is most striking about this person? What is your single dominant impression of him or her?

(Continued)

3. What characteristics or qualities of the person contribute to your dominant impression of him or her? For example, how do the person's looks, clothing, voice, or behavior contribute to your dominant impression?
4. What else about this person's character, personality, or use of language contributes to your dominant impression of him or her?

WRITING ACTIVITY 14

Here is a draft of a paragraph describing a writer's friend. Analyze the effectiveness of this paragraph by answering the questions that follow it.

I have a good friend named Maria Vasquez. One day I lost my wallet. I looked all over my house. I looked under my bed and in my desk. I opened my favorite desk drawer and looked inside. My wallet wasn't there. I needed money to buy some aspirin. I had a terrible headache and I really needed this medicine. So I called Maria. She immediately understood my problem. She went to her bank machine and got money. Then she went to the drugstore. My headache got better. Another time Maria loaned me $100 because my financial aid check was late. I really needed the money. I was afraid I would get closed out of my required courses. Finally, Maria bought me a beautiful coat for my birthday. She must have saved up for months to get this wonderful present for me. But sometimes she's not so generous.

1. Does this draft have a topic sentence? If so what is it? If not, what dominant impression does the writer mention?
2. Write a topic sentence stating what you think the writer is trying to communicate about her friend Maria.
3. Which sentences do not focus on Maria or on the writer's dominant impression of Maria? Cross them out.

4. How can the writer improve this draft? Reread the guidelines "Developing a Topic Sentence and Supporting Details for a Description of a Person" earlier in this chapter. Write down some suggestions for details that the writer might add to support her dominant impression of her friend.

WRITING ACTIVITY 15

Write a paragraph about a person you know well. Begin by freewriting, brainstorming, or clustering about him or her. Decide on your dominant impression of the person: Ask yourself what word best describes this person. Use this word to write a topic sentence about your main impression of the person. Then develop details that illustrate this impression, and shape these details into a paragraph. Use sensory words and images to enable readers to see, hear, and imagine this person.

GROUP WORK 5

Here are eight questions for you and two or three partners to use to help you improve your descriptive paragraphs. Take out the paragraph that you wrote for Writing Activity 15 (or for another activity in this chapter). Exchange papers with a partner, and answer the following questions on a separate piece of paper.

1. What do you think was the writer's purpose in this paragraph?
2. Does the paragraph have a topic sentence? If so, what is it?
3. Which supporting details were most effective in conveying the writer's impression of the person, place, or thing he or she is writing about?
4. Which words helped you see, hear, and sense this subject?
5. Where does the writer need to add more specific sensory words and images?
6. Are any details or sentences unrelated to the topic sentence? If so, which ones?
7. Does the organization and development of this paragraph seem logical to you? If not, which parts are confusing or do not seem logically related to each other?
8. What suggestions do you have for improving this paragraph?

ORGANIZING DETAILS LOGICALLY

The order that you select for organizing your paragraphs depends on the kinds of details you have written. Following are three common patterns of paragraph organization.

Arrange Details Chronologically (in Time Order). Chronological order is effective if your details tell a story, describe a process, or describe a series of actions that take place one after another. Here is a paragraph that a student developed chronologically to support her belief that "lakes are usually not good places for swimming." Note how the writer organized her details according to time order.

Lakes are usually not good places for swimming. I discovered this insight when I was younger, and my family took weekly trips to a nearby lake. Every time we went to Friend's Lake, the first things I noticed were the catfish at the lake's edge. I saw the spiny whiskers around their mouths, and I was sure that they would bite my toes (like cats do). My father would laugh at me and run into the water, splashing right through the catfish. Still I was never convinced. I would stare at the lake's edge and focus on the thick layer of green scum bubbling up from every place my father put his heavy foot. One day, I noticed a thick black head emerge from the scum. It was a snake! Right then and there, I promised myself I would never ever swim in a lake.

WRITING ACTIVITY 16

The events in the paragraph that follows are not organized chronologically. Unscramble the details and rewrite the paragraph so that it develops in logical time order.

Anyone can change a broken light bulb safely if he or she follows a series of steps. Then you can turn on the light switch. Turn off the light switch. That's the most important first step. Next throw away the old bulb. If the light is on the ceiling, get a stable ladder or chair in order to get the light bulb cover off the bulb. Once the bulb cover is off, touch the burned-out bulb gently and quickly to see if it is still hot. Afterwards, screw in the new bulb. If it is hot, use a towel to unscrew the bulb. If everything went well, you should now be staring at your newly glowing bulb. Do not, at this point, stick your finger into the exposed light socket.

WRITING ACTIVITY 17

Write a discovery draft of a paragraph based on one of these topics. Use chronological order to organize your details.

- My first day on a new job
- The time I met my best friend
- My first day at college
- The birth of my child
- An experience I will never forget
- A frightening experience

Arrange Details Spatially (in Order of Location). If your purpose is to describe a person, place, or object, you can arrange your details the way they are arranged in space. Imagine you are a video camera panning the object being described: Move from top to bottom, left to right, far to near, inside to outside, or vice versa. Make sure that your reader can follow the logic of your spatial order. Here is a paragraph in which the writer arranged her details in the order of their location in a room.

Each evening, I retire to my bedroom, feeling as if I am walking into a palace. I open the door and slowly step into the middle of the room. Six feet in front of me is a huge window. Through it I can see the heavy branches of an ancient maple tree which drape across my house. To the left of the window is a fireplace surrounded by two pink and brown Queen

Anne chairs. Next to the chairs is my canopy bed, pushed up tightly against the wall. The bedspread and the canopy are both patterned in dark green and wine-colored brocade. The pattern matches the emerald green carpet covering the entire floor. Behind me, next to the door, is an antique writing table furnished with brass accessories, like an old ink well and a letter opener. Directly above me is a Georgian-style chandelier with four glass candles. This is a room fit for a queen.

WRITING ACTIVITY 18

Look back through your Idea Bank for a topic that could be developed with descriptive details. If you cannot find an idea you want to develop, think about a special place or room and what it means to you. Do some freewriting, brainstorming, or clustering to get started. Ask yourself the five W questions and what-if questions to generate additional details about your topic. Write a discovery draft of a paragraph describing this topic or place. Organize your details spatially.

Arrange Details Emphatically (in Order of Importance). Many paragraphs can be arranged from least important to most important. When you use this organization, you build your details logically, saving the most interesting or important points for the end of the paragraph. (Because this order emphasizes the last detail, it is called ‘‘emphatic.’’) Emphatic organization is appropriate for any paragraph composed of facts, examples, and reasons. Here is a student example.

Last night was one of the most special nights of my life. It was my thirtieth birthday party. Apparently, my family and friends had collected donations from many people since they felt that my first three decades of life deserved special recognition. I am the American Dream come true. Raised in a rat-infested tenement in the South Bronx, I used my gift as the class clown to pursue a comedy career. After graduating from college, I got my first break on the Danny Menello show. I made people laugh by depicting the often comic adventures of my parents trying to feed a family of six on welfare and food stamps. Now those days are over, and I am happy and successful. But the most satisfying part of my life is the love and respect of my friends and my family. I am grateful to them for always encouraging me.

WRITING ACTIVITY 19

Look through your Idea Bank or your freewriting, brainstorming, or clustering notes. Select a topic that could be developed with a series of examples arranged from least important to most important. If you cannot find an idea you want to develop think about a special experience and what it meant to you. Write a discovery draft of a paragraph describing this topic. Organize your details emphatically.

A paragraph that stands alone or a long paragraph within an essay should end with a concluding sentence that restates or comments on the main point. This concluding sentence is often called a ''clincher sentence'' because it lets the reader know that you have decisively ended (''clinched'') your point. One strategy for ending a paragraph is to write a concluding sentence that echoes the idea of the topic sentence *in different words.* Another strategy is to draw a conclusion about the points you developed in the paragraph. You can also make a recommendation based on your points. Or you can end a paragraph with a question for the reader to ponder. Whichever strategy you use, make sure that the final sentence of each paragraph sounds like an ending (rather than as if you simply got tired and stopped writing).

WRITING ACTIVITY 20

Write a discovery draft of a paragraph based on one of the topics below. Use emphatic order to organize your details.

- An important problem that many teenagers have
- An important problem that many parents have
- Reasons you enjoy a particular sport or hobby
- Reasons you do or do not smoke cigarettes

Make sure that you end the paragraph with a clincher sentence that sums up the main idea of the paragraph and lets readers know that the paragraph is finished.

Use the following checklist to help you identify problems in your discovery drafts and to get readers' responses to them. Ask family, friends, and classmates to answer the questions.

DISCOVERY DRAFT CHECKLIST

1. Does the paragraph have a clear topic sentence that expresses the writer's main point or opinion?
2. Is the topic sentence appropriate for the paragraph, or is it too general or too narrow?
3. Are the details appropriate for the writer's purpose and audience?
4. Does the draft have enough details to accomplish the writer's purpose?
5. Are there any details or sentences that don't seem logically related to the topic sentence?
6. Which details include specific and concrete language? Which details are too vague?
7. Can you follow the order in which the details are developed? Is there a more appropriate way of organizing these details?
8. Does the paragraph have an effective clincher sentence?
9. What suggestions do you have for improving this draft?

EXPLORING FURTHER

Recently, the United States Postal Service issued a new stamp commemorating the singer Elvis Presley. Here is a picture of this stamp.

If you were asked to nominate a person for a commemorative stamp, whom would you choose? In your opinion, what person—living or dead—has made the most important contributions to our country or to our society? Who deserves to be memorialized by having his or her picture on a federal postage stamp?

Plan a composition about the person you would nominate for this honor. Use the prewriting activities that you have practiced in Chapter 1 and in this chapter:

1. Think about the person you want to nominate for a commemorative stamp. What feelings and thoughts come to your mind? Why is (or was) he or she so important?
2. Talk about this person with friends, family, and classmates. Write down their reactions and responses. Get feedback from as many people as you can.
3. Explore your feelings and thoughts about your subject's accomplishments or contributions to society by freewriting, brainstorming, clustering, asking yourself the five W questions, and asking yourself what-if questions.
4. Focus your ideas, and develop a topic sentence which identifies the person and states that you are nominating him or her for a commemorative stamp.

WRITING ASSIGNMENT

Write a discovery draft of a paragraph (or several paragraphs) describing the person you think should be honored by the post office with a commemorative stamp. Imagine that your readers are classmates who do not know this person. Your purpose is to help them understand why your nominee's contributions to our society are or were so important.

POINTS TO REMEMBER ABOUT PLANNING AND WRITING STRONG PARAGRAPHS

1. Use prewriting activities to explore your topic. Experiment with freewriting, brainstorming, clustering, asking yourself the five W questions, and asking yourself what-if questions.
2. Choose one main point that you want to describe or support in a paragraph.
3. Write a topic sentence about this main point—a complete sentence that is clear and specific and that is not too general or too narrow for a paragraph.
4. Think about your purpose for writing and about your readers' expectations.

5. Use freewriting or clustering to develop appropriate stories, facts, examples, or reasons to support your topic sentence.
6. Select supporting details that are relevant to your topic sentence.
7. Make sure that you have provided a sufficient number of details to accomplish your purpose (given the audience for whom you are writing).
8. Use specific, concrete language and descriptive words that appeal to readers' five senses.
9. Make sure that your details are organized logically in an order that readers will be able to follow.
10. End with a clincher sentence that sums up the paragraph or that restates the topic sentence in different words.

CHAPTER 3

REVISING AND EDITING

Speaking and writing are similar in many ways. However, one aspect of writing makes it more precise and effective than verbal communication: revision. Once you open your mouth and say something, you cannot ''revise'' your speech. It has been said and heard. However, after you write something, you can always change your words before anyone reads them.

For this reason, almost all successful writers know that good writing requires revision. They recognize that a first draft is closer to speech than to writing because it is spontaneous and not fully thought out. They know that they will have to rethink, reword, and rewrite. Indeed, the novelist James Michener—whose books have sold millions of copies—once said, ''I'm probably the world's worst writer. But I'm the world's best rewriter.''

STEP 6: RETHINK AND REVISE YOUR DRAFT

How do experienced writers shape a draft into a finished, polished piece? They read the draft over and over, each time focusing on a different problem. In their first revision, they may look for ways to clarify the main point and add more supporting details. Next, they might try to identify and cross out words or sentences that are confusing or that don't relate clearly to the main point. When they revise the draft again, they might concentrate on the organization, looking for ways to make the connections between their ideas and sentences clearer. Then, they edit for errors in sentence structure, grammar, diction, spelling, and punctuation. Finally, they proofread for handwriting or typing errors.

Not every piece of writing needs to be revised four or five times. However, any writing that matters to you deserves your attention and your effort at each stage of its planning, drafting, revising, and editing.

WRITING ACTIVITY 1

What are your reactions to what you read in the preceding paragraphs about revising and editing a draft several times? Here are some questions to help you analyze your attitudes toward revising. Write your answers in your Idea Bank or on a separate piece of paper.

1. After you have written a paragraph or an essay, what do you do to it before you hand it in to your teacher? Do you revise it? If so, how?
2. If you do not revise, why not? How did you come to feel that revising is unimportant or unnecessary?
3. Do you think that revising can help you improve your writing? Why or why not?

Try to leave some time between writing a discovery draft and revising it. You may feel drained from composing the draft. Also, the writing is very fresh in your mind, and you may find it difficult to see places where the details and connections are missing or are confusing. Thus, before you revise a draft, you should get some distance from it so that you will be able to read it from the perspective of your intended readers. Here are some techniques for gaining this distance.

TECHNIQUES FOR GAINING DISTANCE FROM YOUR DRAFT

- Put the draft away for several hours (or for a day if you can), so that you forget what you were thinking when you wrote the draft. This makes it easier for you to read and evaluate the actual words you have written (without being influenced by what was in your mind as you wrote).
- Adopt an imagined reader's perspective. Think about this reader's personality, concerns, interests, values. Consider how he or she will respond to your writing.
- Pretend to be the reader for whom you are writing. Reread your draft from this reader's perspective to see if the reader would be confused by any parts.

- Read the draft aloud so that you can hear where it sounds strong and effective and where it is confusing and unclear. Or ask a friend or relative to read it aloud, and take notes on the problems in the draft as you listen to it.

In Chapters 1 and 2, you learned how to plan and write discovery drafts of paragraphs. This chapter shows you how to evaluate, revise, and edit your drafts for the most important qualities of good writing—focus, development, unity, coherence, and correctness.

FIVE IMPORTANT QUALITIES OF GOOD WRITING

- *Focus:* Each paragraph has a clear main point or topic sentence.
- *Development:* Each paragraph supports the main point with enough specific details.
- *Unity:* Each paragraph sticks to its main point.
- *Coherence:* Each paragraph is organized logically and flows smoothly.
- *Correctness:* Each paragraph has complete sentences that are error-free.

Begin revising by looking for strengths in your writing—for sentences and words that you really like. Try to figure out what you did to achieve these effective parts so that you can improve the weak parts. Here are additional strategies for revising.

- Ask a friend, relative, or classmate to respond to your paper.
- Reread your details: Did you provide enough relevant, specific details to support your main point?
- Add new ideas, details, and descriptive words.
- Cross out ideas, sentences, and words that do not sound logical or interesting or that are not clearly related to your main point.
- Cross out sentences or words that are repetitious.
- Use circles and arrows to indicate how sentences or words should be reorganized.
- Use scissors and tape to cut out sentences or parts of sentences and move them to different places in the draft.

The first strategy—asking for feedback from readers—is the most important one. If you want to see how professional writers use this strategy, watch a copy of the film *All the President's Men* (about the Watergate scandal that brought down the Nixon administration). This film profiles the way professional writers work. In one scene, one writer (played by Dustin Hoffman) finishes a draft of a newspaper story and puts it in a bin for publication. Another writer (played by Robert Redford) walks by the bin, picks up the story, reads it, and begins making changes in the story. When the Hoffman character questions the Redford character about what he is doing, Redford answers, "I'm improving it." Then Hoffman reads Redford's changes and says, "You're right. Your version is better."

The point is one that all successful writers know: Sharing your writing and getting feedback on how to revise it is one of the most important parts of the writing process. In the writing activities in the preceding chapters, you have shared your paragraphs with classmates, discussed ways of improving your drafts, and revised your drafts based on classmates' suggestions—just as professional writers do.

REVISING FOR FOCUS: THE TOPIC SENTENCE

As you have learned, the topic sentence helps you and your reader focus on your main idea. Make sure that the topic sentence of each paragraph is appropriate for your purpose and for your intended audience. Ask yourself the following questions about your topic sentence.

1. Is my topic sentence a complete sentence?
2. Does it have key words that limit the topic—that express my opinion or the point that I want to make about the topic?
3. Is my topic sentence too narrow or too broad?
4. Will my readers understand my purpose for writing this paragraph?

If your answer to any of these questions is "No" or "I'm not sure," then rewrite your topic sentence.

Here is an example of a student's attempt to revise a descriptive paragraph that she had written for a school assignment. The topic sentence is in italics. Note that the writer began revising by asking herself the preceding questions.

Draft

Before they printed an Elvis Presley stamp, the United States Postal Service conducted a survey. The post office designed two stamps, one of Elvis in his twenties and one in his late thirties. The survey showed that the public preferred the young Elvis. So they printed a commemorative stamp of the young Elvis. This stamp has a pink background instead of a black velvet background (which would be more appropriate for Elvis art). Also once the stamp goes out of circulation, there will probably be a rash of annoying Elvis-stamp sightings! Most importantly, why has the federal post office put the face of a rock star on a commemorative stamp if he made a mess of his life at the end? He died an alcohol abuser and a drug abuser. Is that what we want young people to look up to?

Here are the writer's answers to the preceding questions about her topic sentence.

1. Yes, my topic sentence is a complete sentence.
2. No, this topic sentence doesn't have key words that limit the topic. It doesn't focus on one main idea, and it doesn't express my disgust with the stamp.
3. My topic sentence is too narrow (it states a fact).
4. Readers will probably be confused because the details in the paragraph don't really relate to my first sentence.

Here is this writer's revised topic sentence and paragraph.

Revision

The new "Elvis" stamp makes me sick. I cannot understand why the United States Postal Service has printed a commemorative stamp of Elvis Presley. The stamp, which has a flashy pink background, shows Elvis at the height of his career when he was young. It does not give any indication of what the singer turned into as he aged. He abused alcohol and drugs, and he died of an overdose of a mixture of drugs. Elvis Presley may have been a world-famous singing star, but he was also an alcoholic and drug addict. Putting a drug abuser on a commemorative stamp sends the wrong message to teenagers. By glorifying Elvis, it glorifies his destructive life-style. Is that really what the post office should commemorate?

The revised topic sentence is more focused than the original, and it lets readers know what to expect from the remainder of the paragraph. Now the topic sentence has key words—''makes me sick''—that helped the writer develop new details to support one main idea.

GROUP WORK 1

Form a group with two or three students, and work together to revise the topic sentence of the following student paragraph.

American space exploration began in the late 1950s with unmanned rocket launches. In 1969, American astronauts landed on the moon. This landing was the crowning glory of the United States space program. The scientific and technological breakthroughs that made this achievement possible became a source of national pride. Unfortunately, this positive feeling did not last too long. After three years, the Apollo moon missions ended, and in the 1970s, there was almost no American space exploration. However, the 1980s saw the beginning of the space shuttle missions, almost all of which were incredible successes. These missions made space exploration a source of national pride. Once again it is a symbol of American determination and ingenuity.

1. What do you think this writer's purpose was in this paragraph?
2. Is the writer's topic sentence appropriate for this purpose? Why or why not?
3. Does the topic sentence have key words that express the writer's attitude and that limit the details that can be used to develop the paragraph?
4. Revise the topic sentence so that it focuses on the details that the rest of the paragraph developed.

WRITING ACTIVITY 2

Take out a paragraph that you wrote for a Writing Activity or a Writing Assignment in one of the preceding chapters. As you reread the paragraph's topic sentence, ask yourself the four topic sentence questions on page 58. Revise your topic sentence to make it more focused and more specific.

REVISING FOR DEVELOPMENT: SUPPORTING DETAILS

After you revise your topic sentence, you will probably have to revise the details that support it. In order to do this, read your draft carefully and critically. Reading critically does not mean tearing your writing apart looking for errors. Rather it means analyzing the paragraph or essay and questioning its effectiveness. (The word *critical* comes from the Greek word for "question.") When we read critically, we examine our writing to see if it makes sense, if it is believable, and if it is logically developed.

The best way to read critically is to reread your writing from the perspective of your intended readers. Here are some questions for you to consider about your purpose and audience.

QUESTIONS FOR CRITICAL READING

1. Was my purpose to *express* my feelings or to *share* something important with my readers? If so, will they find my story or my examples believable and interesting?
2. Was my purpose to *explain* something to readers? If so, will they understand my examples and reasons? Will they find them logical?
3. Was my purpose to *persuade* readers to think or feel or do something? If so, will they be convinced by my reasons?
4. Which details in my paragraph are very specific and convincing? Which images are clear and concrete? How can I build on these strengths to improve the weak parts?
5. Are there places in the paragraph where the reader might respond by saying "Huh? What do you mean?" or "Give me an example"? If there are, what kinds of facts, examples, and reasons should I add?

Experiences, Examples, and Reasons. Most advancing writers underestimate the reader's need for concrete details and for specific examples and reasons. If you suspect that your draft does not have enough specific supporting details to achieve your purpose, ask yourself the five W questions. In addition, do some more freewriting, brainstorming, and clustering to develop new experiences, examples, and reasons. If you think that some of your details are not clearly related to your main point, either cross them out or add words that explain how they relate. Read critically: If a detail is unclear or is not logically related to your main idea, cross it out. No matter how hard you worked to develop a detail or a sentence, if it doesn't clearly support your point, it doesn't belong in the paragraph.

Here is an example of how a student evaluated and revised his draft for focus and development. Note the marginal comments that this writer wrote to himself as he reread his draft. Next, read his answers to "Questions for Critical Reading." Finally, read his revision.

Put "lessons" first??

Draft

Now that a Florida court has acquitted members of the Black rap group 2 Live Crew of obscenity charges, we can learn three important lessons. First people who rush to censor music often end up doing the opposite. *unclear?* Most people would never have even heard of this group if it wasn't for the legal action. The verdict actually helped the group sell more records. The second lesson is that America is a free country. The Russians know that. ~~And~~ *Finally* lesson three is that taking rap music to court is just absurd. It's *What?* so absurd that the jurors complained that they were having physical pain from holding in their laughter, so the judge gave them permission to laugh out loud! *Ending??*

Explain why are you writing about Russians here?

Here are the writer's answers to "Questions for Critical Reading."

1. My purpose is to persuade readers (people interested in rap music) to think the way that I do, that suing rap groups for obscene lyrics is stupid and counterproductive. I don't think readers will be convinced by my reasons.

2. My details seem specific, but I see that I didn't explain my point about America being a free country. I guess I need to be more specific about this.
3. I think my point about censorship having the opposite result is pretty clear.
4. My image of the jury laughing out loud is clear and concrete.
5. My point about Russians and censorship—even if I explain it more—doesn't seem to relate to the topic sentence. Rap has nothing to do with Russians.

Here is the writer's revision.

Revision

We can learn three important lessons from the recent court case in which members of the Black rap group 2 Live Crew were acquitted of obscenity charges. First, the case showed that people who rush to censor music often end up publicizing rather than removing the target of their wrath. Most Americans would never have heard of this group if it had not been for the legal action. Thanks to the publicity it created, this court case actually helped 2 Live Crew sell more records. The second lesson that this case proved is that America is a free country. The Constitution guarantees all citizens—including rappers—the right to free speech. If the public doesn't like the lyrics in a song, they can switch the radio channel, not buy the record, or boycott the record company. Finally, the third lesson is that suing musical groups is stupid. This case was so absurd that the jurors complained that they were having physical pain from holding in their laughter, so the judge gave them permission to laugh out loud. Undoubtedly, 2 Live Crew is laughing all the way to the bank.

This example illustrates the importance of revision. By rereading and rewriting this paragraph several times, the writer clarified and tightened his ideas. The topic sentence of the revision is clearer, and the supporting details are more specific and descriptive. In addition, the writer eliminated unnecessary details and added more specific reasons. This made the revision more focused and more convincing than the draft.

REMINDER

Examine your draft's supporting details to see if they are concrete and specific and if they clearly support your main point. Decide whether you have enough supporting details to accomplish your purpose in writing the paragraph.

WRITING ACTIVITY 3

Take out the prewriting notes or clusters that you wrote for a Writing Activity in one of the preceding chapters. Write a discovery draft of a paragraph based on these notes. When you finish writing, put away your draft for several hours. Then reread it, asking yourself the questions about the topic sentence on page 58 of this chapter and the questions in "Questions for Critical Reading on page 61." If your examples or reasons don't accomplish your purpose, do some more prewriting to develop additional supporting details. Revise the paragraph until you think your intended readers will find it clear and effective.

WRITING ACTIVITY 4

How effective are the topic sentence and supporting details in the paragraph below? Answer the five questions that follow the paragraph.

The first civil rights riot to receive national attention occurred in Harlem, New York City, in the summer of 1964. The riot erupted two days after an off-duty policeman shot a 15-year-old black youth. It was like Rodney King and the riot in Los Angeles. Riots can really be bad. In the 1964 riot, crowds of people roamed the streets, breaking windows, looting stores, and menacing the policemen. The police fired their guns into the night sky. One protestor died and 144 were injured. People always get hurt in these situations. They got hurt in the Rodney King riot. They got hurt in other riots. There has to be a better way to achieve racial justice.

1. What do you think the writer's purpose was?

   ____

2. Does the paragraph have a topic sentence? If so, what is it? If not, what would you suggest as a topic sentence for this paragraph?

   ____

   ____

3. Does each experience, example, and reason support the writer's main idea? If not, cross it out.
4. Does the paragraph accomplish the writer's purpose? If not, where does it need additional or different details? Add these details.
5. Are the details specific enough? Do they contain sensory images that enable readers to experience details from the writer's perspective? If not, circle the places where more specific details are needed and add them.

Write your revision of this paragraph on a separate piece of paper.

WRITING ACTIVITY 5

Think of a television or film star that you admire. For five minutes, close your eyes and become this person. Imagine yourself doing something that this person does very well. What are you doing? What are you thinking? What do you see, hear, touch, smell, and taste? How do you feel? Write a draft of a paragraph describing your imagined experience as this celebrity. You might want to write about "a day in the life" of this person or about an experience that you imagine this person having. Make up specific details, and use concrete sensory language in your description.

WRITING ACTIVITY 6

Take out the draft that you wrote for Writing Activity 5. Find a person you think is a competent *reader* to help you revise this paragraph. Ask your reader to answer these four questions.

1. What do you think was my purpose in this paragraph?
2. Does each experience, example, and reason support the main idea of the paragraph? Which ones do not?
3. In your opinion, does the paragraph accomplish my purpose? If not, where does it need additional or different details?
4. Are the details specific enough? Do they contain sensory images that enable you to experience details from my perspective? If not, where are more specific sensory details needed?

Take notes as the person responds. Repeat this activity with several different readers. Then, reconsider the focus, purpose, and audience for the draft. Decide which of your readers' suggestions you should include in your revision. Revise the paragraph as many times as necessary to accomplish your purpose for writing it.

WRITING ACTIVITY 7

Plan and write a paragraph about your first college registration. Develop a purpose for writing: Do you want to entertain your readers with stories about this experience? Do you want to describe your first registration and explain your reactions to it? Or do you want to persuade readers to believe something based on your experience?

After you finish writing your draft, examine it to identify places where you need additional supporting details. Add additional experiences, examples, and reasons. Then use all the techniques that you have learned in this chapter to determine which parts need to be revised. Revise the paragraph to make it clearer and more specific.

Facts, Statistics, and Testimony. Another strategy for revising the ideas and details in your paragraphs is to add facts and statistics. *Facts* and *statistics* give truths that can be verified. Facts are statements, and statistics are figures, percentages, and measurements. Suppose you state a fact—such as the date of an event—or give a statistic—such as the size of an object. Readers can determine whether what you have written is true or false.

Facts and statistics are effective details for explaining or supporting a topic sentence. For example, which detail in each pair below communicates the writer's point more effectively? Why?

A. The New York City public school system is very big and costs a lot of money.
B. The New York City public school system has about 983,000 students and a budget of about $7.4 billion.

C. The dropout rate in the New York City public school system is pretty low compared with the rate in the Los Angeles system, which is really high.
D. The dropout rate in the New York City public school system is relatively low—17 percent as compared with the high rate in the Los Angeles system—38 percent.

Use facts and statistics to convince your readers of your points.

Another type of supporting detail that achieves this goal is *testimony*. Testimony consists of statements by people you know or by experts you have heard (at lectures, on the radio, or on television). Testimony also includes summaries or quotations from books, newspapers, journals, magazines, and class notes. Here is an example of the use of expert testimony to support a point.

> New York State does not contribute enough money to the education of students in New York City public schools. In 1991, according to the chancellor of the New York City Public School System, Joseph A. Fernandez, New York State spent only about $5,100 per city pupil per year. This was much less than the $8,000 per pupil the state spent each year on students in public schools in suburban counties like Westchester.

Facts, statistics, and expert testimony are all effective material for developing and supporting your points. Below is a student paragraph illustrating the use of facts and statistics to support a topic sentence.

Two of the largest K–12 public school systems in this country are losing the battle against difficult burdens. According to *Newsweek,* the New York City system is educating 982,000 students with a budget of only $7.4 billion a year. Classes are outrageously overcrowded, with 35 to 50 students in a class. Also, there isn't enough money to purchase laboratory equipment or computers for more than half of the secondary schools. The 411,000 students in the Chicago public school system are also suffering. That budget is much less than New York's ($2.6 billion). And more than half the students (51.5 percent) drop out before high school graduation. Both systems lost their chancellors last year. New York's Board of Education did not rehire Joseph Fernandez, and Chicago's Ted Kimbrough resigned. Both public school systems are battling violence. Nearly half the high schools in both systems have weapons detectors to stop students from bringing guns to school. Both systems need new leaders and new money.

GROUP WORK 2

Form a group with two other students. Choose one person to record the group's answers to the following questions about the preceding paragraph.

1. What is the writer's topic sentence and purpose?
2. Which facts or statistics are most convincing in supporting this topic sentence?
3. What source does the writer cite for these facts and statistics?
4. Is this source reliable? Why or why not?
5. The preceding paragraph is a draft. What suggestions do you have for revision?

Here are some guidelines for adding statistics to your writing.

GUIDELINES FOR USING STATISTICS AS SUPPORTING DETAILS

1. Select your statistics from reliable sources and include the exact name of each source.
2. Make sure you understand what your numbers mean.
3. Use statistics sparingly and explain their importance. (Don't pile them up in your paragraph and leave it to your readers to interpret them.)

4. Hyphenate fractions: ''More than *one-half* of the students in Chicago public schools drop out before twelfth grade.''
5. Spell out (and hyphenate) numbers under 100: ''In other words, *fifty-one* out of every *100* students in Chicago public schools drop out before 12th grade.''
6. If a sentence begins with a number, spell out the number, even if it is higher than 100: ''*Two hundred nine thousand* students dropped out in 1991.''

When you use expert testimony to illustrate your points, make sure that the source is telling the truth and is *not* omitting information that doesn't fit his or her belief. Check whether the source is an acknowledged expert in the field that he or she is discussing. Finally, make sure that you write down the source's name or title as accurately as possible. Here is an example of the effective use of expert testimony.

The New York City public school system has accomplished several big improvements in the last five years. Students' attendance in grades K–12 is up, the dropout rate is down, and violent incidents are down. In his 1993 book, *Tales Out of School,* Joseph A. Fernandez (who was chancellor from 1989 to 1993), stated that "school attendance in New York City is the best it has been in twenty-five years, at a citywide high of 86.5 percent and over 90 percent in the elementary schools" (253). Fernandez also noted that "the dropout rate has plummeted to an under 7 percent annual rate, the lowest in school history" (253). Finally, serious incidents of violence in crime "peaked in the mid-'80s (5,233 in 1983–84) and were down to 3,843 in '91 (254)." These numbers are encouraging to parents whose children attend city public schools. They hope that the new chancellor will reinforce these improvements and will help administrators and teachers achieve new ones.

This writer decided that she needed to include Fernandez's exact words and numbers to illustrate her topic sentence. She quoted them as supporting details in her paragraph. If the writer had included Fernandez's words without citing him, she would be guilty of *plagiarism.* Plagiarism is a serious offense. Never borrow someone else's words or ideas and use them in your writing as if they were your own words or thoughts.

Quoting someone else's exact words is one way to add testimony to your writing. You do this by (1) copying the material exactly as it appears in the original, (2) enclosing it in quotation marks, and (3) identifying the source. (See pages 376–379 in Chapter 14 about how to use quotation marks correctly.)

If you want to summarize an important idea or detail that you have read or heard, you can *paraphrase* (write it in your own words). You don't need to enclose a paraphrase in quotation marks. However, you do need to identify the source of the information. Here is how the writer of the paragraph on page 69 revised her work so that she paraphrased her source instead of quoting him.

The New York City public school system has experienced several major improvements in the last five years. Students' attendance in grades K–12 is up, the dropout rate is down, and violent incidents are down. In his 1993 book, *Tales Out of School,* Joseph A. Fernandez noted that attendance in New York City public schools is the highest it has been in twenty-five years—about 86.5 percent (253). He also pointed out that in 1992, the citywide dropout rate was the lowest it had ever been—about 7 percent a year (253). Finally, serious incidents of violence in crime in New York City public schools were down to 3,843 from a high of 5,233 in the mid-1980s (254). These numbers are very encouraging to parents whose children attend city public schools. They hope that the new chancellor will reinforce these improvements and will help administrators and teachers achieve new ones.

GUIDELINES FOR USING TESTIMONY AS A SUPPORTING DETAIL

1. Copy down the words of the source (author or interviewee) exactly as they were said or written.

2. Check that the source is an expert on the topic.
3. When you quote or paraphrase a source in your paper, give the author's last name and the relevant page numbers. (See pages 376–379 in Chapter 14 about how to use quotation marks correctly.)
4. Academic disciplines have different guidelines for citing the source of a paraphrase or quotation. If your instructor doesn't tell you how to cite your sources (and how to write a list of the works that you cited), use the guidelines described in the 1988 edition of the *MLA Handbook for Writers of Research Papers* (Modern Language Association).
5. Interpret or evaluate the testimony you use so that readers will understand why you think it was important enough to be included in your paragraph.

WRITING ACTIVITY 8

Here is a paragraph about a person's use of heroin when he was a teenager. What do you think the writer's purpose was? Did his use of personal testimony help him achieve his purpose?

I thought of myself as a moderate weekend user [of heroin], but soon enough it wasn't uncommon to get high on Friday night, Saturday night, and Sunday night. I was never hooked. I never *had* to have it. But the fascinating thing was nobody knew we were doing it, or if they knew, they weren't saying. My parents didn't know. The schools were deaf, dumb, and blind to the problem in those days. They didn't even talk about drugs in sociology class or "effective living" courses. If a friend or family member was involved, it was swept under the rug. Even at Commerce [High School], where you could see drug deals going down in the hallways, no real concern was voiced about it.

Write your answer to each question in the space below it.

1. What do you think the writer was trying to show or to prove in this paragraph?

____

____

2. In your opinion, did the writer accomplish his purpose? Why or why not?

____

____

____

The author of the preceding paragraph is Dr. Joseph A. Fernandez, who was the chancellor of the New York City public school system when he wrote the book from which this paragraph comes.

3. What is your response to the fact that the preceding paragraph was written by the chancellor of the largest public school system in this country?

____

____

____

____

____

WRITING ACTIVITY 9

Here is Joseph Fernandez's assessment of his teenage heroin use and of drug use in general. How effective is his testimony about his personal experiences in supporting his main point?

You have to know how incredibly dumb that [using drugs] is. If you don't, you know it when the tragedies accumulate around you. . . . In our neighborhood, the tragic stories wrapped together like snakes in a sack. One of the first to go down in our group was a Puerto Rican boy, dead in his teens of an overdose. The only Indian in the group became an addict. A guy we called "skinny," for obvious reasons, went to jail for killing the attendant of a toll station that he tried to rob for drug money. They scuffled and a gun went off.

It was like a killer virus, the drug influence, infecting one life with another. The sister of a good friend of mine was one of the few girls in the neighborhood who used drugs. She married another user, and when they had a baby it was born physically impaired. Her husband became a heroin addict and died of an overdose, and she wound up a prostitute and living with Skinny's younger brother—who got stabbed to death in a bar fight over drugs. Then *she* died of an overdose. The grief caused by drugs still haunts that family.

WRITING ACTIVITY 10

What kinds of details would you write if you were asked to compose a paragraph explaining how or why teenage drug use is "incredibly dumb"? What experiences, examples, reasons, facts, statistics, or testimony would you include in this paragraph? Do some prewriting about this topic, and then develop a paragraph or two about it. When you finish writing your discovery draft, use the techniques that you have learned so far in this chapter to revise your paragraphs.

REMINDER

A strong paragraph has enough relevant experiences, examples, and reasons to develop and support its topic sentence and to achieve the writer's purpose. If the paragraph includes facts, statistics, and testimony as supporting details, the writer must paraphrase or quote them accurately and cite their sources correctly.

REVISING FOR LOGICAL ORGANIZATION

The details in a paragraph are like a house of cards—woven together in a tightly fitting pattern. If you add, delete, or move a detail, you might bring the whole house tumbling down. Thus, as you change the supporting details in your paragraphs, make sure the details fit together logically in an order that readers can follow. One way to do this is to draw circles around words or sentences and use arrows to indicate the places where these should be moved. Another technique is "cutting and pasting"—scissoring out sentences and taping them together in a new order. Writers who use computerized word processing programs can use the Insert, Move, and Replace functions of their programs to add, delete, and move sentences around.

Here are some critical reading questions for you to consider as you evaluate the organization of your drafts and revisions.

1. *If I used chronological (time) order,* did I arrange my details in the order in which they actually occurred? Did I leave out any points or steps?
2. *If I used spatial order,* did I organize my details in a way that will help readers to see what I am describing?
3. *If I used emphatic order (order of importance),* did I arrange my details from least to most important?

Read the following draft of a student paragraph. Are the descriptive details logically organized? Can you tell how they relate to each other?

Draft: My Office

My office at Redco Engineering is a perfect space for me to work in. As you enter the 10 foot by 10 foot square room, you can't help but notice the huge picture window. The only thing on the desk is my IBM computer, which leaves me plenty of room for paperwork. The window looks out onto a spectacular Hudson River view. My desk, a long glass block with brass legs, is in front of the window. To the right of the desk is a sky blue wall which doubles as a communications and entertainment network. On either side of the door are racks and racks of computer printouts. A speaker in the ceiling pipes in any kind of music I select from the channel on the right wall. The communication network is really neat. It has a built-in telephone, modem, and a fax machine. I wish I had a full-time job at Redco so I could spend more hours each day in this room.

After discussing this paragraph with her classmates, the writer realized that the spatial development was not logically organized. She revised the paragraph by imagining that she was standing in the middle of the room and looking from left to right. Here is her revision.

Revision: My Office

My office at Redco Engineering is a perfect space for me to work in. As I enter the 10 foot by 10 foot square room, the first thing I always notice is the huge picture window. This window looks out onto a spectacular Hudson River view. Directly in front of the window is my desk, a long glass block with brass legs. The only thing on the desk is my IBM computer, which leaves me plenty of room for paperwork. To the right of the desk is a sky blue wall which doubles as a communications and entertainment network. It has a built-in telephone, modem, and a fax machine. Next to the communications wall are two high-backed fluorescent blue chairs for people to sit in when we have group meetings. To the right of these chairs is the door through which I entered. On either side of the door are racks and racks of computer printouts, piled up to the ceiling. In the ceiling is a speaker which pipes in any kind of music I select from the channel on the left wall. This office has everything I need to work and to relax. I wish I had a full-time job at Redco so I could spend more hours each day in this room.

The final version is clearer and more interesting than the draft because the examples have been rearranged to improve the paragraph's organization. Now readers can understand the paragraph's organization.

WRITING ACTIVITY 11

This activity will help you improve your ability to identify and revise problems in logical development. The seven sentences below are not developed in a logical order. Rearrange them by numbering each (1, 2, 3, and so on). Then rewrite the sentences (on separate paper) using your new order to form a coherent paragraph.

______ Finally, some students drop out because they become so involved with alcohol or drugs that they can no longer function in school.
______ They simply do not have enough money to pay tuition and to support themselves or their families.
______ Either they lack the academic skills necessary to succeed, or they lack the motivation to do all of the required work.
______ Whatever their reason for leaving, college dropouts are depriving themselves of the opportunity to have fulfilling and rewarding future careers.
______ The major reason most of the dropouts I know left school was that they needed to work full-time.
______ There are several reasons students drop out of college.
______ Another reason people leave school is that they are unable to find satisfactory child care for their children.

WRITING ACTIVITY 12

Do you have children or are you planning to have children one day? Plan and write a paragraph about why you wanted or may want to become a parent *or* about why you do not want to have children. (Or plan and write a paragraph about the reasons people should or should not have children.) When you finish your draft, put it away for a while. Then revise it, using the strategies that you have learned in this chapter. Finally, evaluate your paragraph using "Questions for Critical Reading" (on page 61), and revise the paragraph again.

CHECKING FOR THE FIVE QUALITIES OF GOOD WRITING

So far, you have learned how to identify and revise problems in the two most important characteristics of effective writing—*focus* and *development.* The remainder of this chapter will help you evaluate and revise the *unity, coherence,* and *correctness* of your drafts.

Revising for Unity. *Unity* is singleness of purpose and development. In a *unified* paragraph or essay, all of the sentences work together to support and develop the central focus. Effective writers help readers follow their ideas by ensuring that every detail sticks to the main point. Let's look at how the lack of unity in a paragraph can confuse readers.

Draft

(1) Thurgood Marshall was a great lawyer and judge who made America a better society. (2) He was the first African American justice on the Supreme Court, and his death was a great loss to all Americans. (3) Marshall spent much of his life angry at Jim Crow laws. (4) He began his legal career as one of the youngest lawyers for the National Association for the Advancement of Colored People (NAACP). (5) Throughout the 1930s, Marshall fought—and won—many court cases to force colleges and universities to accept African American students. (6) He believed that "the denial to Negroes of the higher branches of education reflects an attitude and a determination on the part of the whites to exclude Negroes from that preparation which would give them a chance to compete on equal terms with whites in the struggle for existence in America" (53). (7) Marshall became good friends with Eleanor Roosevelt, the president's wife. (8) Marshall believed in "equal justice under the law," and he won twenty-nine of the thirty-two civil rights cases that he argued before the Supreme Court. (9) In 1945, Marshall became the nation's most famous civil rights lawyer when he won the landmark *Brown Versus Board of Education of Topeka* case. (10) This

case outlawed the segregation that existed in public schools in America. (11) Marshall was assisted by his deputy, Robert Carter. (12) In 1967, President Lyndon Johnson nominated Thurgood Marshall to serve on the Supreme Court in recognition of his great efforts to provide justice for all Americans. (13) He served on the Court for twenty-four years. (14) Thurgood Marshall was a great leader who used the law to heal this country's terrible wounds.

This paragraph is not unified. Sentences 3, 7, and 11 do not relate clearly to the main point stated in sentence 1. By breaking up the unity of the paragraph, these irrelevant details confuse readers. Here is the writer's revision.

Revision

Thurgood Marshall was a great lawyer and judge who made America a better society. He was the first African American justice on the Supreme Court, and his death was a great loss to all Americans. Marshall began his legal career as one of the youngest lawyers for the National Association for the Advancement of Colored People (NAACP), working to defeat Jim Crow segregation laws. Throughout the 1930s, Marshall fought—and won—many court cases to force colleges and universities to accept African American students. He believed that "The denial to Negroes of the higher branches of education reflects an attitude and a determination on the part of the whites to exclude Negroes from that preparation which would give them a chance to compete on equal terms with whites in the struggle for existence in America" (53). Marshall believed in "equal justice under the law," and he won twenty-nine of the thirty-two civil rights cases that he argued before the Supreme Court. In 1945, Marshall became the nation's most famous civil rights lawyer when he won the landmark *Brown Versus Board of Education of Topeka* case, which outlawed segregation in American public schools. In 1967, President Lyndon Johnson nominated Thurgood Marshall to serve on the Supreme Court in recognition for his great efforts to provide justice for all Americans. He served on the Court for twenty-four years. Thurgood Marshall was a great leader who used the law to heal this country's terrible wounds.

The revision is clearer and easier to understand than the draft.

WRITING ACTIVITY 13

Evaluate the unity of the paragraph below by answering the questions that follow it.

The domestic and professional lives of women have changed in the twentieth century. Many of my friends disagree about the benefits of these changes. One change is that more women are working in blue-collar jobs and white-collar careers. This is because of recent laws against sex discrimination in the workplace. For example, First Lady Hillary Rodham Clinton has an important position in the White House. She heads a task force to create new health care policies. The number of female police officers and fire fighters continues to increase as does the number of women who work in factories. This has happened even though there has been a recession. The recession may affect our future as an industrial power. Another reason more women are working today is that many companies are creating more attractive part-time jobs with excellent benefits. These kinds of jobs enable women to work and to spend time with their families. Women now make up two-fifths of the American work force.

1. What is the focus or topic sentence of this paragraph?

____

____

2. Which supporting details did you think were most effective in illustrating the writer's main idea?

____

____

3. Is this paragraph unified? If so, why? If not, which sentences should be crossed out or revised? Why?

____

____

____

GROUP WORK 3

Form a group of three. Take out the final version of a paragraph that you wrote for any Writing Activity in this chapter. Exchange paragraphs with a classmate. Evaluate the unity of your classmate's paragraph by answering the following questions (on a separate piece of paper).

1. What is the focus or the topic sentence of this paragraph?
2. Is each sentence related to this focus?
3. What was the writer's purpose, and who was the audience?
4. Do the details accomplish this purpose for these readers?
5. Do any sentences seem unrelated to the focus of this paragraph? If so, which ones? Should the writer omit or revise these sentences?
6. How can this paragraph be made more unified?

Revising for Coherence. Well-constructed paragraphs and essays also have *coherence.* Each idea is clearly and logically related to the one that comes before it and to the one that follows it. *Coherent* means "sticking together," and the details and sentences in coherent writing stick together in an order that flows smoothly.

One way to achieve coherence is to use *transitions*—words and phrases that signal the relationships between your ideas and details. *Trans-* means "across," and transitions reach across sentences to show the connections between ideas in the same sentence, between details in different sentences, and between ideas in different paragraphs. In the chart that follows, some common transitions are arranged according to the type of signal they provide readers.

TRANSITIONAL WORDS AND PHRASES FOR ACHIEVING COHERENCE

- *To signal the time-relationship of the next detail:* first, second, third, next, then, after, before, during, as, now, meanwhile, at last, immediately, finally
- *To signal that the next detail is similar or is an additional example or reason:* also, in addition, furthermore, moreover, similarly, first, next, last, finally
- *To signal that the next detail is an example:* for example, for instance, thus, in particular
- *To signal that the next detail is different:* on the other hand, however, nevertheless, still, but, although, even though, in contrast, on the contrary
- *To signal that the next detail is a consequence:* thus, therefore, consequently, so, as a result, hence
- *To signal that the next detail is a conclusion:* in summary, in conclusion, thus, therefore, on the whole

In addition to the technique of using transitions to signal the connections between ideas, there are two other strategies for improving the coherence of your paragraphs. One is *repeating the key words* that limit the focus of the topic sentence. The other is *using pronouns* to keep your main point echoing throughout the paragraph. Pronouns are words that take the place of nouns (for example, *he, she, it, his, their, that, some, most, another*).

Let's look at a paragraph that does not have coherence. As you read the paragraph that follows, circle each sentence that seems choppy or that doesn't seem logically related to the sentence that precedes it.

Draft

Baseball camps can help people improve their ability to play baseball. This past summer, I went to the All-Star Baseball Camp. I wanted to become a better hitter and fielder. The camp fulfilled my expectations. The camp had great teachers who taught us about the different skills of the game. We analyzed the muscles needed to perform each skill and practiced the skill for hours. I learned how important the catcher's position is. I realized the extent to which the catcher has to guard home plate. The pitcher is important because he or she controls the game. The pitcher is so important. I might want to become a pitcher. I can't wait to return to baseball camp next summer and learn new skills and techniques.

This paragraph has interesting details, but they don't make much sense next to each other. Now read the revised version of this paragraph.

Revision

Baseball camps can help people improve their ability to play baseball. This past summer, I went to the All-Star Baseball Camp because I wanted to become a better hitter and fielder. The camp fulfilled my expectations. It had great teachers who taught us about the different skills of the game. They also helped us analyze the muscles needed to perform each skill. After we studied the skill, we practiced it for hours every day. In addition, I studied catching, and I learned about the importance of the catcher's position. I realized the extent to which he or she has to guard home plate. The teachers also helped me develop a better understanding of how the pitcher controls the game and why he or she is so important to winning or losing. In conclusion, I learned many exciting new things, and I can't wait to return to baseball camp next summer and learn more skills and techniques.

The writer used transitions, repetition, and pronouns to point the reader's attention back to the key words in the topic sentence. The details in the revision are logically arranged, and they stick together—they cohere.

WRITING ACTIVITY 14

Improve the coherence of the paragraph below by (1) adding appropriate transitional words and phrases to show the relationships between the details and (2) substituting pronouns for some of the subjects. Rewrite the paragraph on a separate piece of paper.

Getting my daughter dressed for school is frustrating. The ritual begins at 7 a.m. I wake my daughter up. My daughter opens her eyes. She sits up and asks, "What am I wearing today?" My daughter watches me. I point to a pile of clothes on her night table. My daughter walks over to the pile. She approaches the pile as if it were toxic waste. She pokes a little finger into the pile. Every day, my daughter's first reaction forecasts how the rest of the ritual will proceed. "Yuck," my daughter screams. "Pants. I hate pants," my daughter screams. My daughter jumps back into her bed crying. I take out a skirt. My daughter's next reaction forecasts a more favorable end to the ritual: "Dresses, I love them." My daughter is happy. My daughter lets me finish dressing her. She leaves for school. I always feel bad at the end of this ritual. I feel that I should be in charge. I feel that maybe I should exert more control. After all, I *am* the Dad.

GROUP WORK 4

Form a group of four. Take out a paragraph that you are revising, and exchange paragraphs with one of your classmates. Evaluate each other's paragraphs for unity and coherence by answering the questions that follow on a separate sheet. When you finish, give your written answers to the paragraph's author. Repeat the process with another classmate in your group.

1. Does the revision have a clear topic sentence or main point? If so, what is it? If not, what might it be?
2. Has the writer provided enough specific, relevant details to support his or her points? Why or why not?
3. Is this paragraph unified? Why or why not?
4. Is this paragraph coherent? Why or why not?

REMINDER

Signal the connections between your ideas by repeating the key words in your topic sentence, by using transitions, and by using pronouns that refer back to the main point of your topic sentence.

WRITING ACTIVITY 15

Plan and write a paragraph about one of the topics below. (The key words in each topic are in italics.) When you revise your paragraph, use repetition, and pronouns to refer back to your key word (or words).

- My *favorite friend*
- How to *break a bad habit*
- What *success* means to me
- The *best job* I ever had
- The qualities of a *good parent*
- *Similarities* between two *schools*
- *Differences* between two *cars*
- Reasons people *lie*
- Reasons a *college degree is important*

STEP 7: EDIT AND PROOFREAD THE FINAL VERSION

Revising for Correctness. The fifth quality of good writing is *correctness.* Academic and professional writing should conform to the *conventions of correctness* agreed upon by teachers and experts in the field. In writing, these conventions are followed by authors of books, of articles in newspapers, and of essays in magazines and journals. They include correct sentence structure, grammar, diction, spelling, capitalization, and punctuation. When you finish revising your paragraphs, you must proofread and edit them for these conventions.

Proofreading is the process of reading a final draft to find any errors. *Editing* is the process of correcting errors and unconventional forms in a piece of writing. Writing that has many mistakes or unconventional forms is unclear and difficult to read. You probably discovered this when you worked in groups to help your classmates revise their writing. Group work activities improve your editing abilities because as you identify and correct problems and errors in your classmates' paragraphs, you become more aware of the strengths and weaknesses in your own writing.

Here are some strategies you can use to edit and proofread your paragraphs.

EDITING AND PROOFREADING STRATEGIES

When you finish revising a paragraph, do the following.

- Read each sentence aloud slowly, looking for missing or misused words.
- Read each sentence aloud slowly, looking for errors in sentence structure, grammar, punctuation, and spelling.
- Put a ruler or a sheet of paper under each sentence to force yourself to check one line of writing at a time.
- Look up every word that you are not sure you have spelled correctly.
- Reread your paragraph for the errors that you know you frequently make.
- Type your final copy and examine it for typing errors. It is much easier to identify mistakes in typed copy than in handwriting.

Many writers find it helpful to develop their own checklists of typical errors to refer to every time they edit their writing. Here is an example of a checklist that you might want to copy. Every time you receive a paper back from an instructor, you can use this checklist to help you keep track of your common errors and to correct them.

MY TYPICAL WRITING PROBLEMS AND ERRORS

Problem or Error	Cause	Correction
____________	____________	____________
____________	____________	____________
____________	____________	____________
____________	____________	____________

Read your writing aloud to identify missing words. Check every word to make sure it is the right word for the sentence in which you have used it. Also, examine each word to see if it has the correct ending and is spelled correctly. Finally, don't hesitate to ask family, friends, classmates, and tutors to help you revise and edit your writing.

Here is another checklist for you to use to identify problems in your writing and to get readers' responses to them.

REVISING AND EDITING CHECKLIST

1. Is the topic sentence appropriate for the paragraph?
2. Does the paragraph have enough relevant, specific details to illustrate or support the topic sentence?
3. Where does the paragraph need additional experiences, examples, reasons, facts, statistics, or testimony?
4. Where does the paragraph need more specific words and sensory images?
5. How can the organization of the paragraph be made more logical or more effective?
6. Which sentences should be omitted or rearranged to improve the unity of the paragraph?
7. Where does the paragraph need transitions, repetition, and pronouns to make it more coherent?
8. Does the paragraph have any problems with sentence structure?
9. Which sentences are incomplete or have errors in grammar, spelling, capitalization, or punctuation?
10. What suggestions do you have for further revision?

EXPLORING FURTHER

The following essay was written by a high school student in response to the following question on a college application form.

> If you could spend an evening with any person—living, deceased, or fictional—whom would you choose and why?

The essay is from a collection of students' essays on applications for admission to college—*Essays That Worked: 50 Essays from Successful Applications to the Nation's Top Colleges.*

If I were given the opportunity to spend an evening with any one person, living, deceased, or fictional, whom would I choose and why?

She's about 5′9″, has beautiful blond hair, and a beautiful figure. She's every boy's grade school dream. She's the idol of thousands of young girls around the world. She's been a legend for the past 25 years. And she's the one girl I've always wanted to meet.

Her name is Barbie, and she's been on my mind ever since I saw her at my next door neighbor's house ten years ago. Barbie's been mass produced by Mattel for 20 years. The advertisements have led me to believe that she is the perfect girl. She's beautiful; she lives in a house appropriately enough called a dream house; she has a dream job, and closets and closets full of dream athletic wear, swim wear, evening and casual wear. The woman is supposed to be what all little girls should grow up to be, according to Mattel at least. However, for every lovely feature of Barbie that all little girls want to aspire to and all little boys want to aspire with there are others across America who feel differently. Many women feel she is cheap, ugly, fake, and that she stands for only material things. They believe that Barbie illustrates the idea that beauty is something you put on every morning.

However, if I were ever given the chance to meet anyone in the world, I would pick Barbie. Ever since I was a young kid in the second grade and I saw Barbie on TV in one of her many swimsuits, I've had this urge to meet her. What normal second grade boy wouldn't? She's perfectly proportioned, she has long blond hair, killer blue eyes, long slender legs, and she drives a Corvette! What normal male, for that matter, wouldn't want to meet Barbie!

Yet there is more than just a physical attraction between us. All through history women have been dealt with as mysterious. Fathers tell sons that they will never understand women, that they are too complicated, etc. And from personal experience I can tell you that this is for the most part true. Yet, here is Barbie, the woman who embodies all that is feminine. Barbie has been put at the top of the grand pyramid of women; she is what all women and girls should want to be: ambitious, beautiful, rich . . . perfect. It is my contention that Barbie is the key that will unlatch the years of mystery surrounding women, to unleash all that has gone unbeknownst to the male population since the beginning of time. If I were given a night to speak with Barbie, I'm sure I would wake up the next morning understanding exactly what women throughout the world were all about. Yes, I'm sure there are thousands of women across the United States that would argue that Barbie is nothing but a cheap plastic doll degrading to the whole female population and who was put into production only to excite the hormones of grade school boys all over the world. But what better reason to meet the woman? Here Barbie is at the crux of one of the greatest American debates of all time. Single-handedly this woman we call Barbie has set mothers versus daughters all over the nation. This woman has set the female population on its ear. No one knows what to believe. Is Barbie bleached or was she born blond? Is she incredibly fake and stupid or is she an ambitious working woman? I say it doesn't matter either way. Barbie has received more attention and more debate by the human race than any President, millionaire, or rock star. Anyone who has been talked about and fought over as much as Barbie, certainly will have something worthwhile and interesting to say.

Well, as you can probably tell I am one of those pro Barbie people. I do believe in her and what she stands for and this brings me to the last reason I want to meet her. I don't want to see Barbie make a mistake. She still hasn't married Ken. Now they've been going together for some time now, but to my knowledge, they still haven't tied the knot. I wouldn't be able to stand seeing my Barbie get married to someone as fake as Ken. As far as I can tell, the guy doesn't have a job, he doesn't drive, and Barbie's the only one with a checkbook. I've never seen Ken pick up a tab for Barbie on TV. As far as I'm concerned, he's a gold digger. He doesn't even have real hair; he's got grooved plastic, painted dirt brown for a head.

If I could possibly meet with this woman for one night, just one, and if I told her my feelings towards her relationship with thousands of women and girls throughout the world, and if I could tell her just how big a mistake it would be to marry a guy like Ken, I would feel I had made a great contribution to humanity, as well as to myself, by picking up some valuable information on the way.

Discussion Questions

1. What is the main point of this essay? What do you think was the writer's purpose in writing this essay?
2. What might be another title for the essay?
3. Which details were most effective in helping you understand the writer's feelings about Barbie dolls? Why were these details so powerful?
4. What order did the writer use to develop his ideas? Was this order logical and effective?

5. Why do you think this essay was chosen for a collection of successful college application essays?

WRITING ASSIGNMENT

Write a paragraph or two answering the question that the preceding essay answered: If you could spend an evening with any person—living, deceased, or fictional—whom would you choose and why? Use the prewriting techniques that you practiced in Chapter 1 to plan your composition. Then use the strategies that you learned in Chapter 2 to develop and organize your writing. Finally, use the techniques that you learned in this chapter to revise and edit your draft.

POINTS TO REMEMBER ABOUT REVISING AND EDITING

1. Use "Techniques for Gaining Distance from Your Draft."
2. Examine the topic sentence of each of your paragraphs. It should be a complete sentence that is clear and specific and that is not too general or too narrow for a paragraph.
3. Reread every supporting detail to make sure it is relevant to the topic sentence. If it isn't, cross it out.
4. Make sure every detail includes specific, concrete language. Include descriptive words that appeal to the five senses.
5. Use prewriting strategies to develop new experiences, examples, and reasons to illustrate your topic sentence.
6. Check that your revised details are organized logically in an order that readers can follow.
7. Make sure that the paragraph is unified—that all of the sentences relate to the main idea.
8. Make sure that the paragraph is coherent—that each sentence is logically related to the ones that precede and follow it.
9. Add appropriate transitions to signal the relationships between your ideas.
10. Edit every paragraph to make it relatively free of errors. (If you are writing with a word-processing program, use the *Spell-Check* and the *Grammar-Check* functions.)

The Writer's Handbook

CHAPTER

4

SENTENCE STRUCTURE

When you finish revising your paragraphs for focus, clarity, and logic, it's time to begin editing your writing. Editing is the process of identifying and correcting errors and unconventional forms in a piece of writing. If your writing has many mistakes, readers will find it unclear and difficult to read. Since readers expect to see Academic Written English in academic essays, they will probably react negatively to errors in sentence structure and grammar. Moreover, errors give the impression that the writer doesn't care too much about the readers or about the topic.

Since sentences are the basic building blocks of academic writing, sentences are the first things you should edit. Examine the sentences in your paragraphs to make sure that they are clear, complete, and correct. Can you recognize complete sentences and incomplete word groups?

Read each of the word groups below. In the space provided, write *S* if the word group is a complete sentence or *I* if the word group is incomplete as a sentence.

1. ______ Bo Jackson was the first athlete to make the all-star team in both football and baseball.
2. ______ Jackson (whose real name is Vincent Edward Jackson) always been a spectacular athlete.
3. ______ Born on November 30, 1962, Jackson named after Vince Edwards, the star of the television show *Ben Casey.*
4. ______ Jackson, who has been called the greatest athlete of the century.
5. ______ He became the first athlete to play professional football and major-league baseball at the same time.

Did you identify only 1 and 5 as complete sentences? Then you were correct. If you did not identify the complete sentences, don't worry. This chapter will help you to identify complete sentences and to correct incomplete word groups.

GROUP WORK 1

Form a group with two or three classmates. Take out a piece of writing you did for one of the assignments in this book. Exchange papers with your classmates. After you have read a classmate's paper, write answers to the following questions (on a separate piece of paper). Do not discuss one another's papers until all group members finish writing their comments.

1. What was the writer's main point or focus?
2. What was the writer's purpose in writing about this focus?
3. Which sentences have problems or errors, or seem wrong?
4. Which sentences don't seem to make sense?

Help one another edit and clarify any confusing sentences that have been identified.

As an advancing writer in college you already know how to use sentences to communicate your thoughts and feelings. Now you need to refine and polish much of what you already know. So let's begin with what you know about English sentences. First, as a speaker of the language, you know how to use sentences. You have been speaking them since childhood and writing them since first grade. Second, you know that a sentence expresses a complete thought. Finally, you know how to convey the completeness of your sentences when you speak.

However, knowing how to write clear, complete sentences is more difficult than knowing how to produce them in a conversation. Often it is difficult to know when or how to end a written sentence. Here is an example from a student draft. Can you make sense of it?

My all-time favorite basketball player is Larry Bird when he retired from the N.B.A. professional basketball lost its greatest champion and the fans lost their idol Bird was so intense he worked hard practiced daily and motivated his teammates to work hard too in addition he was so versatile that he could play almost any position also he was a real team player he didn't have to make the great dunks in fact he got great satisfaction from setting up good baskets for teammates Bird was a solid player I really miss watching him.

If you read the preceding paragraph aloud, you will probably be able to determine which words groups belong together (despite the missing end punctuation). This will help you make more sense of the writer's ideas. However, notice how much easier the paragraph is to understand when the writer indicates sentence boundaries (the places where one sentence ends and another begins).

My all-time favorite basketball player is Larry Bird. When he retired from the N.B.A., professional basketball lost its greatest champion and the fans lost their idol. Bird was so intense. He worked hard, practiced daily, and motivated his teammates to work hard too. In addition he was so versatile that he could play almost any position. Also he was a real team player. He didn't have to make the great dunks; in fact he got great satisfaction from setting up good baskets for teammates. Bird was a solid player. I really miss watching him.

English sentences have a number of identifying features, many of which you already know. Here are three of these characteristics.

1. A sentence begins with a capital letter. ''My favorite basketball player is Michael Jordan.''
2. A sentence ends with a mark of final punctuation (a period, an exclamation point, or a question mark): ''Michael Jordan is a phenomenal athlete.''
3. A sentence is a group of words that expresses a complete thought: ''Michael Jordan is the greatest basketball player alive today.''

UNDERSTANDING SUBJECTS AND VERBS

To be complete, a sentence must have two very important elements: a *subject* and a *complete verb.* The subject is the word or group of words that names the person or thing that the sentence is about. (The subject of each sentence below is in italics.)

Michael Jordan dunks.
He flies in the air.
His friends watch him in awe.
Jordan is a phenomenal athlete.

A sentence must also have a word or a word group that serves as its *verb.* The verb is the word or word group that expresses the action of the sentence or that says something about the subject.

Michael Jordan *dunks.*
He *flies* in the air.
His friends *watch* him in awe.
Jordan *is* a phenomenal athlete.

Remember that a complete sentence must have a subject and a verb. Understanding subjects and verbs is an important part of editing sentences. The *subject* is the person, place, thing, or idea that the sentence is about or that is doing the action of the sentence. The *verb* expresses the action that the subject is doing or the condition experienced by the subject. The verb also indicates the *tense* of the sentence (the *time* of the action or condition expressed in the sentence).

If you can speak English, you can identify the subject and the verb of any sentence by using your natural language ability to read sentence clues. For example what is the subject of the "sentence" below? What is its verb?

The mertrons vectralized in the tooger.

What is the subject of this nonsense sentence? To find the subject of this sentence, you probably asked yourself, "Who or what is this sentence about?" The answer is "mertrons." The subject of a sentence is almost always a *noun* (the name of a person, a place, a thing, or an idea) or a *pronoun* ("he," "she," "it," "they," and so forth). (Confused? You can read more about nouns in Chapter 9 and about pronouns in Chapter 11.)

To find the verb of the nonsense sentence, you probably asked yourself, "what word tells what the subject did or experienced?" The answer is "vectralized." Note that the *-ed* ending on "vectralized" tells you that this action took place at some time in the past.

Identifying Subjects. The easiest way to find the subject of your sentences is to ask yourself *who* or *what* the sentence is about. The answer is the subject.

Female professional athletes inspire me. (*Who?* "Female professional athletes" is the subject.)

They serve as my role models. (*Who?* "They" is the subject.)

Role models are very important to young people. (*What?* "Role models" is the subject.)

A subject may appear at the beginning or the end of a sentence.

Magic Johnson deserves his name because he makes magic happen when he plays basketball. Also outstanding is *Patrick Ewing.*

You can even place a subject in the middle of a sentence.

For more than a decade, *Magic Johnson* dominated the world of professional basketball.

A *simple subject* consists of a single word or word group or a name (for example, "basketball," "his teammates," "he," or "Magic Johnson"). A *compound subject* consists of two or more simple subjects joined by the words "and," "but," "or," or "nor." Here are examples of compound subjects.

Shaquille O'Neal and Tom Gugliotta were my favorite N.B.A. rookies last year. *Either Jamal Mashburn or Chris Webber* will be the best rookie of the decade. However, *neither Mashburn nor Webber* will make as much money as O'Neal will.

In three types of sentences, it is difficult to identify the sentence's subject. The first type is questions, which usually begin with a verb or with a question word like "Who," "What," "Where," "When," "Why," or "How" and a verb. In most questions, the subject is the word or group of words that *follows* the verb. In these examples, the subjects are in italics.

Are *you* a basketball fan? Who is *your favorite player*? Are *college basketball games* fun to watch?

The second type of sentence that may cause confusion is the sentence that begins with "there" or "here." In most cases, the subject of a sentence beginning with "there" or "here" comes after the verb.

There are *two games* on television tonight. (*What* is on television? The answer is "two games," so "two games" is the subject of this sentence.)

Here is *my television.* (*What* is here? The answer is "my television," so "my television" is the subject.)

Finally, some sentences have "understood" subjects—subjects that don't appear in the sentences! In requests and commands, the subject is usually not stated or written but most people understand that the subject is "you." Here are examples.

Please watch the basketball game tonight with me. (The understood subject of this request is "you," as in "*You* will please watch the game tonight with me.")

Be here at eight o'clock. (The understood subject of this command is "you"—"*You* be here at eight o'clock.")

GROUP WORK 2

Form a group with two classmates, and work together on this activity. Underline the subject of each sentence in the following paragraph. The first one has been done as an example.

(1) Thousands of years ago, people did not know how to explain things that puzzled them. (2) They were confused by changes in the seasons. (3) Their world was filled with dramatic events that they could not explain. (4) Earthquakes, tornadoes, and eclipses came without any warning. (5) Ancient humans could not turn to scientists for answers to their questions. (6) They answered questions by creating legends and myths. (7) Most myths described powerful gods and goddesses who controlled the human world. (8) There were many myths about the causes of natural events. (9) What was the most famous myth? (10) Ancient people believed that thunder was caused by the gods throwing their lightning bolts. (11) Another popular myth was that thunder was the voice of the gods. (12) Rain, sleet, and snow were tears that different gods cried. (13) In practice, these myths represent early science.

You know that a subject can be a single word or a group of words (also called a *phrase*): "basketball," "the best basketball player," "Christian Laettner and Malik Sealy." However, one word group that *cannot* serve as the subject of a sentence is a *prepositional phrase.* This phrase is a group of words beginning with a preposition and ending with a noun or a pronoun. The preposition shows the relationship of the noun or pronoun in the prepositional phrase to another part of the sentence. There are many prepositions in English. Here are the most frequently used ones:

COMMON PREPOSITIONS

about	around	behind	between
above	at	below	by
across	before	beside	during

for	near	onto	toward
from	of	over	under
in	off	through	with
into	on	to	

A prepositional phrase defines a noun ("the teacher ***in*** *Room 204*") or tells where, when, how, or why the action in the sentence occurs ("***at*** *the front* ***of*** *the room*"). The noun or pronoun that ends a prepositional phrase cannot be the subject of the sentence. The subject is the word or word group *before or after* the prepositional phrase.

A. *One* of my idols is playing ice hockey tonight. (*Who* is playing? "One" is playing, not "my idols," which is part of the prepositional phrase "*of* my idols.")

B. At Brandon Arena, *Manon Rheaume* will be playing goalie during the first period. (*Who* will be playing goalie? "Manon Rheaume" will be playing goalie, not "Brandon Arena," which is part of the prepositional phrase "*at* Brandon Arena.")

C. *Rheaume,* of the Tampa Bay Lightning, is the first woman in professional ice hockey. (*Who* is the first woman? "Rheaume" is the first woman, not "the Tampa Bay Lightning," which is part of the prepositional phrase "*of* the Tampa Bay Lightning.")

The easiest way to identify the subject of a sentence that contains one or more prepositional phrases is to cross out all the prepositional phrases. In the examples that follow, *S* signifies the subject and *V* signifies the verb. The prepositional phrases have been crossed out.

One (S) ~~of my idols~~ is playing (V) ice hockey tonight. ~~At Brandon Arena,~~ Manon Rheaume (S) will be playing (V) goalie ~~during the first period~~.

Rheaume (S), ~~of the Tampa Bay Lightning,~~ was (V) the first woman ~~in professional ice hockey.~~

WRITING ACTIVITY 1

Cross out the prepositional phrases in each of the following sentences. Then identify and circle the subject of each sentence.The first one has been done as an example.

1. ~~In ancient Greek mythology,~~ myths helped people understand the world around them.

2. Through myths, people came to understand the consequences of negative behavior.

3. In the typical myth, gods and goddesses had negative human emotions that caused great problems.

4. One of the most destructive emotions was anger.

5. By causing fights, anger made the gods battle and humans suffer.

6. According to myth, these battles in the sky caused great storms and hurricanes.

7. From these storms, people learned that they should try to control their own anger.

8. Thus, some of the myths taught people lessons about themselves.

Identifying Verbs. The heart of any sentence is the verb. It communicates what is happening in the sentence—what the subject is doing or experiencing. The verb also expresses the time and the action that the sentence is discussing. To identify the verbs in your sentences, ask yourself *what the sentence says* about the subject. The answer is the verb.

Female professional athletes inspire me. (''Female professional athletes'' *do what*? They ''inspire,'' so ''inspire'' is the verb.)

They serve as my role models. (''They'' *do what*? They ''serve,'' so ''serve'' is the verb.)

Role models are very important to young people. (''Role models'' *do what*? They ''are'' important, so ''are'' is the verb.)

If you are still not sure about the verb in your sentence, perform this test on it. Find the word that you think is the verb of the sentence. Put a pronoun (''I,'' ''you,'' ''he,'' ''she,'' ''it,'' ''we,'' or ''they'') in front of this word. Does the verb make a complete thought with the pronoun? Does it make sense? Verbs usually make sense; other parts of speech do not.

Sherry Ross, the first female professional hockey broadcaster. (What word might be the verb? Is it ''broadcaster''? Does ''*She* broadcaster'' sound correct? No, so "broadcaster" is not the verb. This word group is not a sentence because it doesn't have a verb.)

Sherry Ross was the first female professional hockey broadcaster. (What word might be the verb? Is it "was"? Does "*She* was the first female broadcaster" make sense? Yes, so "was" is the verb of this sentence.)

A verb can consist of more than one word. For example, some verb phrases include a verb preceded by a *helping verb* (also known as an *auxiliary verb*). In the examples below, helping verbs are shown in italics.

was working	*has* worked	*had* worked
has been working	*will* work	*will have* worked
can work	*would* work	*might* work

The verb expresses the *tense,* or the time that the action or condition of the sentence is taking place: in the past, in the present (now), or in the future. Helping verbs change the range of time that a verb indicates. Here are examples.

I *worked* as a computer salesperson for a long time. (The verb "worked" by itself indicates that the action took place in the past and it is over—the person no longer works as a computer salesman.)

Actually, I *had worked* for ten years before I retired. (The helping verb "had" indicates that the action of "working" took place at a time in the past before the person retired.)

Since my retirement, I *have been working* part-time as a computer consultant. (The helping verbs "have been" indicate that the action of "working" began in the past and is still going on today, that is, in the present.)

I *could have worked* full-time, but I decided that I wanted to relax more. (The helping verbs "could have" indicate that action was possible but that it did not occur.)

It is important to remember that you cannot use the *-ing* form of a verb (as in "working") as the verb of a sentence unless you include a helping verb. Here are some word groups that are not complete sentences because the helping verbs have been left out.

The hockey star playing goalie. She trying to stop every shot.

Compare the word groups above to the sentences below.

The hockey star *was* playing goalie. She *has been* trying to stop every shot.

HELPING, OR AUXILIARY, VERBS

The words below are always verbs, regardless of how you use them in sentences.

- Forms of the verb "be": am, is, are, was, were, will be
- Forms of the verb "have": has, have, had, has had, have had, will have
- Forms of "be" and "have" combined: has been, have been, had been, will have been
- *Modal* forms (verbs which change the meaning of the verbs that follow them)
  - Modals that express "ability": can, could
  - Modals that express "possibility" or "permission": may, might, can, could, would
  - Modals that express "obligation" or "necessity": shall, should, must

WRITING ACTIVITY 2

Look at the sentences below. If a sentence includes prepositional phrases, cross out these phrases. Then underline the subject of the sentence and circle its verb. The first one has been done as an example.

1. The gods and goddesses ~~of ancient Rome~~ (were) practical figures.
2. They served useful roles in people's daily lives.
3. For instance, many of the gods and goddesses could influence the seasons or the weather.
4. Then Greek culture influenced Roman beliefs.
5. Most of the Romans started to believe in the Greek gods and goddesses.
6. However, these gods and goddesses were given new names by the Romans.
7. Zeus was called Jupiter. Poseidon's name was changed to Neptune. Hades was given the name Pluto.

8. Some people in today's world do not know much about Greek mythology.

9. However, many people recognize the names of Roman gods and goddesses.

10. Do you know any gods or goddesses in Roman mythology?

11. One of the most famous Roman goddesses was Venus.

12. Venus represented romance. She was the goddess of love.

13. In Greek myths, she was called Aphrodite.

14. Greek myths and Roman myths also had gods of love.

15. The Greek god of love was named Eros.

16. The Roman god of love was Cupid. Today, more people recognize the name Cupid than the name Eros.

17. Cupid is still symbolized by an archer with a bag of arrows.

18. The arrows in Cupid's bag are supposed to bring love.

WRITING ACTIVITY 3

Write a paragraph about your ideal career or job. What would you most like to do for a living? Why? Try to use as many of the following helping verbs as you can: *am, have been, could, would, may, might, will be,* and *should.* Write your paragraph on a separate piece of paper. When you finish writing, circle every helping verb that you used.

Descriptive words that separate a helping verb from the main verb are *not* verbs. For example, in "I would not want to work on weekends," the verb is "would want." The word "not" isn't part of this verb even though it appears in the middle of it. The word "not" is an *adverb*—a word that describes the verb. Adverbs that often separate a helping verb and a main verb include "not," "only," "ever," "never," "often," "always," "frequently," and "sometimes." In these three examples, the adverb is in italics and the verb is in bold italics.

Before 1992, no professional hockey team ***had*** *ever* ***drafted*** a female player.

Manon Rheaume ***had*** *always* ***dreamed*** of playing hockey.

In the past year, Rheaume ***has*** *frequently* ***played*** goalie for the Tampa Bay Lightning.

The verb of a sentence can be an *action* verb or a *linking* verb. An action verb expresses the action that the subject is performing. Action verbs include actions that can be perceived by the senses (such as "sing," "dance," "say," and "rot") and those that cannot be perceived (such as "think," "trust," "understand," and "remember").

A *linking* verb (sometimes called a *state-of-being* verb) identifies or describes the subject. Common linking verbs include "be," "appear," "become," "look," "seem," and "feel." Here are additional examples of each type of verb.

Action verbs: Carlos *wrote* two drafts of his paragraph, and later he *revised* the paragraph another time.

Linking verbs: Carlos *is* a good writer, and he *feels* that this course is helping him improve his essays.

GROUP WORK 3

Work on this activity with one or two classmates. Read each sentence below. Underline the subject of the sentence and then circle the verb. The first one has been done as an example.

1. Ancient Greek gods and goddesses (were) not always wise and dignified.
2. Often they performed great deeds simply by trickery or by luck.
3. For example, Zeus became the leader of the Greek gods and goddesses by being lucky.
4. The leader should have been the smartest, strongest god or goddess.

5. Zeus was not smarter or stronger than the rest of them.

6. He won the right to be king by gambling with his two brothers.

7. Zeus had two brothers (Poseidon and Hades). They also wanted to be kings.

8. The three brothers drew lots to decide on their kingdoms.

9. Poseidon won the right to rule all the seas. Hades became the ruler of the underworld.

10. Through luck, Zeus won the lottery. He became the supreme leader of all the gods and goddesses.

WRITING ACTIVITY 4

Underline the subject of each sentence below. Then circle the verb that tells what this subject is doing or experiencing. The first one has been done as an example.

1. Greek mythology presented the gods and goddesses in human form.

2. However, the gods and goddesses were different from human beings.

3. For example, the goddess Aphrodite emerged from the foam of the sea.

4. She walked to the shore, fully grown and amazingly beautiful.

5. Aphrodite became the goddess of love.

6. The goddess Athena was born from an opening in Zeus's head.

7. After being born, Athena stood tall and proud.

8. She was the goddess of wisdom (since she came out of Zeus's head).

9. Aphrodite and Athena had strange births.

10. Obviously, there were many differences between gods and people.

Finally, it is important to remember that the main verb of a sentence is never preceded by the word "to." The "to" form of a verb (also called the *infinitive* form) is the form that you use to look up the verb in a dictionary: to *be,* to *work,* to *emerge.* You can use the infinitive verb form in your sentences, but not as the main verb. Here are examples.

My friend wants to be a professional baseball player. (The verb that expresses the action in this sentence is "wants.")

She has been working hard to become a professional athlete. (The verb in this sentence is "has been working.")

Currently, no professional team is willing to give her a chance. (The verb in this sentence is "is willing.")

REMINDER

The verb tells what the sentence says about the subject. If the verb ends in *-ing,* it must have a helping verb in front of it. Words that separate a helping verb and a main verb are not part of the verb. A verb preceded by *to* is not the main verb of the sentence.

GROUP WORK 4

Work on this activity with one or two classmates. Read each sentence that follows. Underline the subject of the sentence, and then circle the verb. The first one has been done as an example.

1. The story of the Trojan horse was a famous legend in Greek mythology.

2. The war began because the Trojans kidnapped a Greek queen, Queen Helen of Sparta.

3. The Greek soldiers sailed to Troy to get Helen.

4. However, the army of Troy had built a great wall around the city to keep out foreign invaders.
5. The Greek soldiers did not know what to do.
6. Then the Greek leader Odysseus had the idea to build a giant horse.
7. The horse was big enough to hold several soldiers inside.
8. A Greek servant told the Trojans that the horse was a gift from the goddess Athena.
9. The Trojans brought the giant horse in through the gates.
10. At night, the Greek soldiers crept out of the horse.
11. The Greek soldiers opened the city gates.
12. The rest of the Greek soldiers rushed into Troy.
13. They found Helen.
14. Then they destroyed the city of Troy.

WRITING ACTIVITY 5

Use each of the following linking verbs in a sentence. Write the sentence in the space below the verb. For fun, try to make the sentences relate to one another.

1. are

____

____

2. look

____

____

3. sound

____

____

4. feel

____

____

5. seem

____

____

WRITING ACTIVITY 6

In the spaces below, write a topic sentence for a paragraph about each of the topics. (See Chapter 2 for information about how to write a clear topic sentence.) Do not write a paragraph; just write an appropriate topic sentence. Make sure that each topic sentence is a complete sentence. Underline the subject and circle the verb in each topic sentence.

1. a relative

____

____

____

2. a place

____

____

____

3. a current problem in your life

____

____

____

WRITING ACTIVITY 7

Complete each topic sentence below. Then write several sentences that give details to develop or support the topic sentence and its purpose. When you finish writing, check that every sentence expresses a complete thought, has a subject, and has a complete verb.

1. My favorite way to relax is ______________________.

   Audience: Your classmates.
   Purpose: To describe what you do to relax so that readers can experience the activity from your perspective.

   Sentences: ______________________________

   ____

   ____

   ____

   ____

   ____

   ____

   ____

   ____

   ____

2. The best way to make new friends in school is ______________

____.

Audience: Readers who do not know you.
Purpose: To convince readers that your way of making friends is an effective method.

Sentences: ______________________________________

____

____

____

____

____

____

____

____

____

3. Using illegal drugs is ______________________________.

Audience: High school students who do not know you.
Purpose: To convince readers to believe your point about using illegal drugs.

Sentences: ______________________________________

____

____

____

____

GROUP WORK 5

Form a group with two classmates. Take turns exchanging the sentences that you wrote for Writing Activity 7. When it is your turn to read your classmate's work, take notes and be prepared to explain to him or her whether, in your opinion, the details were (1) relevant to the topic sentence and (2) adequate to accomplish the purpose.

EXPLORING FURTHER: DESCRIPTION

Description is a writer's most powerful tool. By describing an object or an issue in detail, you show readers what it means to you and you convey your understanding of it. Thus, much of the writing that you will do at school and at work will require description. For example, you may be asked to describe a person, a place, or an object so that your reader will be able to experience it the way that you do. Or you may be asked to describe an idea, a problem, or a solution in a way that will enable your reader to understand things from your perspective.

Good description has an abundance of specific details that paint vivid pictures for the reader. It also has many words and images that appeal to the reader's senses (sight, hearing, smell, taste, and touch). In addition, a strong descriptive paragraph focuses on a single topic sentence. The main focus of a description should be your dominant impression of the person, object, or place being described. The key words in the topic sentence should limit this impression. Here are some examples.

Martin Luther King, Jr., was *the most famous civil rights leader.*

The *delicious smells* that fill my kitchen remind me of my grandmother.

Our school cafeteria looks and sounds like *a popular dance club.*

If you are describing a place or an object, examine it carefully and jot down notes on your dominant impression of it. If you had to sum up the place or object in one word or a single phrase, what would that word or phrase be? If you are describing a person in one paragraph, you should focus on your dominant impression of the person—the particular feature or quality that you find most striking about the person. Think about your purpose and your intended readers in order to shape your dominant impression into a topic sentence.

Below are questions that you might consider asking yourself if you decide to describe an object or a place. Develop a topic sentence and specific sensory details for your descriptive paragraphs by answering these questions.

1. What is most striking about this place or this object? What is my dominant impression of it?
2. What are its outstanding sights, colors, sizes, and shapes?
3. What are its outstanding sounds, smells, tastes, and textures?
4. What factual and sensory details will help my readers see, imagine, or experience this place or object?

If you decide to describe a person (instead of a place or an object), try answering the questions that follow.

1. Exactly who is this person? What is my relationship to him or her?
2. What is most striking about this person? What is my single dominant impression of him or her?
3. What physical characteristics of the person contribute to my dominant impression of him or her? For example, do his or her looks, clothing, or voice contribute to my dominant impression?
4. What characteristic behaviors or gestures contribute to my dominant impression?
5. What else about this person's character, personality, or use of language contributes to my dominant impression of him or her?

WRITING ACTIVITY 8

Choose a place or an object that you know well or that you would like to describe. Jot down answers to the first set of questions. Examine your answers and develop a topic sentence about this place. Circle all the details that are related to this topic sentence. Do some freewriting or clustering to develop additional details about this topic sentence. Use these details to write a brief description of the object or place.

WRITING ACTIVITY 9

Write a paragraph about a person you know well. Begin by answering the five questions in the middle of page 112. Then do some freewriting, brainstorming, or clustering about this person. Decide on your dominant impression of the person: Ask yourself what word best describes this person. Then develop details that illustrate this impression and write a unified and coherent paragraph. Use sensory words and images to enable your readers to see and hear this person.

Here is an example of how a professional writer uses description to make a point about a period in her life. This excerpt is from *The Heart of a Woman* by the writer, film director, and teacher Maya Angelou.

Laurel Canyon was the official residential area of Hollywood, just ten minutes from Schwab's drugstore and fifteen minutes from the Sunset Strip. Its most notable feature was its sensuality. Red-roofed, Moorish-style houses nestled seductively among madrone trees. The odor of eucalyptus trees was layered in the moist air. Flowers bloomed in a riot of crimsons, carnelians, pinks, fuchsia and sunburst gold. Jays and whippoorwills, swallows and bluebirds squeaked, whistled and sang on branches which faded from ominous dark green to brackish yellows. Movie stars, movie starlets, producers and directors who lived in the neighborhood were as voluptuous as their natural and unnatural environment.

The few black people who lived in Laurel Canyon, including Billy Eckstein, Billy Daniels and Herb Jeffries, were rich, famous, and light-skinned enough to pass, at least for Portuguese. I, on the other hand, was a little-known night-club singer, who was said to have more determination than talent. I wanted desperately to live in the surroundings. I accepted as fictitious the tales of amateurs being discovered at lunch counters, yet I did believe it was important to be in the right place at the right time, and no place seemed so right to me in 1958 as Laurel Canyon.

Discussion Questions

1. What was Angelou's dominant impression of the place she is describing?
2. What was the writer's purpose in this description? What do you think she wanted to show readers?
3. Which details were most effective in enabling you to experience the place? Why were these details so powerful?

4. Circle the verb in each of Angelou's sentences. How do these verbs contribute to her dominant impression?

WRITING ASSIGNMENT

Write a composition describing a famous person you admire (a government leader, a writer, an actor, a musician). You might want to begin by thinking of the one word that best describes this person. Imagine that you are writing this description for readers who do not know you or the person you are describing. Your purpose is to enable readers to "see" and "hear" this person and to understand why you admire him or her.

Begin by using the prewriting strategies that you practiced in Chapter 1. Then revise your paragraph using the Discovery Draft checklist on page 52 of Chapter 2 and the Revising and Editing checklist on page 86 of Chapter 3. When you finish revising your paragraph, examine each sentence to make sure that it has a subject and a verb.

POINTS TO REMEMBER ABOUT SENTENCE STRUCTURE

1. Make sure that each sentence begins with a capital letter and ends with a period, a question mark, or an exclamation point.
2. Read the sentences one at a time to see if each sentence has a subject and a verb.
3. If you use an *-ing* verb to express the action of the sentence, make sure that you have preceded it with an appropriate helping verb.
4. If the word "to" precedes the verb, it is not the main verb of the sentence. (You may have to add another verb that will express the time of the action in the sentence.)

CHAPTER

5

FRAGMENTS

Before you begin this chapter. The aims of this chapter on fragments. Learning how to craft clear, complete sentences.

What's going on here? Can you understand the three "sentences" above? Why not?

In the space below, explain why the "sentences" that begin this chapter are confusing.

____

____

____

The opening paragraph consists of three *fragments*—groups of words punctuated as if they were sentences. In Chapter 4, you learned that a sentence (1) has a subject, (2) has a complete verb, and (3) expresses a complete thought. If any of these three features is missing, the group of words is a fragment, not a sentence. Here is a paragraph with three fragments, each of which is in italics.

> *My father, a high school dropout, but wise and kind.* He was a solid role model. *Realizing how much I learned from my father.* I really appreciate him now. *When my father watched me graduate from high school.* I experienced incredible pride and joy.

Reread the preceding paragraph aloud. Notice that when you read a fragment aloud, often you can't tell that it is a fragment because the sentence that precedes or follows it completes the incomplete thought of the fragment. Look again at the last two groups of words from the preceding example, which are repeated below.

> *When my father watched me graduate from high school.* I experienced incredible pride and joy.

Together, these two groups of words do make up a complete thought. Separately, however, the first one is incomplete. It should *not* be separated from the second word group by a period. The period makes the first word group into a fragment. To correct this fragment, combine the two ideas into one sentence.

> When my father watched me graduate from high school, I experienced incredible pride and joy.

Most people express their ideas in fragments when they speak. Why is it considered wrong when students use them in their writing? The answer is that readers expect writing to be more precise than speaking. Speakers can look at their listeners' expressions and know immediately when they are being unclear, incomplete, or confusing. Writers rarely get this immediate feedback, so they must make their ideas as clear and as complete as possible.

GROUP WORK 1

Form a group with two or three classmates and together answer the following questions. Select one person to record the group's answers.

1. How are speaking and writing similar?
2. In what ways do speaking and writing differ?
3. In what circumstances would it be important for a person to speak in complete sentences?
4. In what circumstances would it be important for a person to write in complete sentences?

One of the advantages that writing has over speaking is that it can be revised and edited until it expresses exactly what you want to communicate. For this reason, writing can be a far more powerful communication tool than speech. However, writing that is filled with fragments does not communicate clearly. When people read fragments, they have to slow down and try to figure out where one idea ends and another begins. This can be frustrating and annoying. Most readers, especially teachers and employers, expect to see complete, correct sentences in a piece of writing. How do you think these readers would react to a paragraph of fragments, such as the one below?

Halloween, always my favorite holiday. Dressing up as Cinderella or Sleeping Beauty. Never a devil or a witch, always a fairy-tale princess. With a face full of my mother's makeup. My hair set into a shower of little pin curls. Wearing one of my cousin's prom dresses. Paraded down the street. The one day of the year I felt beautiful.

Eventually, readers give up trying to make sense of these fragments and decide that the material isn't worth reading. Compare the fragments above with the complete sentences below. Which paragraph is easier to read?

Halloween was always my favorite holiday. I loved dressing up as Cinderella or Sleeping Beauty. Never was I a devil or a witch; I was always a fairy-tale princess. With a face full of my mother's makeup and my hair set into a shower of little pin curls, I'd go trick-or-treating. Wearing one of my cousin's prom dresses, I paraded down the street. Halloween was the one day of the year I felt beautiful.

A sentence communicates a complete idea. It is easier to understand than a fragment. Don't cause readers to give up on your writing. Edit your paragraphs and essays to eliminate fragments.

Remember that a fragment is *not* simply a short sentence. The following sentences are all complete sentences; none is a fragment.

I came. I saw. I conquered.

Here is an even shorter complete sentence: "Go!" The subject of this sentence is not stated, but most speakers of English understand that it is "you."

HOW TO IDENTIFY FRAGMENTS

Find the fragments in your writing by doing the following.

1. Edit for fragments by reading your paragraphs *aloud* from the *last* sentence to the first. If you read the sentences from last to first, you will hear when you have punctuated an incomplete thought as a sentence.
2. Read each sentence from the capital letter to the period, exclamation point, or question mark. Make sure that each expresses a complete thought and has a subject and a verb.
3. If the verb ends in *-ing,* make sure you have preceded it with the appropriate helping verb.

Understanding the different causes of fragments may make it easier for you to identify them in your writing. Here are the four most common types of fragments:

1. Missing-subject fragments: ''With a face full of my mother's makeup.'' (*Who* or *What* has a face full of makeup on? This fragment is missing a subject.)
2. Missing-verb fragments: ''Halloween always my favorite holiday.'' (How can you tell the tense—the time of the idea expressed in this sentence? This fragment is missing a verb.)
3. *-ing, -ed,* or *-en* fragments: ''I wearing a prom dress.'' (Where is the helping verb that indicates the tense or time of this action? This fragment is missing a helping verb that tells when the action occurs: ''*was* wearing.'')
4. Dependent-word fragments: ''When I was a young girl.'' (Where is the rest of this idea? This fragment is missing an idea that would complete the thought.)

You can use the suggestions that follow to find and correct each type of fragment in your own writing.

MISSING-SUBJECT FRAGMENTS

Missing-subject fragments often occur because writers assume that the subject of one sentence applies to the word group that precedes or follows the sentence. Circle the missing-subject fragment in each of the following examples.

A. Hallucinogens are drugs. That can cause users to see, hear, or feel things that do not actually exist.

B. The best-known hallucinogen is marijuana. Causes many users to feel that time is slowing down.

C. The most harmful hallucinogen. LSD can permanently damage brain cells.

Reread the second word group in each of these examples. In *A,* does the word group "That can cause users to see, hear, or feel things that do not actually exist" sound like a complete idea? It does not because it is a fragment that should be connected to the sentence that precedes it. In *B,* the word group "Causes many users to feel that time is slowing down" is also a fragment because it does not tell *what* "causes" this. The drug that "causes" users to feel that time is slowing down is the subject of the preceding sentence ("the best-known hallucinogen"). Thus, this fragment must be connected to the sentence that precedes it. Finally, the fragment in *C*—"the most harmful hallucinogen" —must also be changed. Here are corrected versions of all three fragments.

Hallucinogens are drugs that cause users to see, hear, or feel things that do not actually exist. The best-known hallucinogen is marijuana, which causes many users to feel that time is slowing down. The most harmful hallucinogen is LSD, which can permanently damage brain cells.

There are two ways to correct missing-subject fragments.

HOW TO CORRECT MISSING-SUBJECT FRAGMENTS

1. Attach the fragment to the sentence that precedes or follows it.
2. Add a subject to the fragment. (If you are not sure what a subject is, see pages 96–98 in Chapter 4.)

Here is another sentence followed by a fragment.

Stimulants are drugs that speed up the nervous system. *Cause the heart and lungs to work faster.*

Here are two ways of correcting the fragment.

- *Attach the fragment to another sentence:* Stimulants are drugs that speed up the nervous system and cause the heart and lungs to work faster.
- *Add a subject (a noun or a pronoun) to the fragment:* Stimulants are drugs that speed up the nervous system. They cause the heart and lungs to work faster.

WRITING ACTIVITY 1

In the space below, rewrite the three fragments in the opening paragraph of this chapter (on page 115). Turn each fragment into a complete sentence. (You may have to add words.)

1. ______________________________

2. ______________________________

3. ______________________________

WRITING ACTIVITY 2

Underline the fragment in each numbered set of word groups that follow. Then use one of the two methods noted in "How to Correct Missing-Subject Fragments" to correct each fragment. The first one has been done *both ways* as an example.

1. Landfills are mountains of garbage. Discarded by households and businesses.

   Landfills are mountains of garbage discarded by households and businesses.

   Landfills are mountains of garbage. This refuse was discarded by households and businesses.

2. Many types of garbage in landfills do not dissolve. Staying intact for decades.

____

____

____

3. Some archaeologists study the past by examining this garbage. Left behind by people from earlier times.

____

____

____

4. ''Garbage archaeologists'' have discovered all kinds of household goods from the 1930s and 1940s. In landfills across the country.

____

____

____

5. Some surprising discoveries. Archaeologists finding twenty-five-year-old meals, thirty-five-year-old containers, and fifty-year-old wooden plates and utensils.

____

____

____

6. Based on the findings of archaeologists. People worrying about landfills overflowing with garbage that will never dissolve.

7. Some examples of modern garbage that may be around for decades. These include fast-food wrappers, diapers, and plastic packaging materials.

8. People are beginning to realize that they should use disposable items. That will dissolve in landfills. Without polluting the earth.

MISSING-VERB FRAGMENTS AND RELATIVE PRONOUN FRAGMENTS

As their name indicates, *missing-verb fragments* are word groups that lack a verb. Circle the missing-verb fragment in each example below.

A. Depressants are drugs that slow down the nervous system. Particularly thinking and memory.

B. Barbiturates a type of depressant. They promote sleep and relaxation.

C. Narcotics are another group of depressants. Including opium, morphine, and heroin.

In *A,* does "Particularly thinking and memory" sound like a complete idea? It does not because it does not say anything about "thinking and memory.'' It is missing a subject. This fragment should be connected to the sentence that precedes it. The fragment in *B,* ''Barbiturates a type of depressant,'' needs a verb or needs to be attached to the following sentence, which tells what barbiturates do—''promote sleep and relaxation.'' The fragment in *C,* ''Including opium, morphine, and heroin,'' also needs a verb (as well as a subject). Here are the corrected versions of these fragments.

> Depressants are drugs that slow down the nervous system, particularly thinking and memory. Barbiturates are a type of depressant that promote sleep and relaxation. Narcotics are another group of depressants. These include opium, morphine, and heroin.

Missing-verb fragments can also result from the incorrect use of the following words: ''who,'' ''which,'' ''that,'' ''whose,'' and ''whom.'' These words are called *relative pronouns* because they ''relate'' a descriptive word group to the word that it describes.

> D. Narcotics are drugs *that* cause physical and psychological addiction. (The pronoun ''that'' relates the word ''drugs'' to the word group describing what drugs do.)

Relative pronouns are used to refer back to a noun in the sentence and to begin a word group that gives additional descriptive information about the noun.

> E. Heroin users, *who* need daily fixes of the drug, experience terrible withdrawal symptoms if they stop taking it. (The pronoun ''who'' refers back to the noun ''users'' and gives additional information about it.)

A relative pronoun needs its own verb included in the sentence. In *D* above, the subject is ''narcotics,'' and its verb is ''are.'' The relative pronoun is ''that,'' and its verb is ''cause.'' The subject of *E* above, is ''users,'' and its verb is ''experience''; the relative pronoun is ''who'' and its verb is ''need.''

If you write a word group with a subject and a relative pronoun and only one verb, you will create a missing-verb fragment. Here is an example.

> *People* ***who*** *use drugs such as cocaine and crack.* They can feel very aggressive or anxious.

In the first word group above, the relative pronoun ''who'' is the subject of the verb ''use.'' There is no verb for the true subject of the sentence—''people.'' This fragment specifies particular ''people'' (the ones ''who use amphetamines''), but it does not say anything about these people. It states an incomplete idea. In order to correct it, the writer must add a verb or connect the fragment to a complete sentence. In the two corrected versions that follow, *S* signifies the subject of the sentence and *V* signifies its verb.

S V
People ***who use*** drugs such as cocaine and crack develop personality problems. They can feel very aggressive or anxious.

S V
People ***who use*** drugs such as cocaine and crack can feel very aggressive or anxious.

There are two ways to correct missing-verb fragments.

HOW TO CORRECT MISSING-VERB FRAGMENTS

1. Attach the fragment to the sentence that precedes or follows it. (You may have to cross out the subject of the fragment *or* the subject of the sentence to which the fragment is being connected.)
2. Add a verb to the fragment.

Examples *F* and *G* below each contain a fragment. The examples are followed by both types of fragment corrections.

F. *Crack a deadly form of cocaine.* It can cause seizures, heart attacks, strokes, and coma.

- *Attach the fragment to form a sentence:* Crack, a deadly form of cocaine, can cause seizures, heart attacks, strokes, and coma.
- *Add a verb to each fragment:* Crack is a deadly form of cocaine. It can cause seizures, heart attacks, strokes, and coma.

G. *People who use crack for the first time.* They can experience sudden heart failure and die.

- *Attach the fragment to form a sentence:* People who use crack for the first time can experience sudden heart failure and die.
- *Add a verb to each fragment:* People who use crack for the first time may have a fatal susceptibility to it. They can experience sudden heart failure and die.

WRITING ACTIVITY 3

Underline the fragment in each numbered set of word groups that follow. Then use one of the two methods noted in "How to Correct Missing-Verb Fragments" to correct each fragment. The first one has been done *both ways* as an example.

1. The octopus is a fascinating sea creature. With a soft sac of a body and eight arms covered with suckers.

   The octopus is a fascinating creature with a soft sac of a body and eight arms covered with suckers.

   The octopus is a fascinating creature. It has a soft sac of a body and eight arms covered with suckers.

2. The giant octopus which can have an arm span of more than thirty feet. It has a reputation as a fearsome monster.

   ____

   ____

   ____

3. Scuba divers in octopus territory. They know that they should leave the octopuses alone.

   ____

   ____

   ____

4. Marine biologists who study sea mollusks. They consider the octopus to be one of the smartest underwater animals.

____

____

____

5. Octopuses exhibit a variety of character traits. Curiosity, fear, and aggression.

____

____

____

6. With about the same intelligence as a house cat. An octopus won't bother people unless they bother it first.

____

____

____

7. Octopuses will eat almost any kind of food. If there is not food, even their own arms.

____

____

____

8. The female octopus that gets pregnant. She hatches as many as eighty thousand eggs in her nest.

____

____

____

9. Each egg about the size of a grain of rice. The eggs don't have much chance to survive.

____

____

____

10. The mother octopus who may not leave the nest for more than six months. She often dies of starvation.

____

____

____

FRAGMENTS WITH *-ing, -ed,* and *-en*

In Chapter 4, you learned that every sentence needs a verb that expresses the tense—the time of the action in the sentence. You also learned that some verbs are composed of more than one word. Sometimes writers create fragments by forgetting to use helping verbs. A word group which has a verb that ends in *-ed, -ing,* or *-en* and which is missing its helping verb is a fragment.

Here is a chart of common helping verbs.

HELPING VERBS (ALSO KNOWN AS AUXILIARY VERBS)

am, is	are	was	were	will be
has	have	had		will have
has been	have been	had been		will have been
does	do	did		
can		could		will
may		might		must
shall		should		would

Here are examples of fragments with *-ing, -ed,* and *-en.*

Crack addicts *developing* a tolerance for the drug.

These addicts *depressed* when the drug's effects wear off.

Driven to get more crack in order to feel happy and high again.

Each of these word groups is a fragment because it is missing a helping verb. To correct these fragments, add a helping verb to each *or* change the form of the verb that ends in *-ing, -ed,* or *-en.*

- *Past tense:* Crack addicts *developed* a tolerance for the drug. These addicts *were* depressed when the drug's effects wore off and *were* driven to get more crack in order to feel happy and high again.
- *Present tense:* Crack addicts *develop* a tolerance for the drug. These addicts *are* depressed when the drug's effects wear off and *are* driven to get more crack in order to feel happy and high again.

You have two different ways to correct fragments with *-ing, -ed,* or *-en.*

HOW TO CORRECT FRAGMENTS WITH *-ing, -ed,* and *-en*

1. Add a helping verb before the *-ing, -ed,* or *-en* verb or change the form of the *-ing, -ed,* or *-en* verb.
2. Attach the fragment to the sentence to which it is logically related. (You may have to cross out the subject of the sentence *or* the subject of the fragment when you connect them.)

Below is an *-ed* fragment followed by a sentence.

Many teenagers ***pressured*** *by their peers.* They try drugs to relax or to be accepted.

Here are two ways of correcting the fragment.

- *Add a helping verb before the* -ing, -ed, *or* -en *verb in the fragment:* Many teenagers *are* pressured by their peers. They try drugs to relax or to be accepted.
- *Attach the fragment to another sentence:* Many teenagers, pressured by their peers, try drugs to relax or to be accepted.

WRITING ACTIVITY 4

Underline the *-ing, -ed,* or *-en* fragment in each numbered set of word groups that follow. Then use one of the methods noted in "How to

Correct Fragments with *-ing, -ed,* and *-en*'' to correct each fragment. The first one has been done *both ways* as an example.

1. The Sante Fe Trail winding between Missouri and Sante Fe. It was dug in the early 1800s.

   The Sante Fe Trail was winding between Missouri and Sante Fe. It was dug in the early 1800s.
   The Sante Fe Trail, winding between Missouri and Sante Fe, was dug in the early 1800s.

2. The Trail stretching about 900 miles. It is the oldest trail in the United States.

3. Sante Fe was an important western city. The reason being that it was a frontier market for America's manufactured goods.

4. In Missouri, the economy shaken by the Panic of 1819. Many Missourians were desperate to make money.

5. A Missouri farmer named William Becknell. He decided to travel to Sante Fe to sell his goods.

6. Known as a gambler and a risk-taker. Becknell was the first trader to travel the entire Sante Fe Trail.

7. The Sante Fe Trail launched by Becknell and the other traders who eagerly followed him. The Trail was quite unsafe.

8. Early travelers faced many dangers on the Trail. Thrown by their horses and attacked by rattlesnakes and hordes of insects.

9. Many famous people known to have traveled the Sante Fe Trail. Wild Bill Hickok, General George Armstrong Custer, and Kit Carson being among them.

10. The railroad reaching Sante Fe in 1880. Traffic on the Trail dwindled, and many of the cities along the Trail became ghost towns.

DEPENDENT-WORD FRAGMENTS

Dependent-word fragments occur when writers use a dependent word (such as "when," "because," or "although") to begin a word group *and* forget to connect this word group to a complete sentence. Below is a list of common dependent words.

DEPENDENT WORDS

Here is a partial list of dependent words (also known as *subordinators* or *subordinating conjunctions*).

- *To show time:* after, as, before, once, when, whenever, while, until
- *To show cause:* because, if, since, so that
- *To show concession:* although, even though, though, when
- *To show manner:* how

If a word group begins with one of these dependent words, it cannot be punctuated to stand alone because it represents an incomplete thought. A dependent-word fragment "depends on" the preceding sentence or the following sentence to complete its meaning, so it must be attached to that sentence. For example, look again at the first sentence of this paragraph. If you replace the comma with a period, you create a dependent-word fragment.

If a word group begins with one of these dependent words. It cannot be punctuated to stand alone because it represents an incomplete thought.

Underline the six dependent-word fragments in the following paragraph.

Many teenagers are tempted to try drugs. Because they see others use drugs recreationally without harming themselves. When they watch their peers smoke grass and get high. They wonder whether they should try marijuana too. If they see their friends having fun being high. They may decide that statements about the side effects of marijuana are not true. They may try the drug and not experience any bad side effects. Since it takes several times for the active chemical in marijuana (THC) to build up in the body. Once THC is stored in the body. It can cause long-term physical and mental problems. Although marijuana seems like a safe drug. It can impair a user's fertility, lung capacity, and ability to learn.

These fragments can be corrected by connecting them to the complete sentences in the paragraph. Here is an example, with dependent words in italics.

Many teenagers are tempted to try drugs *because* they see others use drugs recreationally without harming themselves. *When* they watch their peers smoke grass and get high, they wonder whether they should try marijuana too. They see their friends having fun being high, and they may decide that statements about the side effects of marijuana are not true. They may try the drug and not experience any bad side effects, *since* it takes several times for the active chemical in marijuana (THC) to build up in the body. *Once* THC is stored in the body, it can cause long-term physical and mental problems. *Although* marijuana seems like a safe drug, it can impair a user's fertility, lung capacity, and ability to learn.

As the corrected paragraph illustrates, you have two ways to correct dependent-word fragments.

HOW TO CORRECT DEPENDENT-WORD FRAGMENTS

1. Omit the dependent word.
2. Attach the fragment to the sentence to which it is logically related.

Here is a fragment, followed by a sentence.

Although marijuana is not a deadly drug. It can cause very anxious people to suffer nervous breakdowns.

Below are two ways of correcting this fragment.

- *Omit the dependent word:* Marijuana is not a deadly drug. It can cause very anxious people to suffer nervous breakdowns.
- *Attach the fragment to another sentence:* Although marijuana is not a deadly drug, it can cause very anxious people to suffer nervous breakdowns.

Note that you should use a comma to connect a dependent-word fragment to the *beginning* of another sentence.

Although marijuana is not physically addicting, it can cause psychological dependence.

However, you do not need to insert a comma if you connect the dependent-word fragment to the *end* of another sentence.

Marijuana can cause psychological dependence *although it is not physically addicting.*

WRITING ACTIVITY 5

Underline the dependent-word fragment in each numbered set of word groups that follow. Then use one of the two methods noted in ''How to Correct Dependent-Word Fragments'' to correct each fragment. The first one has been done *both ways* as an example.

1. When the book *The Adventures of Huckleberry Finn* was first published in 1885. It did not sell very well.

The book The Adventures of Huckleberry Finn was first published in 1885. It did not sell very well.
When the book The Adventures of Huckleberry Finn was first published in 1885, it did not sell very well.

2. This book is now considered an American classic. Although it was not very popular in its time.

3. While the author, Mark Twain (whose real name was Samuel Clemens), was very famous. His legal problems made it difficult for him to get the book published.

4. The book became enormously popular. After it was banned from the public libraries in Massachusetts in 1885.

5. When we read *The Adventures of Huckleberry Finn* today. We cannot imagine why it was once banned for being too ''coarse.''

____

____

____

6. If the book had not been banned. It might never have become popular.

____

____

____

7. Indeed Mark Twain rejoiced when the book was banned. Because he understood that many people want to read things. That they are not allowed or not supposed to read.

____

____

____

____

8. Twain went to town meetings all over the country, condemning the banning. Whenever he spoke in public.

____

____

____

9. When the Free Trade Club apologized to Twain and offered him an honorary membership. He accepted and made a speech that was reported in all the newspapers.

____

____

____

____

10. Before the end of May, less than three months after the book was banned. *The Adventures of Huckleberry Finn* became a best-seller.

____

____

____

____

REMINDER

There are four different causes of fragments.

- Omitting a subject.
- Omitting a verb.
- Omitting the helping verb for a verb that ends in *-ing, -ed,* or *-en.*
- Beginning a word group with a dependent word.

Correct each fragment using the strategy that seems most logical.

WRITING ACTIVITY 6

Each word group in the paragraph that follows is numbered. Above each word group number, write an *F* if the word group is a fragment or an *S* if it is a sentence.

(1) one of the strongest myths of American history (2) that World War II caused American women to go to work (3) according to

this myth, women who left their homes and went to work in factories (4) patriotically helping their country while their men were away fighting the war (5) going cheerfully home at night to take care of their families (6) however, the images created by this myth are not supported by the facts (7) for example, in 1916—well before the war—approximately eighty thousand women working as teachers (8) and sixty-five thousand women in cotton textile factories (9) nearly half of all African American women and almost all immigrant women worked outside their homes before World War II (10) because they needed the money to survive (11) After World War II, the number of working women remained the same (12) although their jobs changed greatly (13) as men came back and reclaimed the better factory jobs (14) women went back to lower-paying jobs.

GROUP WORK 2

Form a group of three students, and choose one student to record the group's responses. Examine each of the word groups in Writing Activity 6. Then, as a group, decide how to correct each fragment. Write the corrected paragraph on a separate piece of paper.

WRITING ACTIVITY 7

Write a paragraph about a time when you were a child and you realized or learned something important. (Some possibilities include finding out "where babies come from," learning the consequences of lying, or realizing that a parent was not "perfect.") Describe what happened, who was involved, and why this experience sticks in your mind. Begin this paragraph with the words "When I was . . . ," and fill in the age you were when you had this experience. After you finish writing and revising your paragraph, reread it to see if you wrote any fragments. Correct the fragments using one of the methods you learned in this chapter.

GROUP WORK 3

Form a group with two or three classmates. Read the following paragraph, which includes all four kinds of fragments. Together, identify each fragment and decide which method to use to correct it. Choose one person to write the corrected paragraph on a separate piece of paper.

The National Championship of the Women's Professional Billiard Association (WPBA) held last December in a working-class Milwaukee neighborhood. It took place in a pool hall called Ronnie's. Billiards nothing to do with swimming pools. The more commonly used term for "billiards" being "pool." At this championship in Ronnie's. The back room dimly lit. Smoke curling up into hazy clouds above the pool tables. Beer drunk straight from the bottles. The spectators were silent. The only sound in the room. Wooden balls cracking against each other and sinking into deep billiard pockets. The number-two-ranked pool player in the country, Loree Jones. She waited her turn. Propped herself up against an unused pool table. After her turn came and she played her game. Jones tenderly breast-fed her three-month-old baby. Then the woman who was called the best female pool player in the world. Ewa Mataya played next. Mataya winning the Milwaukee event. Mataya had never won. A prestigious national pool championship before. After she got over her shock at winning. Mataya shook hands with her opponent, Loree Jones. Breaking down and clasping Jones and her baby in a teary hug. They are now good friends. As well as great champions.

WRITING ACTIVITY 8

Find and underline all the fragments in the following paragraph. As you find each, decide which method to use to correct it. Write the corrected paragraph on a separate piece of paper.

Did you know that 68 percent of the American people give their pets Christmas presents? Also spend 3.6 billion dollars each year on potato chips. And surveys showing that each American drinks an average of 540 cans of soda a year. These nuggets of information can be found in Lionel Tiger's new book. *The Pursuit of Pleasure.* Tiger, a professor of anthropology at Rutgers University in New Jersey. Dedicated years of his academic life to surveying how people enjoy their lives. This book been called an entertaining exploration of life's delights. In this fascinating book. Tiger who says that he has always wondered why people give so much more attention to suffering. Than to finding things that give them happiness. Wants to make people think more about achieving and maximizing pleasure. Given these objectives, Tiger is enthusiastic. Makes a strong pitch for people to look actively for pleasure. Feeling strongly that we ignore the pleasure that families can give us. Especially new parents. Who are often overwhelmed by the difficulties of caring for an infant. May forget how much fun a baby can be. Whether you read Tiger's book, or not. Try to find more pleasure in your life.

WRITING ACTIVITY 9

Below is a paragraph with all *four* kinds of fragments. After you find each, decide which method to use to correct it. Then write the corrected paragraph on a separate piece of paper.

For centuries, the Yuqui Indians have kept their ancient lifestyle in the jungles of the Bolivian Amazon. Choosing to live in a world of strangler vines, bush rattlesnakes, and jaguars deep in the jungle's recesses. Each evening, they have foraged. For leaves, berries, and roots to feed their families. Each evening, they have carried their smoldering embers to their fireplaces. Wrapped in leaves in order to start their camp fires. To cook the howler monkeys that they hunted and captured for food. The Yuquis have lost the art of making a fire. The reason that they must keep several embers smoldering all the time. The Yuquis believing that they are the only human beings on earth. They ignore other people. Sometimes, they have seen airplanes. Flying above the jungle. To the Yuquis, airplanes considered flying spirits of people who have died in the tribe. When commercial loggers started to appear in the jungle. The Yuquis thought the loggers were the spirits of the dead sent back to torment the tribe. The Yuquis had been battling the spirits to save their world. Only to find that more and more spirits keep coming. And will one day drive all the Yuquis out.

GROUP WORK 4

Form a group with two classmates, and exchange your corrected version of the paragraph in Writing Activity 9. Examine the differences between how you and your classmates corrected each fragment. Explain why you chose the correction method that you used.

WRITING ACTIVITY 10

Write a paragraph about your favorite friend or relative. Why do you like this person? What makes him or her special? As you write, try to use the word "who" in as many sentences as you can (for example, "My cousin Gloria is a person *who* always makes time for the people she cares about"). After you finish writing and revising your paragraph, reread it to see if you wrote any fragments. If you did, correct them using one of the methods you learned in this chapter.

HOW TO CORRECT FRAGMENTS: A REVIEW

- Reread each sentence in your paragraph or essay, starting with the *last* one first. Does each one make sense as a complete idea and sentence?
- Make sure each sentence has a subject and a verb that expresses what the subject is doing or experiencing.
- Check to see that each time you used a verb ending in *-ing, -ed,* or *-en,* you also used a helping verb.
- If a word group begins with a dependent word, make sure that the word group is connected to a complete idea.

EXPLORING FURTHER: NARRATION

Narration is storytelling. If someone asks us "What happened?" we narrate a sequence of events, selecting the specifics that seem most important at that given moment. When we put these narratives down on paper, we can reflect on their meaning, reorganizing them according to our purpose and our focus. Writing about the events in our lives helps us understand them better and learn from them.

Effective narration has qualities similar to those of good description: a clear focus and purpose, abundant details that enable readers to visualize exactly what happened, an explanation of the writer's thoughts and feelings about the experience so readers can share the writer's perspective and reactions, and a logical organization. In order to write a strong narration, you must decide on your focus and your purpose. You might want to tell a story in order to share an unforgettable or important experience you had, to explain why you hold a particular belief, or to support a theory or a point of view.

Narrative writing closely resembles the stories we tell in speaking. Because of this, you have to be sensitive to the structure of the sentences in your narratives. As you revise your written stories, look for fragments and correct them.

The key to narration is attention to detail. The more specific details you include, the richer and more interesting your narration will be. However, as with all writing, the details that you develop and select to support your points depend on your purpose and your readers' needs. How much do your readers already know about you and about the event you are recounting? If they know very little, then you have to include details that answer the five W questions plus "how."

Who? What? Where? When? Why? How?

Your answers to these questions will help readers understand what happened and why it was important to you.

As you freewrite or brainstorm notes for narrative paragraphs, remember to include details that appeal to all five senses. Think about the people and the places that you are narrating: What do (or did) they look like and sound like? What smells remind you of them? If you are narrating an experience that occurred in the past, close your eyes and replay the events in your mind as many times as you need to in order to remember specific details.

In addition, don't forget to include details about your responses and reactions to the experience that you are relating. How did you feel when it occurred? Why? How do you feel about it now? Why? Let your emotions and your voice come through so that readers can understand the significance of the experience for you. Developing a draft of a narrative may help you understand the events or experiences more clearly. Share your reflections with readers. Explain why the experience was so meaningful, or how it changed you, or what it taught you.

WRITING ACTIVITY 11

Write one or two narrative paragraphs about the most serious problem you experienced during your first semester at your current school. Imagine that the reader is someone who does not know you. Think about what this reader will need to know about you in order to understand your narrative and your point of view. Use the five W questions above to help you generate details for this narrative. Your paragraph (or paragraphs) should (1) describe the problem, (2) explain how you felt about it, (3) explain how you solved or did not solve the problem, and (4) explain how you feel about it now or what you learned from it. When you finish writing and revising, edit your paragraph for fragments.

If you are having difficulty developing details for narrative paragraphs, use the questions below to generate information.

1. Exactly what happened?
2. Where and when did it happen?
3. How did it happen?
4. Who was involved, and what did they do and say?
5. What *exactly* did you see, hear, smell, and feel?
6. What were your reactions to the people and events?
7. How did this experience affect you (and others)?
8. Now that time has passed, what meaning does this experience hold for you? Can you interpret the experience in different ways? (Does it hold more than one meaning for you?)
9. What did you learn from this experience?
10. What would you do differently if this experience happened again?

WRITING ACTIVITY 12

Write a paragraph about an unforgettable experience—one that was so wonderful or so terrible that you will always remember it. Revise your narrative until it describes exactly what happened, why it happened, and how you felt and reacted. You might also want to explain what you learned from this experience. When you finish writing and revising your paragraph, edit it for fragments. Correct the fragments using one of the methods you have practiced in this chapter.

The following narrative, ''Sustenance of My Life,'' was written by Marcy Donohue when she was an undergraduate at Hunter College in New York City. In this essay, Ms. Donohue uses narration to explain how she learned about herself and her strengths and limitations.

Food is not mere sustenance to me; no, food is a joy, a comfort, a way of life. When I am frightened and anxious, I eat the foods that soothe me, usually something from childhood: cereal, milk, cheese. When sadness overcomes me, I crawl into bed with a good book and some candy treats that remind me of Halloween and the Easter Bunny. When some occasion arises to celebrate, it's off to my favorite restaurant with friends for a five-course food orgy.

Freudians and psychoanalysts would say that I have been starved for maternal love as a child and so still have an oral fixation at age thirty-one. I say baloney to the shrinks. Why was Beethoven obsessed with music and

Einstein with relativity? No one questions these geniuses. All this leads me to how I found happiness in life.

For the last ten years I have spent much time and energy trying to figure out what career I should pursue. First I experimented with the Garment Industry. I attended the Fashion Institute of Technology and worked as an assistant buyer for Lerner Shops. This took about four years. I was very unhappy with the screaming buyers, the cheating salesmen, and the sleazy environment.

My second career was in Investment Management on Wall Street. So I switched from F.I.T. to Baruch College for business classes. The brokerage firm I worked for was beautiful and no one screamed, but I just could not grasp the concept of stock purchasing. It was too abstract for me; I needed to work with a more tangible product.

My third professional testing ground was the law. I felt I could effect change in America like Al Pacino did in ''And Justice for All.'' I got a job with a prestigious law firm and switched to Hunter College for a degree in English. This time I felt I was on the right track.

Once I started attending Hunter, though, I couldn't concentrate on any of my classes. I was only getting B's in school when I should have been getting the A's needed for law school entry. I cut class, did papers at the last minute, and when I did show up for class, I made up crazy games to count down the minutes until the period ended. Most of my notetaking consisted of menu planning and grocery lists for my next dinner party.

At this point I started to seriously question my judgment. Why couldn't I stick to one thing? While realistically examining my life, I realized that only one part of me had never changed: love of food. Grocery shopping, cooking, reading cookbooks, hours of experimenting and serving people my creations were the only things I was really passionate about. Work and school never thrilled me; I'd rather be watching the Frugal Gourmet. It took me such a long time to connect food with a career choice.

All of my life I had been conditioned to choose a ''traditional'' career. I was very unsure about turning something I considered fun into a paying job. I was taken over by confusion. The only thing I was sure I loved was food. Buying it, washing it, cutting it, cooking it, and eating it. I was crazy for it. So I called all the cooking schools in Manhattan and asked for their brochures. It all seemed exciting, but could I really depend on food for my career? Not until someone recommended that I investigate the famous Culinary Institute of America in Hyde Park, New York, did I realize just how serious a career in food preparation could be.

The Culinary Institute was overwhelming! Thirty-nine kitchens, including an Oriental kitchen and a fish kitchen, classes in garde manger, charcuterie and culinary math: this school meant business. CIA students learn how to prepare gourmet extravaganzas and build a successful restaurant. Would I really be able to make it through the rigorous 21-month program that CIA required? Far away (75 miles) from my family and friends, how would I survive?

I was mortified at the prospect of telling my co-workers and family that I was bagging my Yuppie dream of Manhattan and law school so that I could move to the wilderness and learn how to cook. My mother said, "I'll never see you, Joe will never see you." My grandmother said, "You already know how to cook." My office said that I would at least make more money as a chef than as an attorney in the glutted law field.

I was happier than I had been in years. I was so excited about the idea of attending a cooking school in the country that I couldn't sleep. I fantasized constantly about being a master chef and owning a four-star country inn. I would become so famous that I would publish a line of cookbooks, and be so rich that Joe would give up practicing law to aid me in my preparation to fulfill these dreams.

Finding out who I was and learning how to be true to my passions gave me freedom, freedom to move ahead in life and accept my strengths and limitations. In September I begin training at the Culinary Institute. This time I feel confident that my career choice reflects my true desires. No longer will I flounder around in areas that I am not interested in; now I am motivated to push myself to do my best. I know that I'll be successful because I will be doing what I love most in the world: cooking and eating.

Discussion Questions

1. Which paragraph begins the actual narration? How do you know?
2. What might be another title for this narrative?
3. Why do you think Donohue was "mortified at the prospect of telling my co-workers and family that I was bagging my Yuppie dream of Manhattan and law school so that I could move to the wilderness and learn how to cook"?
4. What did Donohue find out about herself through this experience?
5. In the eighth paragraph, the author includes a fragment: "Buying it, washing it, cutting it, cooking it, and eating it." (This fragment should have been connected with a colon to the sentence that precedes it: "The only thing I was sure I loved was food: buying it, washing it, cutting it, cooking it, and eating it.") Fragments like this one appear in nonfiction, especially when the writer is trying to sound informal or conversational. Do you think this writer would have included this fragment if she were writing a paper for her English instructor? Why or why not?
6. What did you like best about this narrative?

WRITING ASSIGNMENT

Write a composition about an event that helped you understand yourself better. Explain what your view or perception was *before* the event and how the event caused you to change your mind about yourself (or your future or your goals). Provide enough details so that readers who do not know you will understand exactly what happened and how it changed you.

Begin by using the prewriting strategies that you practiced in Chapter 1. Then decide on a purpose for writing, and write a topic sentence about the main point that you want to make in this narrative. Use sensory details to make the participants and the experience come alive for your readers. When you finish writing, revise your paragraph using the Discovery Draft checklist on page 52 of Chapter 2 and the Revising and Editing checklist on page 86 of Chapter 3. When you finish revising your paragraph, examine each sentence to make sure that it has a subject and a verb. Finally, check to see if you have written any fragments. If you have, correct them using one of the methods you learned in this chapter.

✔ POINTS TO REMEMBER ABOUT FRAGMENTS

1. Make sure that each sentence begins with a capital letter and ends with a period, a question mark, or an exclamation point.
2. Read each sentence individually to see if it has a subject and a verb.
3. If you use an *-ing* verb to express the action of the sentence, make sure that you have preceded it with an appropriate helping verb.
4. If the word "to" precedes the verb, it is not the main verb of the sentence. (You may have to add another verb that will express the time of the action in the sentence.)
5. Correct missing-subject fragments by adding a subject or by connecting the fragment to the sentence that precedes or follows it.
6. Correct missing-verb fragments by adding a verb or by connecting the fragment to the sentence that precedes or follows it.
7. Correct fragments with *-ing*, *-ed*, or *-en* by adding an appropriate helping verb or by changing the verb to a form that communicates the tense—time of the action in the sentence.
8. Correct dependent-word fragments by deleting the dependent word or by connecting the fragment to the sentence that precedes or follows it.

CHAPTER

6

RUN-ONS AND COMMA SPLICES

RECOGNIZING RUN-ONS

Read the following sentence. Why is it so confusing?

That that is is that that is not is not.

What does the writer of this sentence mean? It is difficult to tell because the writer has not provided any punctuation to show readers where one idea ends and another begins. If the writer had edited this sentence and supplied the appropriate punctuation, it would make more sense: "That that is, is. That that is not, is not." Without punctuation, these two sentences form a confusing run-on.

A *run-on* consists of two or more sentences (complete subject-verb units) incorrectly punctuated as one sentence. It is the opposite of a fragment. *Fragments* contain too little to be a complete sentence; run-ons contain too much. Like fragments, run-ons confuse readers, who have to read them over several times to figure out where one idea ends and another begins. For example, compare the run-on in word group *A* below with the sentence in word group *B*. Which is easier to read? Why?

A. I am doing very well on all my essay tests now I have learned how to write more efficiently in my composition class.

B. I am doing very well on all my essay tests now. I have learned how to write more efficiently in my composition class.

In *A*, two complete ideas are punctuated as if they were one sentence. This creates a problem for readers. Seeing no punctuation after the word *tests* or after the word *now,* readers continue without pausing. However, when they get to the verb *learned,* they are confused. Here comes a new idea without a signal that the writer is no longer developing the first idea. Readers then have to go back to the first idea and try to figure out if the word *now* belongs with the first idea or with the second idea.

In *B,* the two ideas have been divided into separate sentences. The writer has done the work of indicating where one idea ends and where the next idea begins. Thus, the reader does not have to work hard to interpret the sentence. The two sentences in *B* are clearer than the run-on in *A*.

Can you recognize run-ons? Read each of the word groups below. In the space provided, write *S* if the word group is a complete sentence or *RO* if it is a run-on.

1. ______ Students take many tests in school including multiple-choice, true-false, matching, and essay tests.
2. ______ Essay tests are different from the other types, they require writing.
3. ______ An essay test requires students to show what they have learned, it also requires them to write clearly.
4. ______ It is best to be clear and direct on an essay test that way teachers will understand your ideas.
5. ______ The keys to doing well on essay exams are knowing the material, understanding the question, budgeting time carefully, and editing for errors.

Did you correctly identify only the first and the fifth groups of words as sentences? In the second and the third sentences, two complete ideas are incorrectly joined with a comma—creating a run-on that is called a *comma splice.* The fourth sentence is also a run-on (the words "*that way*" begin a new sentence). If you were not sure whether these word groups were sentences or run-ons, don't worry. The remainder of this chapter will help you identify run-ons and correct them.

Length does not determine whether a word group is a sentence or a run-on. Remember that a run-on is two (or more) complete sentences that are run together without appropriate punctuation between them. Here are examples of short run-ons. Each subject is indicated by an *s* and each verb by a *v*.

1. College (s) is (v) fun it (s) is (v) a challenge.
2. I (s) go (v) to Hunter it (s) seems (v) great.
3. I (s) like (v) the school I (s) hate (v) the commute.

If you insert a comma between each complete idea in the run-ons on the bottom of page 148, does that correct them?

1. College is fun, it is a challenge.
2. I go to Hunter, it seems great.
3. I like the school, I hate the commute.

Inserting a comma does *not* correct these run-ons. It simply turns each run-on into a *comma splice*. A comma cannot be used to correct a run-on, because a comma by itself is not an acceptable mark of punctuation for separating two complete sentences.

Just as a fragment is not simply a short sentence, a run-on is not merely a long sentence. A sentence can also be hundreds of words long and be perfectly correct, so long as it is punctuated correctly. For example, here is a correct sentence that is 64 words long.

> A college degree can benefit graduates in many more ways than just financially: It can improve a person's capacity for self-discovery, increase knowledge and intellectual tolerance, lead to greater achievements, increase adaptability, promote a greater interest in political and civic affairs, and lead to a greater feeling of self-worth; college can have all these impacts and also help people make and save more money!

The writer of this paragraph used commas, a colon (:), and a semicolon (;) to combine all these ideas into one sentence.

Many writers have difficulty identifying run-ons because they sound like complete ideas when they are read aloud. For example, read the following paragraph aloud. As you are reading, try to identify each run-on.

My best friend Susan wanted to ice-skate she wanted to join her college's varsity skating team, so she bought a pair of ice racers with razor-sharp blades. She had skated a few times when she was younger, she was a "natural" ice-skater. Susan never had any lessons, skating lessons were very expensive, and Susan's family didn't have the money to pay for them. Last year, Susan decided to earn money for lessons, she waited on tables and she did typing for friends. In the morning she attended classes, in the afternoon she practiced skating, at night she worked to earn money. Susan's family was proud of her, they supported her goal, they tried to help her financially and psychologically. Susan practiced hard, she skated every day, racing around the track for five or six hours. She wanted to succeed—for her family and her friends, she also wanted to prove that she could accomplish her dream. Susan made the team, she won two medals in the divisional championship.

Each word group that ends with a period in the preceding paragraph is a run-on.

Let's examine the first run-on in this paragraph: "My best friend Susan wanted to ice-skate she wanted to join her college's varsity skating team, so she bought a pair of ice racers with razor-sharp blades." Note that this run-on consists of two complete sentences, even though it expresses three ideas:

> My best friend Susan wanted to ice-skate. She wanted to join her college's varsity skating team, so she bought a pair of ice racers with razor-sharp blades.

The ideas containing the subject-verb units "she wanted" and "she bought" are correctly combined into one sentence with the word *so.* (You'll read more about this later in the chapter.)

Here is one way to correct the run-ons in the paragraph about Susan:

My best friend Susan wanted to ice-skate. She wanted to join her college's varsity skating team, so she bought a pair of ice racers with razor-sharp blades. She had skated a few times when she was younger, and she was a "natural" ice-skater. Susan never had any lessons. Skating lessons were very expensive, and Susan's family didn't have the money to pay for them. Last year, Susan decided to earn money for lessons. She waited on tables and she did typing for friends. In the morning she attended classes, in the afternoon she practiced skating, and at night she worked to earn money. Susan's family was proud of her. They supported her goal; they tried to help her financially and psychologically. Susan practiced hard: She skated every day, racing around the track for five or six hours. She wanted to succeed—for her family and her friends. She also wanted to prove that she could accomplish her dream. Susan made the team, and she won two medals in the divisional championship.

Did you notice that many of the sentences in this paragraph now begin with "she"? The writer probably wrote most of the run-ons in the original version of this paragraph because she assumed that the word *she* should be part of the preceding idea, since this word was referring to the same person ("Susan"). However, the fact that two statements are about the same subject doesn't mean that you can put them together in the same sentence. Here is an example of this kind of run-on (in which the second statement begins with a pronoun that refers to the subject of the first statement):

> Susan is a strong-willed woman, she is willing to work hard to get what she wants.

The word group above is a comma splice. It has two complete thoughts (two subjects and two corresponding verbs):

> S V S V
> Susan is a strong-willed woman. She is willing to work hard to get what she wants.

REMINDER

When you begin a word group with a pronoun (*he, she, they,* or *it*) that refers back to a noun in a preceding word group, check to make sure that you haven't written a run-on.

CORRECTING RUN-ONS AND COMMA SPLICES

There are four methods of correcting run-ons:

1. Separate the two sentences with a period and a capital letter.

   Susan is a strong-willed woman. She is willing to work hard to get what she wants.

2. Separate the two sentences with a semicolon (;).

   Susan is a strong-willed woman; she is willing to work hard to get what she wants.

3. Insert a comma and a *coordinator* after the first complete subject-verb unit. (The seven English coordinators are *and, but, yet, for,*

or, nor, and *so.* They are discussed on pages 154–155 of this chapter.)

Susan is a strong-willed woman, *and* she is willing to work hard to get what she wants.

4. Insert a *dependent word* (or *subordinator*) where it seems most logical. (Subordinators are discussed on pages 159–160 of this chapter.)

   Because Susan is a strong-willed woman, she is willing to work hard to get what she wants.

How do writers decide which method to use to correct run-ons that they discover in their drafts? Experienced writers often try out all four methods and select the one that best conveys the relationship between the ideas in the two sentences. For example, here is a comma splice:

Many teachers give essay exams, they want to test students' ability to express their knowledge.

In your opinion, which of the four methods of correcting this run-on best expresses the relation between the two ideas?

A. Many teachers give essay exams. They want to test students' ability to express their knowledge.

B. Many teachers give essay exams; they want to test students' ability to express their knowledge.

C. Many teachers give essay exams, for they want to test students' ability to express their knowledge.

D. Many teachers give essay exams because they want to test students' ability to express their knowledge.

All four methods are correct. None is "better" than the other three. All these solutions express the same meaning, but they differ in emphasis. The coordinator "for" in sentence *C* and the semicolon in sentence *B* signal a close relation between the two ideas (and give each the same emphasis). The subordinator "because" in sentence *D* also signals a closeness in ideas, but the word *because* moves the sentence's emphasis to the idea that precedes it. The period in sentence *A* signals that the writer feels that the relation between the two ideas is not close enough to justify combining them into one sentence.

Here is another run-on, followed by each type of correction. Which correction communicates the meaning most clearly?

Essay tests are difficult for students these tests enable teachers to determine what students have and have not learned.

E. Essay tests are difficult for students. They enable teachers to determine what students have and have not learned.

F. Essay tests are difficult for students; these tests enable teachers to determine what students have and have not learned.

G. Essay tests are difficult for students, but these tests enable teachers to determine what students have and have not learned.

H. Although essay tests are difficult for students, these tests enable teachers to determine what students have and have not learned.

Sentence *H* probably communicates the meaning most clearly because it uses the word *although* to show the relation between the two ideas. The word *although* indicates that the writer is admitting the first point in order to contrast it with the second point in the sentence.

GROUP WORK 1

Work on this activity with one or two classmates. Read the following paragraph. Together, identify each run-on and comma splice and underline it. The first one has been done as an example.

I have always had difficulty taking tests in school, especially essay tests. When I was in elementary school, I had problems with reading and writing, I did both things very slowly. When I had to take tests that involved writing, I would panic, I would get so nervous that I would simply freeze up. My fifth-grade teacher realized that I was intelligent but that I had difficulty dealing with tests. He did not know how to help me, so he sent me to see Dr. Cardoza, the school's language specialist. Dr. Cardoza was wonderful, she taught me how to relax and handle the stress. To this day, I practice her techniques I use them before every essay test I have to take in college. First I relax my head, I loosen my neck muscles until my head droops. Then I relax each muscle in my body, working from my neck down to my toes. Finally, I picture myself doing well on the test, I form a mental image of myself writing the answers smoothly and easily, and I tell myself that I can do well on the test. And I usually do!

Coordination. Coordination involves combining two or more complete sentences using a comma and a *coordinator* (sometimes called a *joining word* or a *coordinating conjunction*). Combining two sentences with a coordinator does not change their meaning. It does, however, show readers the relationship between the two ideas. Here is an example:

> **Run-on:** Essay exams have strict time limits they require students to budget their time carefully.
>
> *Corrected with a period:* Essay exams have strict time limits. They require students to budget their time carefully.
>
> *Corrected with a semicolon:* Essay exams have strict time limits; they require students to budget their time carefully.
>
> *Corrected with a coordinator:* Essay exams have strict time limits, *so* they require students to budget their time carefully.

The first correction (separating the two ideas with a period) fixes the run-on by making it into two complete sentences. However, the third way of correcting the run-on—by joining the two ideas with a comma and the coordinator *so*—tells readers that the second idea is a result of the first. The coordinator reveals the relation between the two ideas.

English has only seven coordinators, listed below and on the next page.

COORDINATORS

and — Indicates that the second idea provides additional information or information similar to the first idea:

Essay exams test students' knowledge, *and* they assess students' ability to apply this knowledge to new problems.

but and *yet* — Indicate that the second idea provides contrasting or different information with respect to the first idea:

Multiple-choice exams test students' knowledge, *but* they cannot test students' ability to apply this knowledge to new problems.

for	Indicates that the second idea provides reasons for the information in the first idea: Essay exams can assess students' ability to apply their knowledge, *for* these exams require students to solve problems using the theories and ideas they have learned.
or	Indicates that the second idea provides an alternative to or consequence of the information in the first idea: Teachers can use essay exams to test students' ability to memorize material, *or* they can use these exams to test students' ability to think about the material.
nor	Indicates that the second idea continues a negative statement begun in the first idea: Multiple-choice tests cannot test students' thinking skills, *nor* can they assess students' ability to use their new knowledge.
so	Indicates that the information in the second idea is caused by the information in the first idea: An essay exam assesses memory and interpretive skills, *so* most teachers give this kind of exam at least once a semester.

REMINDER

Note that you should insert a comma after the first complete idea, *before* the coordinator. (See pages 368–377 for more information about commas.)

WRITING ACTIVITY 1

In the space beneath each of the following run-ons, try out the following methods of correcting it: First, separate the two complete thoughts with a period. Then rewrite the ideas again, this time separating them with a comma and the appropriate coordinator. The first run-on has been corrected both ways as an example.

1. The movie *Jurassic Park* was enormously popular, it tapped into people's fascination with dinosaurs.

The movie Jurassic Park was enormously popular. It tapped into people's fascination with dinosaurs.

The movie Jurassic Park was enormously popular, for it tapped into people's fascination with dinosaurs.

2. Dinosaurs were once the major life-form on earth they ruled the planet long before people did.

3. Dinosaurs roamed the earth millions of years before human life developed, they were not the earliest form of animal life.

4. Tiny shelled animals existed more than 200 million years before the dinosaurs, then came fish and small reptiles about 100 million years later.

5. Many scientists think that dinosaurs evolved from small reptiles, they hypothesize that the first dinosaurs were very small turtles and crocodiles.

6. Gradually, larger dinosaurs developed, during the Jurassic Period huge dinosaurs such as apatosauruses and stegosauruses lived all over the world.

7. The records left by dinosaurs are footprints and fossils, these are bits of bone or shell preserved in stone or amber.

8. Scientists who study fossils are called *paleontologists,* the word *paleontology* means the ''study of ancient forms of life.''

9. One of the most famous paleontologists is Dr. Luis Alvarez, he won the Nobel Prize in physics.

10. Dr. Alvarez studied dinosaur fossils with his son Walter together they found evidence to show that the dinosaurs were wiped out by a huge asteroid that struck the earth.

Subordination. In Chapter 5, you learned about dependent-word fragments. These fragments occur when writers use a dependent word to begin a word group and forget to connect this word group to a complete sentence. Another name for a "dependent word" is a *subordinator.* You can use subordinators to combine related ideas into a single sentence: Subordinate a sentence by adding a subordinator (a *subordinating conjunction*) to its beginning and then attaching it to another sentence. Here are two examples:

> A huge asteroid struck the earth about 65 million years ago. It spewed tons of dust into the air. This thick dust cloud blocked the sun's rays. Many plants and animals were wiped out forever.

There are many subordinators in English. Below is a brief list of common ones, arranged according to the relation that they indicate between ideas. You will probably recognize these subordinators as the "dependent words" that were discussed on page 131 in Chapter 5.

SUBORDINATORS

Although, even though, and *unless* indicate that the idea that follows provides contrasting or different information from the other idea:

> *Although* essay exams are difficult, they help students learn the material more thoroughly.

Because, since, in order that, and *so that* indicate that the idea that follows provides reasons for the information in the other idea:

> Many students worry that they won't do well on essay exams *because* they know that these exams require excellent writing skills.

If, provided that, and *once* indicate that the idea that follows explains on what condition the action or condition expressed in the other idea is dependent:

(Continued)

> Students who know the material will get good grades on essay exams *if* they write clearly and logically.
>
> *Before, while, when, during,* and *after* indicate that the idea that follows explains the time of occurrence of the other idea:
>
> Students should leave time to find and correct errors *after* they finish writing their essay exams.

Like coordination, subordination connects ideas so that readers can understand the relationships between them. However, when you coordinate two ideas, you are presenting them as equally important:

A. Dinosaurs were able to adapt to different environments, but they could not live without energy from the sun.

To "subordinate" means to treat something as less important than or as dependent on something else. When you subordinate the two ideas in example *A,* the idea that begins with the subordinator gets less emphasis (and readers perceive it as less important):

B. *Although* dinosaurs were able to adapt to different environments, <u>they could not live without energy from the sun</u>.

The idea that is stated as a complete sentence ("they could not live without energy from the sun") gets emphasized.

If you wanted to emphasize the first idea that occurs in a sentence, you would make that idea the complete sentence (and place the subordinator at the beginning of the second idea).

C. <u>Dinosaurs could not live without energy from the sun</u>, *although* they were able to adapt to different environments.

Read sentences *A, B,* and *C* aloud. All three express the same ideas and the same relationship between the ideas, but they differ in pausing and in emphasis.

Note that when a sentence begins with a subordinated word group, you should put a comma after this word group. However, when the sentence begins with the complete subject-verb unit, you do *not* need to put a comma after it.

Because dinosaurs had body temperatures that changed with the surrounding temperatures, paleontologists think that these animals were cold-blooded. (comma after the subordinated word group)

Paleontologists think that dinosaurs were cold-blooded because these animals had body temperatures that changed with the surrounding temperatures. (*no* comma before the subordinated word group)

WRITING ACTIVITY 2

Correct each of the following run-ons in the space provided by adding an appropriate subordinator to the beginning of one of the ideas. The first one has been done as an example.

1. The word *fossil* used to mean any old or interesting object dug out of the earth, it comes from the Latin *fodere,* which means "to dig out."

   The word fossil used to mean any old or interesting object dug out of the earth because it comes from the Latin fodere, which means "to dig out."

2. Scientists started to study fossils around the sixteenth century, the word *fossil* got its current meaning (evidence of prehistoric life-forms).

   ____

   ____

3. The term *prehistoric* sounds as though it means "before history" it actually means the time before any written records were kept.

   ____

   ____

4. Fossils are often discovered by accident, construction crews dig out old riverbeds.

   ____

   ____

5. Fossils are often made of stone, the shapes of animals, shells, and bones have been preserved for millions of years.

____

____

6. Scientists can estimate the approximate age of fossils they can figure out the age of the rocks in which the fossils were found.

____

____

7. Fossils can provide many clues about ancient dinosaurs they cannot indicate the color of the dinosaurs' skin.

____

____

8. A fossil can show tiny marks in skin textures, it cannot preserve any indication of color.

____

____

9. Fossils cannot indicate the color of dinosaurs, scientists who study dinosaurs have to guess what they looked like.

____

____

10. Dinosaurs developed from reptiles the dinosaurs in *Jurassic Park* were painted with the colors of today's lizards and crocodiles.

____

____

WRITING ACTIVITY 3

In the space beneath each run-on below, correct it two times: First, use a comma and a coordinator; then rewrite it using an appropriate subordinator. The first one has been done as an example.

1. Paleontologists get much information from fossils, there are no answers to many of their questions.

   Paleontologists get much information from fossils, but there are no answers to many of their questions.

   Although paleontologists get much information from fossils, there are no answers to many of their questions.

2. Fossils cannot preserve noise, scientists have no way of knowing what dinosaurs sounded like.

3. Dinosaurs evolved from different reptiles, they probably made a variety of roars and squeaking noises (as reptiles do today).

4. Fossilized dinosaur teeth differ in many ways scientists know that some dinosaurs ate meat and others ate plants.

5. Fossils show how dinosaurs changed over time, they provide evidence for theories about how dinosaurs finally disappeared.

6. Scientists like Luis Alvarez can develop theories about why the dinosaurs died out, they cannot prove these theories.

GROUP WORK 2

Form a group with two classmates. Choose one person to write the group's responses on a separate sheet of paper. Together, correct the following run-ons four times, using *all four* methods to correct each one: (1) period, (2) semicolon, (3) comma and a coordinator, and (4) subordinator.

1. Most fossils contain only bits and pieces of ancient creatures, figuring out how they go together is like doing a giant jigsaw puzzle.

2. Putting together pieces of broken dinosaur bones is very difficult, so many of the pieces are missing.

3. Most fossils are broken and filthy, they have to be cleaned and repaired before scientists can figure out what animal they come from.

4. Scientists who put together dinosaur bones have to know how bones and muscles work they have to fill in the missing pieces with plaster parts.

5. So many dinosaur skeletons are missing bones, scientists have to put together pieces from different fossils.

6. Dinosaur skeletons in museums look real, they are actually a mixture of different fossilized bones and pieces of plaster.

WRITING ACTIVITY 4

Correct the following run-ons four times, using *all four* methods to correct each one: (1) period, (2) semicolon, (3) comma and a coordinator, and (4) subordinator.

1. Fossils are usually bones or shells sometimes an entire prehistoric animal is discovered.

   Period: ______________________________

   ____

Semicolon: ____________________

____

Comma and a coordinator: ____________________

____

Subordinator: ____________________

____

2. In 1900 a Russian hunter was ice-fishing in Siberia he made a frightening discovery under the ice.

Period: ____________________

____

Semicolon: ____________________

____

Comma and a coordinator: ____________________

____

Subordinator: ____________________

____

3. The hunter thought he found a huge woolly elephant, the creature he dug up had a long trunk and two gigantic ivory tusks.

Period: ____________________

____

Semicolon: ____________________

____

Comma and a coordinator: ______________________________

____

Subordinator: ______________________________

____

4. The animal was a woolly mammoth it was an ancient relative of today's elephants.

Period: ______________________________

____

Semicolon: ______________________________

____

Comma and a coordinator: ______________________________

____

Subordinator: ______________________________

____

5. The mammoth had been under the ice for about 40,000 years its skin and fur were perfectly preserved by the ice.

Period: ______________________________

____

Semicolon: ______________________________

____

Comma and a coordinator: ______________________________

____

Subordinator: ____

____

6. This mammoth probably fell in the ice and got stuck it had a broken hip and a broken leg.

Period: ____

____

Semicolon: ____

____

Comma and a coordinator: ______________________________

____

Subordinator: ____

____

HOW TO CORRECT RUN-ONS: A REVIEW

- Reread each sentence in the paragraph or essay that you are revising, starting with the *last* one first. Is each one a complete idea and sentence?
- Check to see if you accidentally combined two sentences together (with or without a comma).
- Check each word group that begins with a pronoun that refers back to the subject of the previous word group. Make sure you have not created a run-on.
- Decide which of the four correction methods is most appropriate for correcting each run-on that you find in your writing.

GROUP WORK 3

Form a group with two other students. Decide which person will record the group's decisions on a separate sheet of paper. Together, identify and correct every run-on and comma splice in the following paragraph.

At Lumahai Beach in Hawaii, there is an odd-shaped black rock that sticks out into the water, it looks like a big tongue. Actually it is an ancient black rock its shape was created by the waves beating against it. The islanders have a legend about this rock, they say it is the tongue of a giant that once lived on the beach. The giant was always screaming and sticking out his tongue at people. One day another giant killed the screeching giant, he threw his body into the ocean. The sharks ate the giant they would not touch his tough black tongue. The tongue washed up on the beach, it turned to stone. The black tongue looks as though it is lapping the water, it always amazes new visitors to the island. They cannot believe that a rock could be shaped like a tongue simply by the forces of nature.

WRITING ACTIVITY 5

Identify and correct every run-on and comma splice in the following paragraph. Rewrite the paragraph (with your corrections) on a separate sheet of paper.

The Inca Indians ruled Peru more than 400 years ago, they built great cities near the tops of mountains. Legends about these cities spread around the world. As time passed, explorers came from all over to look for the Inca cities. People spent many years and hundreds of dollars looking for the cities, they looked for centuries without any success. One explorer who was obsessed with the cities was an American his name was Hiram Bingham. He tried to find the cities many times, he wanted to know what ancient Inca civilization was like. In 1911, he began his fifth expedition up the mountains of Peru, this time he went with Indian guides. Finally he found an ancient city of stone he was amazed at its grandeur. Stone buildings stood on carved streets, a whole stone city had been built on the top of the mountain. Bingham did not find any written records about the city he named it after a nearby mountain, Machu Picchu. *Machu Picchu* is an Indian word, it means "old peak." Bingham had found an old peak indeed.

EXPLORING FURTHER: PROCESS ANALYSIS

Coordination and subordination are wonderful tools for showing relationships between your ideas. Combining ideas through the use of coordinators and subordinators is very helpful to advancing writers who are trying to explain or analyze issues or processes. Probably the most common form of academic analysis is *process analysis*—explaining how to do something, how something works, or how something happens.

You already have learned the two writing strategies needed to write a process analysis—describing and narrating. To explain how and why something works or occurs, you can *describe* its parts or the events in clear, precise language. To explain how to do or to make something, you can *narrate* a series of steps or instructions in a logical sequence.

An effective process analysis explains each step clearly and completely, and it shows the reader why this process is important. In addition, it also exhibits the other qualities that you have been developing in your writing, including a clear focus, concrete and sensory language, unity, coherence, and correctness.

The first step in developing a how-to analysis is choosing a suitable topic and a purpose for writing. Possible purposes for writing a process analysis include the following:

- To give directions or instructions about how to do something or how to make or prepare something
- To explain how something works
- To explain how to accomplish or achieve something

Here is a student's analysis of how to catch fish. If you had never been fishing, do you think you could catch a fish by following this writer's explanation?

Good fishing results from good planning. Fancy rods and bait won't get you a boat full of fish, but careful planning might. Begin planning your wonderful day out on the lake by figuring out what equipment you will need. If your goal is to catch food fish like trout, you will need a fishing rod (with a reel of fishing line on it), several painted fishing hooks and lures, and some live bait (like wiggly worms or frisky shrimp). Choose a day that is clear and bright so that you can be comfortable and you can see the fish in the water. Go early (around 5:00 in the morning) because that is when most fish come up to the surface of the water for their own breakfast. Now here is the disgusting part: You must spear the live bait with the hook at the end of your rod. If you simply cannot bear to put a live creature onto a hook, then attach a lure onto the hook (but remember that nothing attracts fish like a moving piece of bait). Next, unreel the line so that the hook is about two feet under the water and wait. And wait and wait and wait until you finally feel a tug on the line. Then, slowly reel in your catch and hope that it is a fish and not a boot or a can. Even if you don't catch fish your first time out, you can still have a relaxing day on the water.

Do you think that this writer accomplished his purpose? Why or why not?

____

____

____

WRITING ACTIVITY 6

Reread your Idea Bank or your journal and put a check next to an entry that you might use to develop an analysis of how to do something or of how something works. If you do not want to use the ideas in your Idea Bank, possible topics for this activity include how to cook something, how to fix something, how to break something, how to find and check out a book from your school's library, or how to impress someone on the first date. Do some freewriting, brainstorming, or clustering about this topic.

If you were going to develop a paragraph about this process, what would your purpose be? What would you want readers to know or be able to do? Also, write down who you think might be interested in reading about this process. How much do these readers already know about the process? What exactly might they need to know about it?

Keep your purpose and your readers in mind as you brainstorm and answer the "reporter's questions" (what? who? where? when? why? how?) about the process you are analyzing. As you write down details, think about the information your readers will need in order to understand the process. Here are some guidelines for drafting these details.

GUIDELINES FOR DEVELOPING DETAILS FOR A PROCESS ANALYSIS

1. Describe any equipment, materials, or tools that readers will need to do the process successfully.
2. Define any key terms or technical words that readers might not fully understand.
3. Divide the process into manageable steps, each of which you can explain in a sentence or paragraph.
4. Tell the reader exactly what to do at each step and how and when to do it.
5. Explain the importance of each step.
6. Describe what the reader should *not* do (and why not).
7. Conclude by briefly stating the advantages, value, or importance of learning how to do this process.

WRITING ACTIVITY 7

Trace the figure on the next page with a pen or a pencil, so that you can get the "feel" of drawing the shapes in this figure. Next, write a paragraph explaining how to draw this figure. Give your set of written instructions to a friend or relative (or classmate), but do *not* show this person the figure. Ask him or her to draw the figure by following the directions in your paragraph. If the person has difficulty, ask him or her which directions were unclear and revise your paragraph in light of the responses.

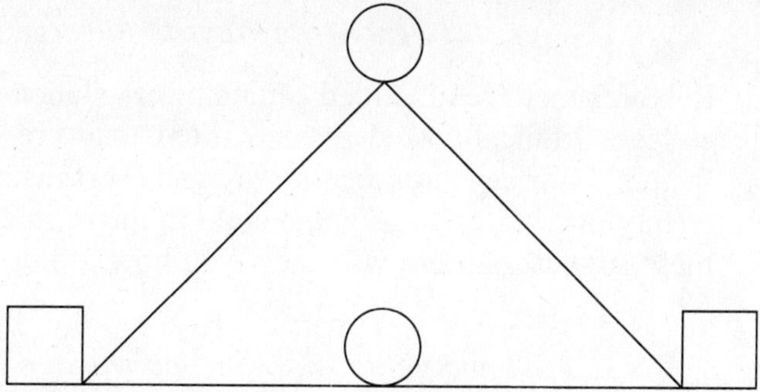

WRITING ACTIVITY 8

Write a how-to paragraph about *one* of the following topics:

Preparing your favorite meal
Forgiving someone who has hurt you
Buying a new car
Breaking up with a girlfriend or boyfriend
Playing an instrument
Picking fruit from trees
Learning another language

Develop your idea by prewriting—freewriting, brainstorming, or clustering. Then decide on a purpose for writing, and write a topic sentence about the advantages or importance of knowing the process you have chosen. Explain any materials or equipment that the readers will need, and define any terms they may not know. Then explain each step—in clear, specific language—in the order in which the steps are to be performed. When you finish writing, reread your paragraph from the point of view of an unknown reader:

1. Will my details enable this reader to carry out the process?
2. Will the reader be able to follow the development of my ideas?
3. Will the reader understand why the process is important or useful?

The reading that follows is an analysis of the process of succeeding in college. It is an excerpt from a book titled *Your College Experience: Strategies for Success,* by A. Jerome Jewler and John N. Gardner.

Twenty-One Ways to Succeed in College

Researchers have identified certain things students can do to ensure success in college. Ironically students are often unaware of what these "persistence factors"—or keys to success—are and how much they really matter. Here are twenty-one basic things you can do to thrive in college. This book is built on these suggestions and will show you how to implement them.

1. *Find and get to know one individual on campus who knows you are there and who cares about your survival.* One person, that's all it takes. It might be the leader of your orientation seminar or some other instructor, . . . an academic advisor . . . , or someone at the career or counseling center. . . . Like the orientation seminar on most campuses, this book is designed to help you get out on campus and meet that person.
2. *Learn what helping resources your campus offers and where they are located.* Follow the suggestions throughout this book for how to get in touch with the people who are there to serve you. Most campuses have career planning offices, personal counseling centers, and academic skills centers, as well as many other resources.
3. *Understand why you are in college.* Your college experience will be much more productive if you can identify specific goals you wish to accomplish. . . .
4. *Set up a daily schedule and stick to it.* If you can't do it alone, find someone on campus or at home who can help—perhaps someone in your academic skills or personal counseling center. [Assign] sufficient time for study, work, sleep, and recreation. If you have family or work obligations, find ways to balance them with time for study. A serious talk with family members may be in order.
5. *If you're attending classes full-time, try not to work more than 20 hours a week.* Most people begin a downhill slide in the quality of learning beyond 20 hours. Don't be one of them. If you need more money, borrow it from a reliable source or talk to a financial aid officer. Try to work on campus. Students who work on campus tend to do better in classes and are more likely to stay enrolled than those working off campus. . . .
6. *Assess and improve your study habits.* An integral part of your success in college involves assessing your own learning style, taking better notes in class, reading more efficiently, and doing better on tests. If your campus has an academic skills center, by all means visit it. . . .
7. *Choose teachers who involve you in the learning process.* Attend

classes in which you can actively participate. You'll probably learn more, more easily and more enjoyably. . . .

8. *Know how to use your campus library.* The library isn't as formidable as it might seem, and it offers a wealth of information and resources. . . .
9. *Improve your writing.* Your writing skills will serve you well throughout life if you take some pains now to improve and secure them. Write something every day—the more you write, the better you write. Remember, writing is for life, not just for English 101. . . .
10. *Develop critical thinking skills.* Challenge. Ask why. Look for unusual solutions to ordinary problems and ordinary solutions to unusual problems. There are few absolutely right and wrong answers in life, but some answers come closer to being ''truthful'' than others.
11. *Find a great academic advisor or counselor and fight to keep him or her.* The right advisor can be an invaluable source of support, guidance, and insight throughout your college years. . . .
12. *Visit the career center.* Even if you think you have chosen your academic major, the career center may offer valuable information about careers and about yourself. . . .
13. *Make one or two close friends among your peers.* College represents a chance to form new and lasting ties. It also offers great diversity in terms of the people on your campus. Choose your friends for their own self-worth, not for what they can do for you. Remember that in college, as in life, you become like those with whom you associate.
14. *If you're not assertive enough, take assertiveness training.* It's never too late to learn how to stand up for your rights in a way that respects the rights of others. . . .
15. *Get involved in campus activities.* Work for the campus newspaper or radio station. Join a club or support group. Play intramural sports. Yes, most campus organizations do welcome newcomers—you're their lifeblood. . . .
16. *Take your health seriously.* How much sleep you get, what you eat, whether you exercise, and the kinds of decisions you make about drugs, alcohol, and sex all contribute to how well or unwell you feel. Get into the habit of being good to yourself and you'll be both a happier person and a more successful student. . . .
17. *If you can't avoid stress, learn how to live with it.* Although stress is an inevitable part of modern life, there are ways of dealing with it. Your counseling center can introduce you to techniques that will help you worry less and study more. . . .
18. *Show up at class.* Better yet, participate. Instructors tend to test on

what they discuss in class, as well as grade in part on the basis of class attendance and participation. Don't abuse your new freedom. Being there is your responsibility. Simply being in class every day (unless you are sick) will go a long way toward helping you graduate.

19. *Remember that you are not alone.* Thousands of other new students are facing the same uncertainties you now face. Find strength in numbers.
20. *Learn to appreciate yourself more.* Hey, you got this far!
21. *Try to have realistic expectations.* At first you may not make the grades you should be making or made in high school. Even if you were a star athlete in high school, you might not be anything special in college. . . .

Do most of these suggestions sound simple? We guarantee that if you follow them, they can make a difference in your life, as they already have for thousands of graduates.

WRITING ASSIGNMENT

What do you know how to make or do well? Write a process analysis of your "specialty." (It could be a meal, a basketball shot, or a study skill.) Imagine that you have been asked to write about your specialty for your school newspaper. Write an analysis that explains how to do or make something for a reader that has never tried doing or making this thing.

POINTS TO REMEMBER ABOUT RUN-ONS AND COMMA SPLICES

1. Make sure that each sentence expresses a complete idea and that it begins with a capital letter and ends with a period, a question mark, or an exclamation point.
2. Read each sentence, one at a time, to see if it has a subject and a verb.
3. Check each sentence, one at a time, to determine that it is a complete sentence and not a fragment or a run-on.
4. Correct every fragment, using one of the methods you learned in Chapter 5.
5. Correct each run-on by (1) separating the two complete ideas with a period, a semicolon, or a comma and a coordinator or (2) inserting a dependent word in front of the appropriate word group.

SENTENCE VARIETY AND STYLE

Now that you have learned how to identify and correct errors that distort the meaning of your sentences, it's time to have fun playing with sentences. Crafting effective sentences requires writers to move beyond correctness and consider matters of length, balance, emphasis, and variety. In order to write interesting sentences, you need to become more aware of the many possibilities that you have every time you shape a sentence. Here are four possibilities to consider when you try to make your sentences more lively, varied, and precise:

1. Add adjectives and adverbs (words that modify and describe other words in a sentence) to clarify your exact meaning.
2. Add descriptive phrases (groups of words), such as prepositional phrases, phrases that begin with verbs of the *-ing, -ed,* and *-en* type, and appositive phrases.
3. Vary sentence beginnings.
4. Combine sentences by coordinating or subordinating them.

This chapter will show you how to experiment with sentences until they communicate your exact meaning and emphasis.

ADDING ADJECTIVES AND ADVERBS

The easiest way to improve your sentence variety and style is to expand your sentences by adding *adjectives* and *adverbs* to them. An adjective is a word that is used to modify (describe) a noun or a pronoun by telling "what type," "which one," "how many," "what color," "what size," and so forth. An adverb is a word used to modify a verb, an adjective, or another adverb; it tells "how," "when," "how often," "where," and "to what degree." Here are some examples of how writers use adjectives and adverbs to clarify meaning:

A. I have a shiny new Chrysler Jeep. (The adjectives "shiny," "new," and "Chrysler" modify the noun "Jeep.")

B. It is fiery red. (The adjective "red" modifies the pronoun "it" and the adverb "fiery" modifies the adjective "red.")

C. I drive it slowly and carefully. (The adverbs "slowly" and "carefully" modify the verb "drive.")

D. Driving this car is a consistently enjoyable experience. [The adverb "consistently" modifies the adjective "enjoyable" (which is modifying the noun "experience").]

E. The car hugs the road extremely well. [The adverb "extremely" is modifying the adverb "well" (which is modifying the verb "hugs").]

Adjectives and adverbs enable readers to experience your ideas from your unique perspective. Here is an example to illustrate this point.

Draft: I have always wanted to drive a car.

Revision 1: As far back as I can remember, I wanted to drive a Jeep.

Revision 2: As far back as I can remember, I wanted to drive a flaming red Jeep.

In the revisions, the writer tried to show what he meant by "always wanting a car." First he explained what he meant by "always." Then he used adjectives to describe precisely the car he wanted. This helps readers understand his meaning, and it makes his sentences more interesting.

WRITING ACTIVITY 1

Here are five pairs of words. The first word in each pair is an adjective, and the second is an adverb. Write a sentence using each word (in the space provided). The first one has been done as an example.

1. Good My new contact lenses are quite effective.

Well These lenses help me see well.

2. Careful ______________________________

____

Carefully ______________________________

____

3. Confident ______________________________

____

Confidently ______________________________

____

4. Joyful ______________________________

____

Joyfully ______________________________

____

5. Serious ______________________________

____

Seriously ______________________________

____

Here is another example of how adding adjectives and adverbs clarifies a writer's meaning and makes a sentence more interesting. Below is a short, simple sentence. What image or mental picture does it communicate to you? Does it help you "see" the "sunset"?

People in my area enjoy seeing the sunset.

This sentence is confusing. Where is this "area"? Why do people who live there enjoy the sunset? Let's add some adjectives to clear up the confusion.

At sunset, from my apartment on a cliff above the Pacific Ocean, neighbors and friends gaze at the sun slowly dipping into the azure sea.

Now the sentence creates a visual image for readers to experience. We can all paint word pictures with adjectives and adverbs. All we have to do is tune in more closely to our senses.

> **REMINDER**
> Expand your sentences with adjectives and adverbs that make your ideas clearer and more precise. Use specific concrete words that let readers see, hear, smell, taste, and feel the things and actions you are describing.

You can add adjectives and adverbs to just about every place in an English sentence. Let's expand a simple sentence to illustrate this point. Here is the sentence.

The sun was magnificent.

First, we can add details before and after the subject so that we specify exactly what we mean.

The *setting* sun *drifting down like a melting candy* was a magnificent sight.

We can also add details at the end of the sentence to give more information.

The setting sun drifting down like a melting candy was a magnificent sight *at the rim of the ocean.*

The added sensory details clarify the meaning and make the sentence more interesting.

WRITING ACTIVITY 2

Here is a simple sentence.

From my room, I can see an interesting sight.

Expand this sentence by following the directions below.

1. Rewrite the sentence, adding adverbs that describe *what* exactly it is that you can see from a window in your room.
2. Rewrite either the original sentence or sentence 1 from above, adding adjectives and adverbs that describe what this sight looks like. (What shape? Dimensions? Size? Colors?)
3. Rewrite either the original sentence or sentence 1 or 2 above, adding adjectives and adverbs describing how this sight makes

you feel. (Why is it interesting? What emotions does it evoke in you?)

GROUP WORK 1

Form a group of three students. Together, expand each sentence below by adding adjectives and adverbs before and after the subject and the verb. Choose a recorder to write the group's revision on a separate sheet of paper. See how many words you can add to each blank place in the sentence, but you do *not* have to add words to every blank space. The first one has been rewritten two different ways as an example.

1. ______ I watched ______ the sun set ______.

   Yesterday, I watched with awe as the sun set on the horizon.

   Last night, I watched the sun set slowly into the pocket between the earth and the sky.

2. ______ my neighbors and I ______ gathered ______.
3. The ______ sun was ______ as it slipped ______ down to the earth.
4. The sky ______ changed colors, from ______ to ______.
5. ______ people stood ______ and watched the ______ scene.
6. ______ the sun disappeared ______.

Here are some questions to consider as you decide where to add adjectives and adverbs to the sentences in your drafts:

1. What adjectives can I add to describe the subject of this sentence more fully?
2. What adjectives and adverbs can I add to clarify what the subject is doing or experiencing?

3. What adverbs can I add to clarify where and when (or for how long) the action of this sentence is occurring?
4. What adverbs can I add to clarify how and why the action of this sentence is taking place?

WRITING ACTIVITY 3

Choose *one* of the topics below to develop into a paragraph or a brief essay. When you finish composing and revising your writing, examine every sentence—one at a time—to see where you can expand it by adding more adjectives and adverbs.

Describe your favorite food and explain why it is your favorite. Use adjectives and adverbs to help readers see, smell, and taste this food.

Describe your favorite music and explain why it is your favorite.

Describe something that you find particularly ugly or revolting and explain why it is so disgusting.

Describe your favorite place to relax and explain why you like it so much.

ADDING DESCRIPTIVE PHRASES

Another way to make your sentences more interesting and varied is to add groups of descriptive words such as prepositional, participial, and appositive phrases. Each type of phrase is explained in this section.

Prepositional Phrases. A *prepositional phrase* is a group of words beginning with a preposition and ending with a noun or a pronoun. It can be an adjective phrase (telling who or what the subject or object is) or an adverb phrase (telling where, when, how, or why the action in the sentence occurs or occurred). Here are some examples of prepositional phrases.

A light-year is a unit **of** measurement used **by** astronomers **for** measuring distance **in** space. It represents the number **of** miles that light travels **in** one year. This distance is about 6,000,000,000,000 miles.

There are many prepositions in English. Some of the most frequently used ones are listed on the top of page 183.

COMMON PREPOSITIONS

about	between	off
above	by	on
across	during	onto
around	for	over
at	from	through
before	in	to
behind	into	toward
below	near	under
beside	of	with

To vary your sentences, add prepositional phrases that describe the sentence's subject (and object) and that describe where, when, and how the action in a sentence occurred. Here is an example of using prepositional phrases to add these details to a sentence:

Draft: Proxima Centauri is near the earth.

What? Proxima Centauri is the name **of** a star near the earth.

Where? Proxima Centauri is the name **of** the star nearest **to** the earth.

Where? Proxima Centauri is the star **in** our galaxy that is nearest **to** the earth.

WRITING ACTIVITY 4

Expand each of the following sentences by adding one or more prepositional phrases to each of the blanks. Rewrite them on a separate sheet of paper. The first one has been done as an example.

1. Many young children swim competitively ________.
(how or where?)

Many young children swim competitively on a swimming team at their local pool during the entire year.

2. Often, their entire family is affected ________.
(how or why?)

3. Young swimmers have to practice ________, so a family member
(when or where?)

has to drive the child ________.
(where?)

4. Swim meets (races) are usually held ________ ________.
(where?) (when?)

5. Swimmers ________ must warm up ________ ________ before
(who?) (where?) (when?)

the beginning of ________.
(what?)

6. The audience sits ________ ________ waiting for each race.
(where?) (how or when?)

7. The swimmer's family often gets nervous ________.
(when?)

8. After each race, the swimmers sit and wait ________.
(where or how?)

9. Some of the swimmers get up and pace ________.
(where or how?)

10. A young swimmer's family usually spends long hours ________.
(where or why?)

Another way to vary your sentence patterns is to shift prepositional phrases to different places in your sentences. Here is an example.

Original: Proxima Centauri, the star **in** our galaxy that is nearest **to** the earth, is about four light-years away.

Shift 1: **In** our galaxy, the star that is nearest **to** the earth, Proxima Centauri, is about four light-years away.

Shift 2: About four light-years away is Proxima Centauri, the star **in** our galaxy that is nearest **to** the earth.

Shift 3: The star **in** our galaxy nearest **to** the earth, (about four light-years away) is Proxima Centauri.

Which one sounds best to you? Which one communicates the idea most precisely? The answer really depends on what the writer wants to emphasize. Shifts 1, 2, and 3 all express the same idea, but they emphasize different parts of the sentence. Shift 1 emphasizes how far away the star is from the earth. Shift 2 emphasizes the fact that this star is the nearest to the earth, and shift 3 emphasizes the name of the star.

WRITING ACTIVITY 5

On a separate sheet of paper, rewrite the ten sentences from Writing Activity 4, shifting the prepositional phrases to different places in the sentence. For example, here is one possible revision of the first example in Writing Activity 4.

1. Many young children swim competitively *on* a swimming team *at* their local pool *during* the entire year.

During the entire year, many young children swim competitively on a swimming team at their local pool.

REMINDER

Add adjectives and adverbs before and after your subjects and verbs to make your sentences clearer and more precise. Then add prepositional phrases and experiment with shifting these phrases to different places in your sentences.

WRITING ACTIVITY 6

Plan and write a paragraph describing what you do in your free time. Do you have a favorite hobby or recreational activity? If so, what is it? How do you do it? Where do you do it? What materials or things do you need to do it? How does doing this activity help you relax?

Revise your draft using the techniques that you practiced in Chapter 3. When you finish revising the ideas, organization, unity, and coherence of your draft, examine every sentence. Where can you add prepositional phrases to clarify your meaning or to vary your sentence patterns? Rewrite the paragraph and underline every prepositional phrase that you added.

Participial Phrases (Phrases Beginning with *-ing, -ed,* and *-en* Verbs). A *participial phrase* is a group of words beginning with a participle—a verb that ends in *-ing, -ed,* or *-en* (also called a *verbal*). In Chapter 5, you learned how to use helping verbs and verbs that end in *-ing, -ed,* or *-en* to write clear correct sentences. You learned that if you leave out the helping verb, you create a fragment:

A. The professor *entertaining* the class.

B. Many students *interested* in his description.

C. *Taken* in by his funny stories.

In Chapter 5, you learned that one way to correct these fragments was to add a verb (or a subject and a verb):

D. The professor *entertaining* the class *described* his enjoyment of roller-blading.

E. Many students *interested* in his description *gave* him their full attention.

F. They were fascinated, *taken* in by his funny stories.

In sentences *D, E,* and *F,* the participial phrases that begin with *-ing, -ed,* and *-en* verbs are functioning as adjectives *not* as verbs. In sentence *D,* the phrase ''*entertaining* the class'' is describing the ''professor.'' Similarly, in sentence *E,* the phrase ''interested in his description'' describes the ''students.'' In sentence *F,* the phrase ''taken in by his funny stories'' also describes the students (''they'').

One way to add variety to your sentences is to add participial phrases to them and experiment with moving these phrases to different places in the sentences. Here is an example of moving *-ing, -ed,* and *-en* phrases to the beginning of these sentences to make them more interesting.

G. *Entertaining* the class, the professor described his enjoyment of roller-blading.

H. *Interested* in his description, many students gave him their full attention.

I. *Taken* in by his funny stories, they were fascinated.

A simple way to practice using participial phrases to expand and vary your sentences is to write pairs of sentences with the same subject and then combine them using an *-ing, -ed,* or *-en* phrase. Here are some examples.

Draft: Matchbox cars were first produced in 1953. They are still being made today.

Possible revisions:

First produced in 1953, Matchbox cars are still being made today.

Matchbox cars, first produced in 1953, are still being made today.

Still being made today, Matchbox cars were first produced in 1953.

Matchbox cars, still being made today, were first produced in 1953.

Which is best? It's up to the writer to decide which version communicates his or her meaning and emphasis most clearly.

WRITING ACTIVITY 7

Practice using participial phrases by combining each pair of sentences that follow. You may have to change some verb endings; others already are in the appropriate *-ing, -ed,* or *-en* form. The first one has been done two different ways as an example.

1. Matchbox cars are tiny copies of real vehicles. They were first produced in 1953.

   First produced in 1953, Matchbox cars are tiny copies of real vehicles.
   Matchbox cars, first produced in 1953, are tiny copies of real vehicles.

2. People were fascinated by these tiny replicas. They collected dozens of them.

3. Matchbox cars looked like their life-size versions. They were made in many different car models.

____

____

4. Matchbox collectors have spent hundreds of dollars on the cars. They have huge collections.

____

____

5. A Connecticut man owns the largest collection. He has more than 14,000 Matchbox vehicles.

____

____

6. Matchbox collectors have formed associations. They share information about the vehicles.

____

____

7. Collectors are fascinated by these miniature machines. They buy magazines and books about the vehicles.

____

____

8. The Matchbox Company is keeping customers happy. It is still producing new vehicles.

____

____

WRITING ACTIVITY 8

Take out a paragraph that you wrote for another class or for an earlier chapter in this book. Circle the sentences that seem to have the same pattern or that seem to begin in the same way. On a separate sheet of paper, rewrite these sentences. Add descriptive words and prepositional phrases to expand them and vary their structure. See if any sentences can be changed to *-ing, -ed,* or *-en* phrases and inserted into other sentences. When you finish experimenting with revising your sentences in different ways, rewrite the final version on another sheet of paper.

Appositive Phrases. An appositive is a word or phrase that renames (gives another name for or a brief definition of) the noun or pronoun that it follows. Here are two sentences that include appositive phrases:

1. Aliens, *imaginary creatures from other planets,* are popular characters in movies. (The phrase ''imaginary creatures from other planets'' is an appositive that explains what ''aliens'' are.)
2. The most famous film alien, *E.T.,* was a sweet, friendly creature. (The noun ''E.T.'' is an appositive that identifies the ''most famous film alien.'')

How are appositives formed? If you examine the sentences above, you can see that each is created from two ideas:

1. Aliens are *imaginary creatures from other planets.*
   Aliens are popular characters in movies.
2. The most famous film alien was *E.T.*
   The most famous film alien was a sweet, friendly creature.

Appositive phrases function like *-ing, -ed,* and *-en* phrases. For example, suppose you wrote the following sentence.

Superman is a famous alien.

Now suppose that you want to add information to this sentence explaining who Superman is. You can do this several ways.

1. Add a word group that begins with a relative pronoun (*which, that, who, whom,* or *whose*):

   Superman, *who was a comic book character from the planet Krypton,* is probably the most famous alien in history.

2. Add a participial phrase (that starts with an *-ing, -ed,* or *-en* verb):

   Superman, *created as a comic book character from the planet Krypton,* is probably the most famous alien in history.

3. Add an appositive phrase:

   Superman, *a comic book character from the planet Krypton,* is probably the most famous alien in history.

All three sentences communicate the same idea and emphasis, but the third one does it with the fewest number of words. This does *not* mean that the third sentence is the ''best'' one. Deciding which strategy is best for a particular sentence depends on one's meaning and on the patterns of the surrounding sentences. A series of sentences with appositives can be just as repetitive and tedious to read as a series of short simple sentences. As you revise your drafts, play with your sentences. Experiment with adding different phrases in order to select the one that sounds best and that communicates your meaning most clearly.

WRITING ACTIVITY 9

Combine each of the following pairs of sentences into a single sentence by changing one of them into an appositive and inserting it into the other sentence. The first one has been done as an example.

1. Aliens are imaginary creatures from somewhere other than Earth. Aliens are popular characters in movies.

   Aliens, imaginary creatures from somewhere other than Earth, are popular characters in movies.

2. The most famous alien is Superman. He is a heroic alien from the fictional planet Krypton.

   ____

   ____

3. Superman has devoted his life to helping human beings. He is a strong, compassionate alien.

____

____

4. Klaatu was another heroic alien. He was a character in *The Day the Earth Stood Still.*

____

____

5. Klaatu came to warn humans not to wage war in space. He was an alien with human emotions.

____

____

6. *2001: A Space Odyssey* was another popular movie about aliens. It did not show the aliens, but it did reveal their signs.

____

____

7. In *Close Encounters of the Third Kind,* the aliens wanted to get to know human beings. These aliens were curious and friendly.

____

____

8. One of the world's favorite movie aliens was E.T. E.T. was an ugly but appealing creature.

____

____

VARYING SENTENCE BEGINNINGS

If most of the sentences in your paragraphs begin the same way, they will bore your readers. You can vary your sentence beginnings by using all the techniques that you have learned in this chapter. As you revise your sentences, add adjectives, adverbs, prepositional phrases, participial phrases, and appositives. Then experiment with shifting these descriptive words or phrases to the front of your sentences. Here is an example of this experimental process. First the writer added descriptive words and phrases.

(1) A warlock is a witch, wizard, or sorcerer. (2) A warlock is a fictional creature. (3) A warlock has many powers. (4) These powers are evil. (5) Warlocks can do magic. (6) A warlock's magic destroys people. (7) Only one warlock did good things. (8) He was famous. (9) His name was Merlin. (10) Merlin was an assistant. (11) He helped King Arthur.

Next, the writer moved parts of sentences around, combining the eleven draft sentences into six revised sentences. (Note, for example, how the writer combined the first and second sentences and the third and fourth sentences.)

The fictional creature known as a warlock is a male witch, wizard, or sorcerer. A warlock has many supernatural powers, most of which are often evil. Just by waving their hands, warlocks can do magic. Warlocks' magic is often deathly, destroying people and things. Only one warlock was famous for doing good things to help humans. Named Merlin, this warlock was a kind and generous assistant to King Arthur.

Another way to expand the variety of your sentences is to revise any *dummy subject* openers such as "there" and "it." Some English structures do require a dummy subject. For instance, English-speaking people use "it" to describe the weather ("It's cold outside" or "It's raining"). The "it" has no meaning; it simply provides a dummy (a meaningless) subject. However, often we use dummy subjects to begin sentences that already have a "real" subject: "*There are* four movies playing at the Cineplex" (instead of "Four movies are playing at the Cineplex").

Beginning with an unnecessary dummy subject weakens a sentence because it moves the focus away from the actual subject. A series of sentences with dummy subject openers is also boring to read:

There is a movie that I really enjoyed. It was called *Hocus Pocus.* It was about three witches who are sisters. It was obvious that the movie was a Halloween spoof. It did not have an intelligent plot, but I was impressed by the acting. There were three of my favorite actresses in the movie: Bette Midler, Kathy Najimy, and Sarah Jessica Parker. There also were many wonderful special effects in the movie.

Look for dummy sentence openers that deaden your writing style, and revise them.

WRITING ACTIVITY 10

Rewrite the following sentences as a paragraph on a separate sheet of paper. Delete every unnecessary dummy subject and make whatever other changes are necessary to make each sentence complete and correct. The first one has been done as an example.

1. ~~It was~~ About a week ago ~~that~~ my husband and I decided to go camping.
2. There was a state park nearby that had campgrounds.
3. It was clear that we were going to have a problem.
4. There was not enough time for us to practice setting up our new tent.
5. It was quite late and dark when we arrived at the campsite.
6. It was obvious that we didn't know how to pitch the tent.
7. There was a paper in the tent box that explained how to set up the tent.
8. It was a set of directions for a different kind of tent.
9. There were many problems that we had trying to get the tent set up.
10. It was a long and uncomfortable night that the two of us spent sleeping in our car.

GROUP WORK 2

Form a group with two other students. Together, revise the paragraph below by varying the sentence beginnings and by deleting unnecessary words. Choose one student to record the group's final version on a separate sheet of paper.

It is fun to think about the stars in the sky. Stars are actually clouds of shining gases. They look like twinkling dots of light. They look this way because they shine in the night sky. They are much farther away from the earth than the other planets in our solar system. They are many light-years away. Stars are not fixed in space. They move at different speeds. They also vary in size and color. It seems that stars appear to be white. They really are yellow, orange, or red. They vary in color because their temperatures are different. Stars that are the hottest are almost white. They have gases with a temperature of several hundred thousand degrees. Stars that are cooler are orange and red. They are 2,000 to 3,000 degrees. Stars are beautiful to look at in the night sky. They are mystical points of faraway light.

COMBINING SENTENCES

Many advancing writers worry so much about making sentence errors that they try to keep their sentences short and simple. They think that short simple sentences are clearer than long complicated ones. Are they correct? Is sentence clarity related to sentence length? Here is an experiment that will help you answer this question. Ask three people whether the sentences in *A* or *B* below are easier to read and to understand.

A. A solar eclipse is a planetary phenomenon. An eclipse occurs when the moon passes. It goes between the sun and earth. It blocks our view. Our view is of the sun.

B. A solar eclipse is a planetary phenomenon that occurs when the moon passes between the sun and the earth and blocks our view of the sun.

Each of the sentences in passage *A* has seven or fewer words. Each is shorter and simpler in structure than the single sentence in *B,* which has twenty-six words. Yet probably everyone will say that the sentence with twenty-six words is clearer than the five short sentences. One long sentence that omits repeated words and that spells out the relationships between its ideas is often easier to understand than are several short sentences.

Combining short simple sentences into longer ones helps you express the relations between your ideas more precisely. It also makes your sentences clearer and more interesting to read. This chapter has provided you with opportunities to practice combining sentences by changing them into prepositional phrases; *-ing, -ed,* and *-en* phrases; and appositives. Here is an example of each strategy:

> **Uncombined sentences:** I am attending seminars. The seminars are in my field. My field is astronomy. I am learning fascinating facts.
>
> *Combined with prepositional phrases:* I am attending seminars **in** my field **of** astronomy and learning fascinating facts.
>
> *Combined with an* -ing, -ed, *or* -en *phrase:* **Attending** courses in my field of astronomy, I am learning fascinating facts.
>
> *Combined with an appositive phrase:* I am attending seminars in my field, astronomy, and learning fascinating facts.

Which sentence is "best"? Only the writer of these sentences could answer this question, since the answer depends on the writer's intended meaning and emphasis.

Coordination and Subordination. In Chapter 6, you practiced two other sentence-combining techniques: coordination and subordination. Remember that coordination involves combining two or more complete sentences, using a comma and a coordinator (*and, but, yet, for, or, nor,* or *so*). Subordination involves combining related ideas into a single sentence by adding a subordinator to the beginning of one of the ideas. (Subordinators include words like *although, even though, because, since, if, before,* and *when.*) Here are examples of both methods of combining sentences.

> *Coordination:* In a solar eclipse, the sun looks completely covered, *but* the moon does not block all the sun's rays. People should not look directly at an eclipse, *for* the sun's rays can burn their eyes.
>
> *Subordination:* In a solar eclipse, *even though* the sun looks completely covered, the moon does not block all the sun's rays. People should not look directly at an eclipse *because* the sun's rays can burn their eyes.

Remember that you have to decide which idea you want to emphasize when you combine sentences. You have to decide precisely what you are trying to say. Also, you have to experiment with coordinating and subordinating your clauses until they emphasize the idea that you want to stress.

WRITING ACTIVITY 11

Below are six sets of sentences. On a separate sheet of paper combine each set into one sentence. You will have to decide whether to use a coordinator or a subordinator to combine the two ideas. You might want to try combining each set both ways and decide which way makes more sense or sounds better to you.

1. Juneteenth is a holiday observed mostly in Texas and Louisiana. It celebrates the freeing of the slaves in those states.
2. The Emancipation Proclamation was created in September 1862. It was not signed by the President until January 1, 1863.
3. Texas and Louisiana were southern states. Slaves in several southern states were not freed until the Emancipation Proclamation became an amendment to the Constitution.
4. Many slaves were released almost two years after the Emancipation Proclamation. The Proclamation was ratified as Amendment 13 in 1865.
5. Today, people in Texas and Louisiana want to celebrate the liberation of the slaves. They hold huge festivals and parades.
6. African Americans plan many of the festivities. People of every ethnic background celebrate Juneteenth.

Subordination with Relative Pronouns. In Chapter 5, you learned about using relative pronouns (*who, whom, that, which,* and *whose*) to correct fragments. Relative pronouns are used to begin a word group that gives additional descriptive information about the subject:

The sentences *that* I am writing now need more adverbs.

Relative pronouns can also be used to subordinate ideas. If you want to combine two sentences that have the same subject, replace the second subject with the appropriate relative pronoun. Here is an example of this technique for combining sentences:

Abraham Lincoln was a great president, whose ~~His~~ goals were to end the Civil War and to create support for the Emancipation Proclamation, which ~~This proclamation~~ made slavery illegal.

Combining the three sentences above with relative pronouns links the ideas together more closely and reveals the relationships between them. It also makes the writing flow more effectively by eliminating words that are repeated unnecessarily.

WRITING ACTIVITY 12

Here are eight sets of sentences. Combine each set into one sentence, using a relative pronoun. The first one has been done as an example.

1. Space exploration has provided us with exciting discoveries. These discoveries have benefited people in many ways.

   Space exploration has provided us with exciting discoveries which have benefited people in many ways.

2. America's space program took us to the moon and to other planets. The program also changed the materials that we use for sports.

   ____

   ____

3. For example, the Easton Company produced aluminum to cover spacecraft. They then used this metal to make baseball bats.

   ____

   ____

4. Polyurethane foam was invented to insulate spacecraft. This foam is now used to keep baseballs firm and solid.

5. The inventor of the popular Ping golf clubs was a research engineer. He worked on spacecraft in the 1950s.

6. His understanding of design problems helped him shape a new golf club. This new shape makes the game easier to play.

7. Space engineers also developed pressurized gas cushioning systems. These systems were used to make space suits.

8. Gas cushioning systems use pressurized gas inside rubber containers. Today these systems can be found in Nike Air sneakers.

REMINDER

Relative pronouns cannot be used interchangeably. Use *who* to refer to people and use *that* and *which* to refer to other nouns or pronouns.

How do experienced writers decide whether or not to combine their sentences? They experiment with combining them in different ways, and they evaluate the results of their experiments. They also ask themselves the following questions:

- Would the reader understand my ideas more clearly if I wrote them as separate sentences?
- Which way of combining my sentences communicates my meaning and my intended emphasis most clearly?
- If two (or more) sentences should be combined, which strategy for combining them sounds best?

GROUP WORK 3

Form a group of three students and choose one person to record the group's revisions. Below is a student paragraph that was rewritten as a series of simple, short sentences. Together, try out different ways of combining these sentences to make longer, clearer ones. Delete repeated or unnecessary words. Two possible combinations for the first set have been done as an example.

1. Neil Armstrong was a person.
   He was the first person to do something.
   Neil Armstrong walked.
   He walked in outer space.

   (1) Neil Armstrong was the first person to walk in outer space.

   (2) Neil Armstrong was the first person who walked in outer space.

2. Neil Armstrong stepped onto a surface.
   The surface was on the moon.
   The date was July 21, 1969.

   ____

   ____

   ____

3. Armstrong was not the first person to do something.
   He was not the first person to take a journey.
   The journey was to outer space.
   The journey was in a spacecraft.

   ____

   ____

   ____

4. Yuri Gagarin made the flight.
   The flight was the first manned space flight.
   Yuri Gagarin was from the Soviet Union.
   Yuri Gagarin made the flight in April 1961.

   ____

   ____

   ____

5. Neil Armstrong walked on the moon.
   Neil Armstrong said words.
   The words were his first words.
   The words were "That's one small step for man, one giant leap for mankind."

   ____

   ____

   ____

   ____

WRITING ACTIVITY 13

Here is a paragraph that was rewritten as a series of short simple sentences. On a separate sheet of paper, try out different ways of combining each set of sentences to make a single, clearer sentence. Then delete repeated or unnecessary words.

1. I have always wanted something.
   I have wanted to be an astronaut.
   I have wanted to be this for a long time.
   I have wanted to be this for as long as I can remember.
2. I dream about something.
   I dream frequently.
   My dreams are about flying in outer space.
   My dreams are about walking on other planets.
3. An astronaut ventures into space.
   An astronaut leaves something behind.
   That something is the safety of the atmosphere.
   The atmosphere is the earth's.
4. Outer space differs from something.
   This something is the earth's atmosphere.
   Outer space lacks the air we need to breathe.
   Outer space lacks the pressure our blood needs to keep moving.
5. An astronaut has to wear something.
   This something is a space suit.
   A space suit supplies oxygen and air pressure.
   A space suit provides protection from extreme temperatures.

■ EXPLORING FURTHER: DEFINITION

Like a good sentence, a good definition clarifies the meaning of a term, a concept, or an issue. An effective definition communicates what you mean by the word or the concept and distinguishes it from all other words or ideas. Why is it important to know how to write clear definitions? Why not simply look up unfamiliar terms in a dictionary and quote the dictionary's meanings? The answer is that dictionaries provide only the *denotations* of a word—its objective, literal definitions at the particular time that the dictionary was written.

For example, the dictionary definitions of the word *frugal* include "not wasteful or not spending freely" and "economical." These denotations are neutral; neither implies that *frugal* is a good or a bad way to be. In addition to having denotative meaning, a word can have *connotations*—emotions or feelings that people associate with the word. For example, for some people, *frugal* has a positive connotation ("thrifty, economical, careful"). For others, the same word has a negative connotation ("cheap, stingy, miserly").

WRITING ACTIVITY 14

Look up the dictionary definition of each of the following words:

unassuming, humble, meek, submissive

What meanings do these words have in common?

____

____

____

How do their connotations differ?

____

____

____

WRITING ACTIVITY 15

Here is a list of six terms. Look up the dictionary definition of each one. Write the dictionary's first definition in the appropriate space. Then write what the word means to *you.* The first one has been done as an example.

1. Intelligence
   Dictionary definition: *the ability to learn or to understand from experience; the ability to respond successfully to new situations*

   My definition: *the ability to understand people and things and to learn from experience and from mistakes*

2. Truth
   Dictionary definition: ______________________________

   ____

   My definition: ______________________________

   ____

3. Freedom
   Dictionary definition: ______________________________

   ____

   My definition: ______________________________

   ____

4. Racism
   Dictionary definition: ______________________________

   ____

   My definition: ______________________________

   ____

5. Loyalty
   Dictionary definition: ______________________________

   ____

   My definition: ______________________________

   ____

6. Disability
   Dictionary definition: ______________________________

   ____

My definition: ______________________________________

____

How long should a definition be? You know the answer—as long as you need to accomplish your purpose for your intended readers. Sometimes a sentence is sufficient to define a term:

> A dictatorship is a type of government in which one person has absolute control over all the people and the powers.

A sentence definition may be appropriate when you are writing for readers who are familiar with your topic and with the vocabulary you are using. Often, however, you will need to write a paragraph to define a word or a term, especially if your readers do not have background knowledge about your subject.

Writing a Formal Definition

A *formal* definition has three parts: (1) the word, term, or subject that the writing is defining, (2) the general class or category to which the term belongs, and (3) the features or characteristics that distinguish the object, person, or idea from all others in this class or category. A formal definition can be as brief as a single sentence or as long as an essay. Here are some examples of sentence-length formal definitions.

Word or term	Category or class	Distinguishing features
A dictatorship	is a type of government	in which one person has absolute control over all the people and the powers.
A convocator	is a person	who calls together other people for an academic or religious assembly.
A saxophone	is a single-reed wind instrument	that has a curved metal body and a range of about three deep octaves.
A sanctuary	is a building or a place	set aside for worship of a god or gods.

REMINDER

Do *not* use a word to define itself. For example, do not write "A dyspeptic is a person who suffers from dyspepsia." This kind of definition is known as a *circular definition* because it sends readers around in circles trying to figure out what the term means. A better definition of this word might use synonyms: "A dyspeptic is a person who suffers from indigestion and stomach problems."

When you write a formal definition, use precise, clear language to state the general class or category to which the word you are defining belongs *and* to describe its distinguishing characteristics. If your category or your characteristics are vague, readers may not understand your meaning. Here is an example of a formal definition that is too vague.

> A hectogram is a measure used to weigh things.

Do you understand what a *hectogram* is from this definition? How does a hectogram differ from an ounce or a pound? Here is a more precise revision of this definition:

> A hectogram is a metric measure of weight equal to 100 grams (or 3.527 ounces).

WRITING ACTIVITY 16

Plan, write, and revise a paragraph-length formal definition of the word *frustration.* Think about this word. How would you define frustration? What general category or class does it belong to? (Is it a "thing"? If not, what is it?) What characterizes frustration?

In the space below, write a formal definition of this term. Remember that *frustration* is *not* a *when* or a *where.* (*When* refers to a time, and *where* refers to a place; *frustration* is neither.)

____

____

____

____

____

____

As with all writing, the topic sentence and the details you develop for your definition paragraphs depend on your topic, your purpose, and your readers' knowledge and expectations. Here are some questions to consider as you plan your definitions.

1. Do I want readers to understand an unfamiliar term or subject?
2. Do I want readers to get a new or fresh understanding of a familiar word or topic?
3. Do I want to explain how the meaning of a word has changed over time (or from one generation to the next)?
4. Do I want to explain why a term is often misunderstood or used incorrectly?
5. Do I want to argue for a particular definition of a word or a subject?
6. How much do my readers already know about the term or subject I am defining?
7. What else do readers need to know about the subject or about me in order to understand my definition?
8. What examples and explanations would best accomplish my purpose in writing this definition for these readers?

Strategies for defining words or terms vary. Depending on your purpose and readers, you might simply write a synonym for the term. Or you could look up a word in a dictionary and quote its definitions—its dictionary meanings. You might write a subjective definition that communicates your personal interpretation of the term. Or you could write a formal definition that identifies the class or category to which the term belongs and explains how it differs from others in that class.

Definition paragraphs can be organized from the least important example to the most important one—or vice versa. You can also try organizing your details or examples in order of their general familiarity (from best known to least familiar). If you are using narration to develop a definition paragraph, then chronological order is probably the most appropriate way of organizing your stories and examples.

Here is an essay in which the writer uses definition to explain an activity that taught her a lesson. It was written by a high school senior, Celia E. Rothenberg, on her application for admission to Wellesley College.

Detasseling, simply defined, is the removal of the tassel from a corn stalk so that pollinization of the plant can occur and hybrid seed corn can grow. Among midwestern high school students detasseling is infamous because it requires extremely long hours in the July heat, tolerance of "corn rash" and bugs, and a lot of physical strength. I signed up in response to a dare from someone who believed that I would not be able to last the full six weeks. Perhaps it was the growing recognition of my own strength, my pride in being one of the twelve detasselers (out of the original seventy) who were asked to work the entire detasseling season, or the antagonistic nature of the dare that propelled me through all six weeks, but what I learned from that experience has changed me as a person.

Detasseling helped me to look beyond the surface of people who are different kinds of achievers from those I encounter every day. Attending University High School, I have learned to respect academic accomplishments above other types of achievement. Yet many of my fellow detasselers had completely different sets of values and goals that I came to admire. Many of them were working in order to eat, or to buy essential books and supplies for school. Being singled out as a "brain" from the first day because of the stereotype the students held of students from my high school was difficult. Yet I earned the respect of my crew by working hard, and we developed a friendly, working relationship.

My partner, Josh, told me that the money he was making from the summer would be his only money for the rest of the year and would enable him to finish high school; college for him was an impossibility. Yet he never lost his sense of humor. Walking the three-quarters of a mile down each row, he would "rap," "I don't like to pick this corn, but I'm still glad that I was born." He gave me a true sense of what it means to make the most out of very little.

Speaking little English and understanding even less, two Thai girls who detasseled that summer never complained; together they could outwork the strongest and most experienced of the detasselers. Their determination to adjust to new surroundings and to work hard earned the respect of all of us.

The dynamics of the crew reflected the responsibility most of the crew felt toward the job and the farmer whose corn we detasseled. There were days when we stayed after dark working by flashlight to finish a field so that it would not have to be plowed under, which would have meant a significant monetary loss for the farmer as well as a waste of three acres of good corn. Only after we finished did I realize that we had worked since 5 A.M. Since detasseling, I have not been a part of a group that requires every member to be as responsible as each crew member had to be then.

While discovering the strengths of so many different kinds of people, I also discovered some of my own strengths. I discovered my ability to respond to physical as well as academic challenges. I realized that I am able to depend on my own inner resources. This discovery of my own physical strength and my ability to endure came as a revelation to me.

Learning to judge people by different standards carried over into the school year when I realized that I did not have a date to the Junior Prom. Not used to staying home, I considered my options and discovered someone who was also dateless. A gifted math student, PLATO programmer, and someone who always carried a calculator, he seemed to have little in common with me. Even so, I asked him to Prom. Detasseling proved to me that different types of people can learn from each other, and we did. A very special friendship evolved after Prom, perhaps partly because of our differences and partly because we had taken the time and effort to discover that beneath the surface we share many things in common.

The concept of detasseling and what it requires is understood by few; yet those who have experienced it share a special bond. After detasseling we did not see each other again as a group, but we parted with respect for one another. I left valuing new things about myself and other people. And I also won the dare.

Discussion Questions

1. What is ''detasseling''? Can you define it in your own words?
2. What was the writer's purpose in this essay? What did she want to show or convince readers of?
3. Did the writer accomplish this purpose? Why or why not?
4. How did detasseling help the writer learn about herself and about other people?
5. Which sentences in this essay were particularly effective or interesting?

WRITING ASSIGNMENT

Plan, write, and revise a paragraph or two defining the ideal spouse (husband or wife). What qualities or behaviors characterize the ''perfect'' husband or wife? Develop your details and examples using one or more of the strategies that you practiced in this chapter. Decide on a logical order for your details, and end with a conclusion that sums up your personal interpretation of this word. When you finish writing your paragraph, revise it using the techniques you learned in Chapter 3 (and use the Revising and Editing Checklist on page 86). Then examine each sentence and answer these questions:

- Does it communicate my meaning and my emphasis clearly?
- How can I make this sentence more interesting?
- Are my sentences varied?

Use the strategies that you practiced in this chapter to improve your sentence style.

✔ POINTS TO REMEMBER ABOUT SENTENCE VARIETY AND STYLE

1. Be willing to ''play'' with your sentences. Experiment with rewriting them in different ways for a different focus or different emphasis.
2. Examine every sentence for places where you might add descriptive words and phrases in order to communicate your ideas more precisely.
3. Add adjectives and adverbs that enable readers to share your perceptions and experiences.
4. Vary the lengths of your sentences.
5. Add prepositional phrases that explain ''where,'' ''when,'' ''why,'' and ''how.''
6. Add participial phrases (that begin with *-ing, -ed,* or *-en* verbs) and appositive phrases.
7. Vary your sentence beginnings. Try shifting a phrase within a sentence to the beginning of the sentence.
8. Combine sentences with a comma and a coordinator.
9. Combine sentences by changing one sentence into a prepositional phrase, a phrase that begins with an *-ing, -ed,* or *-en* verb, or an appositive phrase.
10. Combine sentences by changing one sentence into a relative clause.

CHAPTER

8

MODIFICATION AND PARALLELISM

Here is a sentence that is not a fragment or a run-on. Read it and figure out why it sounds funny:

> We learned that Malcolm X asked Alex Haley to help him write his autobiography in our English class.

Did Malcolm X write his autobiography while he was in this student's English class? That is what the sentence above states. Do you see the problem? Where should the writer have put the descriptive phrase ''in our English class'' in this sentence? What does this phrase modify (describe)?

In Chapter 7, you practiced using descriptive words and phrases to add interesting details to your sentences and to make them lively and varied. Another name for a descriptive word or phrase is a *modifier.*

TYPES OF MODIFIERS

The following parts of speech are descriptive modifiers.

- *Adjectives* modify nouns. They tell *who, what kind, how many,* and *which ones*: ''*Five brown* leaves drifted down, stirred by the *light* winds.''
- *Adverbs* modify verbs, adjectives, or other adverbs. They tell *how, when, where, to what extent,* and *why*: ''*Today,* some birds chirped *very loudly outside* my window.''
- *Participial phrases* are groups of words that act as adjectives: ''*An-*

noyed by the noise, several squirrels climbed down the tree, *hoping for quiet.*''

- *Appositive phrases* are also groups of words that act as adjectives: ''The birds, *four sparrows and two cardinals,* dived toward the squirrels.''
- *Prepositional phrases* are groups of words that can act as adjectives or adverbs: ''The squirrels *on the ground* (adjective) burrowed *under the leaves* (adverb).''

Here is a sentence with several types of modifiers.

> *Resting in the middle of the road,* we saw a *large gray* wolf *coming home from the movie theater.*

Can you tell what is wrong with this sentence? Who or what is in the road? Who or what is on the way home from the movies? The two participial phrases (descriptive word groups that begin with *-ing* verbs) sound funny because they are not next to the noun or pronoun they are describing. They are both *misplaced modifiers*—awkward or confusing phrases that are not placed next to the word they are describing. If we move a misplaced modifier next to (or near) the word it is modifying, we clear up the confusion:

> *Coming home from the movie theater,* we saw a *large gray* wolf *resting in the middle of the road.*

Here are two possible corrections of the sentence in the first paragraph of this chapter:

1. *In our English class,* we learned that Malcolm X asked Alex Haley to help him write his autobiography.
2. We learned *in our English class* that Malcolm X asked Alex Haley to help him write his autobiography.

The prepositional phrase ''in our English class'' should be next to or near the word it is describing—the pronoun ''we.''

IDENTIFYING AND CORRECTING MISPLACED MODIFIERS

Here is another example of a sentence with a misplaced modifier. Can you correct it?

> *Shining brightly in the night sky,* I gazed at the moon.

Do you see why the modifier (the *-ing* participial phrase) is misplaced? Who or what is ''shining brightly in the sky'' in this sentence? We can correct this sentence by moving the modifier:

I gazed at the moon *shining brightly in the night sky.*

As you can see from this example, a misplaced modifier can give a meaning to a sentence that the writer did not intend. Here are more sentences with modifier errors in them. As you read them, figure out why they sound awkward or confusing.

A. Elena realized that meditating helps her perform better in her races *the evening before.* (*When* does Elena run in races?)

B. Elliot *almost* answered all the questions on the graduate school admissions questionnaire. (Did he answer *any* questions?)

C. Charlotte saw several research papers *standing near the librarian's desk.* (Can research papers *stand*?)

All three sentences have misplaced modifiers. The descriptive words are not next to the words they are describing. They should be rewritten as follows:

A. Elena realized that meditating *the evening before* helps her perform better in her races. (Now the sentence makes sense: Elena meditates the evening before she races.)

B. Elliot answered *almost* all the questions on the graduate school admissions questionnaire. (This correction says that he answered ''almost all the questions'' rather than he ''almost'' responded to them.)

C. *Standing near the librarian's desk,* Charlotte saw several research papers. (Now this sentence makes it clear that it was Charlotte who was ''standing near the desk,'' not the research papers.)

When you edit your sentences, make sure that every modifier is next to the word it is describing. If you begin a sentence with a modifier, make sure that the word it is describing follows directly after the modifier.

In addition, as you reread and edit your drafts, check for the modifiers *almost, only, just, hardly,* and *finally.* These modifiers should be placed immediately *before* the word that they are describing. If you move one of these modifiers to a different place in a sentence, you create confusion. For example, examine the differences in meaning among the following sentences.

1. *Only* I said that you are cute. (Nobody else said it.)
2. I *only* said that you are cute. (I did not mean it.)
3. I said *only* that you are cute. (I didn't say anything else.)

4. I said that *only* you are cute. (No one else is cute.)
5. I said that you are cute *only*. (I said that you are simply cute, nothing else.)

The misplacement of modifying words and phrases can result in confusing (or unintentionally funny) sentences. Put modifiers next to—or as near as possible to—the words they describe.

GROUP WORK 1

Work on this activity with two or three classmates. Together, examine each of the sentences below. Decide whether the modifier in each sentence makes sense or is misplaced. Circle every misplaced modifier and draw an arrow pointing to its proper position next to the word it is supposed to modify. The first one has been done as an example.

1. I love to go see animals in zoos that roam free.
2. Instead of cages, many zoos keep animals fenced in large ranges.
3. I particularly enjoy watching the wild animals sitting on a bench outside the fence.
4. The big cats pace back and forth near the fence from Asia.
5. As the lions stare at me, I feel as though they could reach out and devour almost my hand.
6. The panthers look at me sitting up straight at the edge of the range.
7. The tigers come right up and glare at people with piercing yellow eyes at the fence.
8. An endangered wild cat, my zoo has a Bengali tiger.

WRITING ACTIVITY 1

Circle the misplaced modifier in each of the following sentences. Rewrite the sentence correctly on a separate sheet of paper.

1. I wrote an essay about my father in my English class.
2. I was overwhelmed as I wrote down my ideas with love.
3. When I was about six, I wrote about an experience that I remember.
4. It happened when my mother and sister were at the mall who liked to go shopping.
5. I was sleepy, so I decided to take a nap in my room on the bed.
6. When I woke up, the house was silent which should have been filled with the sounds of cooking.
7. I searched through the entire house anxious and afraid.
8. I saw my father finally sleeping on the sofa in the den.
9. Snoring away, I watched and listened to my father.
10. I woke my father with hugs feeling gratitude and love.

WRITING ACTIVITY 2

Think about a time in your life when you realized what someone meant to you. Did you ever have an experience that revealed your true feelings about a special relative or friend (or that revealed the person's feelings toward you)? Write a paragraph or two describing this experience. What happened? When? Where? How? What did you learn?

When you finish planning and writing your paper, revise it and edit it. Look for places in each sentence where you can add descriptive words and phrases. Then reread your sentences to see if you have written any misplaced modifiers. If you have, correct them.

GROUP WORK 2

Form a group with two or three other students, and choose one person to record the group's answers. Read the student paragraph that follows. Then, together, identify the misplaced modifier in each sentence and decide where it belongs.

Loved by many teenagers as the best new rap-and-blues singers, my brothers took me to hear Bell Biv De Voe. Waiting in line to get in, the street was filled with people of every age and color. I bought a poster from a man with a picture of the group selling souvenirs. Clapping their hands for the concert to start, the club was filled with people. When the show started, four handsome young men jumped onstage carrying microphones dressed in black. I was excited that I was going to hear them finally sing. My favorite song suddenly the notes of "Above the Rim" came booming from the stage. This song is about basketball as a metaphor for making love which has complex harmonies. Sounding better than on the album, the audience went crazy as the group sang "We're living life above the rim." Then the group, which is about not having casual sex, sang the ballad "Situation." I was watching Ricky Bell dance standing and clapping in my seat. When the concert ended, I was overwhelmed as we walked out of the club with pleasure.

IDENTIFYING AND CORRECTING DANGLING MODIFIERS

Another kind of sentence error that writers may have difficulty with is a *dangling modifier.* This is a descriptive word or phrase that does not clearly or logically modify another word in the sentence. The most frequent type of dangling modifier is a participial phrase that comes at the beginning of a sentence:

Glancing at my computer, the screen was blurry.

A computer screen cannot glance at anything! This sentence is confusing because it is missing the subject that the dangling modifier is supposed to describe. Who or what was "glancing at my computer"? We can correct this sentence by inserting the appropriate subject right after the modifier:

Glancing at my computer, I saw that the screen was blurry.

A descriptive word or phrase that begins a sentence must be followed by the word (or words) it is meant to describe. Here are two more examples of dangling modifiers:

A. *Despite sketching for weeks,* errors were made on the final design. (Is there a *person* in this sentence who did the sketching and made the errors?)

B. *While gazing at the sky,* her foot hit a rock and stumbled. (*Who* gazed at the sky and *who* stumbled?)

In both sentences, the word that each modifier is describing is missing from the sentence. The sentences have to be rewritten so that the subject is present, not merely implied:

A. *Despite sketching for weeks,* Chun-Mo made errors on the final design. (This correction adds a person who is taking the actions.)

B. *While gazing at the sky,* Liz hit a rock with her foot and stumbled. (This correction adds a person who did the hitting and then stumbled.)

The only type of dangling modifier that is *not* confusing to readers is a modifier that is describing the "understood" subject *you* in a command sentence:

To get to the cafeteria, use the west staircase to go to the eighth floor.

In the sentence above, the phrase "to get to the cafeteria" is modifying the implied subject, "you."

WRITING ACTIVITY 3

Circle the dangling modifier in each of the following sentences. Add a subject for it to modify, and rewrite the sentence correctly in the space below. The first one has been done as an example.

1. An insane day, I am thinking of staying in bed tomorrow.

   I had an insane day, and I am thinking of staying in bed tomorrow.

2. While cooking breakfast this morning, the water boiled over onto the floor.

3. Piled with dirty dishes, I didn't even try to clean the coffee pot.

4. After eating two fruits, my stomach started to ache.

5. Closed into a tight parking spot, I had difficulty pulling the car out of the garage.

6. Being late for work, stopping for the newspaper and coffee was impossible.

7. Hitting the rear bumper at a red light, my new Pontiac Trans-Am was dented.

8. Rushing to the garage, the mechanics could not work on the car for at least a week.

9. Having gotten to the office late, the boss yelled at me.

   ____

10. To get home from work tonight, a cab must be taken.

   ____

WRITING ACTIVITY 4

Each of the sentences below has a misplaced or dangling modifier. Circle the error in each sentence and rewrite it correctly on a separate sheet of paper.

1. Misunderstood for years, scientists are now able to explain how an embryo becomes a fetus.
2. By examining ultrasonic pictures, many important discoveries were made.
3. Eight weeks after conception, scientists call the developing mass of cells a *fetus.*
4. At the age of about twelve weeks, the size of a bar of soap.
5. Rapidly growing and changing, we can see the fetus's organs when it is about fifteen weeks old.
6. The mother by the end of six months can feel the fetus moving in her womb.
7. Before birth, the mother's body is changing.
8. As her uterus gets ready to give birth, the baby turns upside down.
9. To be born, the muscles of the mother's uterus must contract against the baby.
10. Lasting anywhere from twenty minutes to twenty hours, the baby is born at the end of labor.

GROUP WORK 3

Form a group with two or three other students, and choose one person to record the group's answers on a separate sheet of paper. Read the following sentences. Then, as a group, identify the misplaced or dangling modifier in each sentence and correct the sentence.

1. While sleeping last night, a horrible nightmare ended my dreams.
2. I was dreaming about my house sleeping peacefully.
3. My husband shifted his weight to one side of the bed who was snoring loudly.
4. Hearing the noise and feeling the bed shake, the dream changed.
5. Much more scared than usual, the dream turned into a nightmare.
6. Flashing bolts of lightning, I dreamed that a terrible storm ripped apart my house.
7. Starting with the roof and tearing out the bedrooms, the destruction was awful.
8. My husband's snoring sounded like giant claps in my head of thunder.
9. I felt like Dorothy when my bed shook violently in *The Wizard of Oz.*
10. Shaking me to wake up, the nightmare finally ended.

REMINDER

Read each sentence, looking for each word that describes a noun, pronoun, or verb. Make sure that every modifier has a logical subject (not an implied one). Also make sure that every modifier is next to (or as close as possible to) the noun, pronoun, or verb that it is describing.

IDENTIFYING AND CORRECTING FAULTY PARALLELISM

Another type of sentence error is faulty parallelism. *Parallel* means ''matching'' or ''corresponding.'' Parallel lines run in the same direction (and stay the same distance apart); parallel words or phrases are written in the same grammatical form. When you write a sentence that discusses a series of words or ideas, these words or ideas must be in the same—parallel—parts of speech. For example, here is a sentence with a series of three parallel phrases, each consisting of an *-ing* verb and a noun.

> Roberto's favorite activities include *playing volleyball, reading autobiographies,* and *building model cars.*

If one of the phrases had been written in a different grammatical form from the others, it would create an awkward-sounding error in parallelism:

> Roberto's favorite activities include *playing volleyball, reading autobiographies,* and *to build model cars.*

The second sentence sounds unbalanced. Each of the verbs should be in the same (parallel) grammatical form (''playing,'' ''reading,'' and ''building'').

Sentences are a bit like songs. Misplaced modifiers or faulty parallelism affects readers the way untuned instruments or off-key notes affect listeners. Parallelism errors are jarring because they break the rhythm of a sentence. Effective parallelism, on the other hand, is a repeating pattern that reinforces the writer's meaning. For instance, here is a sample of the dramatic effect of using parallelism correctly. It is an excerpt from the speech that Winston Churchill, the prime minister of England, gave during World War II to inspire the British troops (the parallel structures are shown in italics).

> *We shall fight* on the beaches, *we shall fight* on the landing grounds, *we shall fight* in the fields and on the street, *we shall fight* in the hills; *we shall never surrender,* and even if, which I do not for a moment believe, this island or a large part of it were *subjugated and starving,* then our Empire beyond the seas, *armed and guarded* by the British fleet, would carry on the struggle, until, in God's good time, the new world, with all its *power and might,* steps forward to the *rescue and liberation* of the old.

In each set of sentences below, the first sentence has a parallelism error, and the second sentence illustrates one way of correcting the error.

1. An effective teacher is intelligent, sensitive, and shows consideration. (The first two descriptive words are adjectives, but the third is a verb phrase.)

   An effective teacher is intelligent, sensitive, and considerate. (All three modifiers are adjectives.)

2. I want to be a teacher in order to have a good career, to help others, and for sharing knowledge. (The first two descriptive phrases in this series begin with *to* verbs; the third one should also.)

   I want to be a teacher in order to have a good career, to help others, and to share knowledge. (Now all three phrases consist of *to* verbs followed by nouns.)

3. My favorite teachers were those who seemed enthusiastic, friendly, and who listened carefully. [The first and the third descriptive phrases have the same pattern (the word *who* followed by a past tense verb and an adjective or adverb). The second descriptive word in this series should follow this pattern.]

   My favorite teachers were those who seemed ethusiastic, who were friendly, and who listened carefully. (All three modifiers have the same pattern.)

4. Not only do I hope to become a teacher, but also get an M.A. degree in education. (The first goal is a complete sentence, but the second goal is simply a verb phrase.)

   Not only do I hope to become a teacher, but I also want to get an M.A. degree in education. (Now both goals include a subject and a verb.)

   I hope to become a teacher and get an M.A. degree in education. (In this sentence, both goals are stated as verb phrases.)

Keep your sentences balanced by using the same grammatical form or part of speech to express related words and phrases that you have combined using the word *and* or *or*.

WRITING ACTIVITY 5

Circle the faulty parallelism in each sentence below and rewrite the sentence correctly in the space provided. The first one has been done as an example.

1. I enjoy working in my garden because it provides me with regular exercise, fascinating, and enabling me to be creative.

   I enjoy working in my garden because it provides me with regular exercise, it is fascinating, and it enables me to be creative.

2. Gardening helps people exercise their arms and legs as they pull out weeds and to dig up the soil.

   ____

   ____

3. An effective gardener is three things: careful, creative, and has a knowledge of plants and flowers.

   ____

   ____

4. The best rewards of planting and growing flowers are seeing beautiful things grow, relaxation, and to get in touch with nature.

____

____

5. My children suggested that we grow vegetables and maybe some fruits can be planted.

____

____

6. I prefer planting flowers because they are easy to grow, need little attention, and flowers add beauty to their surroundings.

____

____

7. Whether to plant vegetables or growing flowers is a crucial decision that gardeners must make unless they have acres of space for their garden.

____

____

____

8. My garden is calm and peaceful in contrast to my life, which is nerve-racking and it can be very busy.

____

____

9. On rainy days, I either take care of plants indoors or finding some other chore or ways to exercise.

____

____

10. For me, gardening represents an escape from my problems, it is a relaxing hobby, and exercising comes from gardening.

WRITING ACTIVITY 6

Here are five quotations that illustrate how the rhythm of parallelism emphasizes the writer's meaning. In the space below each quotation, write a sentence imitating its parallelism. The first one has been done as an example.

1. "Ask not what your country can do for you—ask what you can do for your country." (John Fitzgerald Kennedy)

   Think not about how your friends can help you—think about how you can help your friends.

2. "Whoever is loved is beautiful, but the opposite is not true, that whoever is beautiful is loved." (Jelaluddin Rumi)

3. "The reward rests not in the task but in the pay." (John Kenneth Galbraith)

4. "The love of liberty is the love of others; the love of power is the love of ourselves." (William Hazlitt)

____

____

5. ''We are not built like a ship to be tossed, but like a house to stand.'' (Ralph Waldo Emerson)

____

____

GROUP WORK 4

Form a group of two or three people. Together write a sentence for each of the quotations. Your sentence should imitate the parallel structure of the quotation.

1. ''It is easier to love humanity as a whole than to love one's neighbor.'' (Eric Hoffer)
2. ''I came; I saw; I conquered.'' (Julius Caesar)
3. ''There is only one thing in the world worse than being talked about, and that is not being talked about.'' (Oscar Wilde)
4. ''You don't learn to hold your own in the world by standing on guard, but by attacking and by getting hammered yourself.'' (George Bernard Shaw)

> **REMINDER**
> Experiment with your sentences to determine which method of correcting errors in parallelism communicates your meaning most clearly *and* provides the best rhythm.

GROUP WORK 5

Work with one or two classmates on this activity. Choose one person to read the following passage aloud (quietly). It is the text of Abraham Lincoln's Gettysburg Address, the 1863 speech that he made to dedicate the National Cemetery at the site of a battlefield in Pennsylvania. In this speech, President Lincoln eloquently proclaimed the goals of a democratic country.

When you have finished reading (or listening to) this speech, identify every example of parallelism and be prepared to discuss why you think it is or is not effective.

In a larger sense, we cannot dedicate—we cannot consecrate—we cannot hallow—this ground. The brave men, living and dead, who struggled here, have consecrated it far above our poor power to add or detract. The world will little note nor long remember what we say here, but it can never forget what they did here. It is for us, the living, rather, to be dedicated here to the unfinished work which they who fought here have thus far so nobly advanced. It is for us to be here dedicated to the great task remaining before us—that from these honored dead we take increased devotion to that cause for which they gave the last full measure of devotion; that we here highly resolve that these dead shall not have died in vain; that this nation, under God, shall have a new birth of freedom; and that government of the people, by the people, for the people shall not perish from the earth.

WRITING ACTIVITY 7

Combine each set of sentences into a single sentence. Make sure that the ideas you combine are in parallel grammatical form. The first one has been done as an example.

1. We left to go to the beach. Dark clouds were beginning to form. It was starting to drizzle.

   When we left to go to the beach,

dark clouds were beginning to form, and it was starting to drizzle.

2. We consoled ourselves. We did this by saying that the rain would stop by the time we got to the beach. We also said that the dark clouds would disappear.

3. We were looking forward to seeing something. We wanted to see clear blue skies. We wanted to see water that was calm and cool.

4. The beach is a place that is wonderful. It is a place for having fun. It is a place to forget your troubles.

5. We arrived at the beach. The sun was beginning to peek through the clouds. The air started to get warmer.

6. We did some of our favorite activities, which include playing beach volleyball. We swim in the ocean. We like to jog on the sand.

7. After a day by the sea, we went somewhere. We went to a park nearby. We went to shower. We went to empty the sand from our belongings.

 ____

 ____

8. We all felt hungry. We were also tired. We were also feeling exhilarated.

 ____

 ____

9. The adults cooked a meal at a campfire. The children were setting the table.

 ____

 ____

10. A little planning makes a day at the beach seem like a real vacation. A little cooperation helps too.

 ____

 ____

■ EXPLORING FURTHER: COMPARISON AND CONTRAST

Parallelism involves balancing words or ideas in a sentence; comparison and contrast involve balancing ideas in paragraphs and essays. Parallelism and comparison require the same critical thinking skill—the ability to recognize the similarities between words, phrases, and ideas.

People use comparison and contrast in almost every decision they make—from deciding what to wear to choosing a husband or a wife. When you think about the similarities between two people, things, places, or points of view, you are comparing them. When you think about their differences, you are contrasting them. How often do you compare and contrast things—consciously or unconsciously—every day? For instance, when you purchase an item, often you have compared and contrasted it with all the other things you could have bought.

If a teacher assigns a "comparison" paper, find out whether you are to compare *and* contrast the subjects. Some teachers do not state the direction "contrast" in their assignments, assuming that comparison papers analyze *both* similarities and differences.

Once you have chosen two subjects and decided whether to write about their similarities, their differences, or both, you have to think about your purpose and your audience. Here are some questions to consider when you are planning a paragraph that compares, contrasts, or does both.

- What exactly do I want to explain or illustrate or prove?
- Who are my readers? Who would be interested in reading this paragraph?
- How much do my readers already know about the two subjects that I am comparing or contrasting?
- What else do they need to know about these subjects?
- What unfamiliar terms should I define or explain?
- What details will support the point I am making about the subjects that I am comparing or contrasting?

WRITING ACTIVITY 8

Here are some topics for a comparison or contrast paper: two jobs, relatives, classes, teachers, musical groups, songs, movies, or problems. Choose one of these topics, and do some brainstorming and clustering about it. Then ask yourself the questions above and write down your answers. Use these notes to develop a paragraph or two comparing or contrasting your two subjects.

When you finish writing your draft, examine each sentence. Is it a complete sentence? Where can you add modifiers to help readers understand your points?

Developing a Comparison or a Contrast Paragraph

One way to develop details for a comparison or contrast paper is to write a chart of similarities, differences, or both between your two subjects. Here is an example of a student's chart for the topic "Jobs and Professions":

Comparison-Contrast Chart: Jobs Versus Professions

Jobs	Professions
minimum wage	excellent salaries
no pension	good pension (and benefits!)

physical labor	mental work
set time for vacation	responsibilities often require professionals to miss vacations
punch a clock and go home	work until the objectives are accomplished (and take work home to do at home)
	Professions provide more emotional and financial rewards
you can prepare for a job in a few months	You need to attend college and (usually) to get degrees to be a professional
Job skills don't change (unless the technology changes)	Professionals need to keep up with changes in their fields (read books and journals and go to conferences to learn new things)

After examining this chart, the writer decided that she had more details about differences than about similarities. She revised her notes so that they focused on the differences between jobs and professions. Here is her revised list.

Differences	**Jobs**	**Professions**
Salary	Often minimum wage	Higher starting salary and pay scale

Responsibilities	Physical work Punch clocks Don't take home work	Mental work Work long hours Take work home
Preparation	Some college or learn on the job	Many years of college Books, journals, conferences

This list provides the writer with a blueprint for a paragraph contrasting her two subjects. It also helps her develop a topic sentence for her paragraph:

> When we examine the differences between jobs and professions, we can see that studying for a professional career is well worth the effort.

In this topic sentence, the writer identifies her two subjects (''jobs'' and ''professions''), and she indicates that she will focus on their differences. The topic sentence of a comparison or a contrast paragraph should identify the subjects being compared and should state your opinion about these subjects or about the similarities or differences between them.

GROUP WORK 6

Form a group with two or three classmates, and choose one person to write down the group's responses. For each pair of subjects below, decide whether you think they are more similar or more different. If the group decides that the subjects are more similar than different, prepare a comparison chart for the two subjects. If the group decides the subjects have more differences than similarities, prepare a chart of their contrasts.

1. High school and college
2. Mothers and fathers
3. City children and rural (or suburban) children
4. A bicycle and a motorcycle
5. Typewriters and computers

You can organize comparison and contrast paragraphs for the two subjects in two ways. One strategy is to develop details subject by subject; this is often called *block* order (because you are blocking out the important features of one subject and then of the other subject). With block order, you discuss all the features of one of the subjects you are comparing or contrasting before going on to discuss the next subject. Here is an example of a contrast paragraph organized by block order. The writer has selected five points of contrast, which she describes for each of her subjects.

Jobs
Salaries
Advancement
Preparation
Responsibilities
Requirements

Professions
Preparation
Responsibilities
Requirements
Salaries
Advancement

When we examine the differences between jobs and professions, we can see that studying for a professional career is well worth the effort. Most nonprofessional jobs pay only minimum wage, and the salary scale is not large. There is not much room for advancement (financially or on the job). Nonprofessionals often master the essentials of their jobs in a few days or years. Some even learn on the job. Finally, people who work in blue-collar jobs know when and where they have to work, usually punching clocks, leaving at the same time every day, and never taking home work. Professionals, on the other hand, need years of education to acquire the skills and degrees for their work. When they begin their careers, they work long hours, often taking work home at night and on the weekends. Professionals assume many responsibilities, but their salaries usually increase in relation to their responsibilities. People in professional careers know that their years of education and preparation frequently result in high incomes, excellent benefits, and great satisfaction.

Another strategy for organizing comparison and contrast paragraphs is to develop ideas point by point, in *alternating* order. Here you alternate from one subject to the other. In an alternating pattern, first you decide on the points of comparison or contrast, and then you compose the paragraph or essay point by point, indicating how each point relates to both the subjects you are comparing or contrasting. In the paragraph that follows, the writer of the preceding paragraph reorganized the information into alternating order.

When we examine the differences between jobs and professions, we can see that studying for a professional career is well worth the effort. Most nonprofessional jobs pay only minimum

Salaries	wage, whereas professional careers offer the potential for very high
	starting salaries and even higher retirement incomes. Professionals
Advancement Responsibilities	are also able to advance and to take on more responsibilities (for more money). Most jobs do not offer these opportunities. However,
Preparation	professionals must pay for the years of education to acquire the
	skills and degrees for their work. Finally, people who work in blue-
Requirements	collar jobs know when and where they have to work, usually
	punching clocks, leaving at the same time every day, and never
	taking home work. Professionals usually work long hours, often
Hours	taking work home at night and on the weekends. Still, people in
	professional careers know that their years of education and
	preparation frequently result in high incomes, excellent benefits, and
	great satisfaction.

WRITING ACTIVITY 9

Think about two courses that you took recently. Do some brainstorming about the ways in which these courses were similar or different. Then decide on the important points you want to compare and contrast (for example, the types of knowledge you were expected to learn, amount and difficulty of required reading and writing, and so forth). Prepare a chart comparing *or* contrasting these courses, using the points of comparison or contrast that you think are most important.

WRITING ACTIVITY 10

Choose a pair of subjects from any of the preceding writing activities in this chapter. Develop a chart that compares them and a chart that contrasts them. Decide whether you want to emphasize their similarities or their differences. Write a topic sentence indicating the emphasis you have chosen. Then write a paragraph based on the corresponding chart.

The following comparison and contrast essay has no title. It was written by a high school student named Heather L. Nadelman on her application for admission to Yale University. In this essay, the writer describes two sides of her personality by comparing them to coffee and tea and then by contrasting coffee and tea.

"Coffee or tea?"

A simple enough question, a question that seemingly requires an absent-minded, automatic reply. Clearly, in this world one is either a coffee or a tea drinker. I, however, am an exception to this rule; I constantly vacillate between coffee and tea. My enjoyment of both drinks does not stem merely from flexible tastebuds, nor does it originate in a desire to be as little trouble as possible by drinking whatever is available. Rather, this ambivalence depicts two distinct sides of my personality.

Coffee is lively, exuberant, and extroverted: a wild, wet dog show, complete with pouring rain, whipping winds, and a dog who simply will not behave. The ring has become a sea of oozing mud, turning the dog you so perfectly groomed last night into a mud-splattered, bedraggled horror who resembles an alley cat more than a purebred show dog with a pedigree going back to the *Mayflower.* Animals who never before had shown signs of unstable temperament suddenly decide to be terrified of the wind's flapping their handlers' yellow rain slickers. All dogs are quick to take advantage of the fact that their handlers, with fingers numbed from cold and eyes half-blinded from rain, have very little control over them. On such a day, a steaming cup of well-brewed hot coffee is one's only salvation; only coffee can transform such misery into a memory that will be laughably, almost fondly, recalled.

Tea is sedate, thoughtful, and introverted: a cold November afternoon with a friendly fire crackling in the background. One sits in an overstuffed armchair with an open copy of *Wuthering Heights,* reading, dreaming, and listening to music that plays softly from the stereo. The novel and music flow into each other, transporting the room to a time that perhaps was, perhaps never was, or perhaps always is. The world's worries are locked outside, flung to the chilly winds; inside, all is peaceful and relaxed. On such an afternoon, one feels able to solve every riddle that the greatest minds have pondered. Yet oddly, on such afternoons one never attempts solutions. So near the point of understanding, one allows all answers to escape; if the mysteries of life were solved, much of the pure pleasure of thinking would be lost forever. At such moments of partial meditation it is tea, the world's most civilized drink, that is one's only conceivable companion.

Although often contradictory, my need for coffee and my need for tea balance each other nicely. The freneticism of the world of dog shows is as important as the quiet reflection of a peaceful afternoon. Perhaps I will originate a new personality classification, the "coffeetean," roughly equivalent to an introverted-extrovert or extroverted-introvert. Unlike the simple lives of people wholly shy or wholly exuberant, the life of a coffeetean, if a bit complicated, cannot fail to be varied and exciting.

Those who drink coffee, tea, and hot chocolate, however, are far too schizophrenic for their own good.

Discussion Questions

1. What is the main point of this essay? What was the writer's purpose in writing this essay?
2. Which details, comparisons, and contrasts were most effective in helping you understand the writer's perception of herself?
3. What order did the writer use to develop her ideas? Was this order logical and effective?
4. Which sentences show interesting uses of parallelism?

WRITING ASSIGNMENT

Plan, write, and revise a paragraph or two comparing or contrasting yourself with an object (a plant, an animal, a book, a movie, a food, a house, and so forth). First, make a chart of the similarities and differences. Decide whether you want to write about similarities only, differences only, or both. Then use the strategies that you learned in this chapter to develop a topic sentence and supporting details for your paragraphs.

✔ POINTS TO REMEMBER ABOUT MODIFICATION AND PARALLELISM

1. Make sure that each sentence expresses a complete idea and that it begins with a capital letter and ends with a period, a question mark, or an exclamation point.
2. Read each sentence, one at a time, to see if it has a subject and a verb.
3. Check each sentence, one at a time, to determine that it is a complete sentence and not a fragment or a run-on.
4. Make sure that every modifier is next to the word or words that it is describing.
5. Make sure that words in a pair or in a series are in the same grammatical form.

CHAPTER 9

GRAMMAR: NOUNS AND VERBS

What is *grammar*? Most of us think that grammar means the rules for using words and sentences correctly. Most people also assume that every language has one clear set of rules for correct or "good" grammar. This is not true. The rules for "correct" grammar can differ from community to community. For example, the rules for correct American English usage differ from those for correct British English usage. Moreover, the rules for correct Appalachian American English are different from those for correct Los Angeles Urban Black American English.

The way in which a community uses its language is called a *dialect,* and there are more than a dozen dialects of American English, each with slightly different grammatical rules. The grammar and usage rules in this chapter describe the dialect called *Academic Written English* (sometimes called *Standard Written English*), which is the dialect generally used for writing in schools, business, the government, and the news media.

In writing, as well as in speaking, grammar and usage depend on one's subject, purpose, and audience. For instance, someone might say the following sentence to a friend:

> My friend Tania, she ain't goin' to work anymore 'cause she's got to finish college this semester.

The speaker has communicated her message without worrying whether her grammar was "correct." If the listener didn't understand the speaker, he or she would probably respond with "What do you mean?" However, if the speaker had written this sentence in the final version of an academic paragraph, her teacher would probably find it unacceptable. The writer would need to edit the sentence so that it follows Academic Written English conventions:

> My friend Tania isn't going to work anymore because she has to finish college this semester. (The writer might have made the statement even more formal by omitting the contractions: "My friend Tania is not going to work anymore because she has to finish college this semester.")

Effective writers examine their writing from the perspective of their intended readers. As you revise your paragraphs and compositions, think about the Academic Written English conventions that your readers will expect. If you don't follow these conventions, readers may not understand your ideas and may get distracted by or annoyed at your unconventional words or grammar. In school and at work, edit your writing so it conforms to the basic conventions of Academic Written English.

You have already learned how to edit your sentences for correctness and for variety. As you learned in Chapter 4, the building blocks of sentences are nouns and verbs. A *noun* is a word that names a person, place, thing, concept, or quality (such as *child, biology, tables*). A *verb* is a word that expresses an action, a condition, or a state of being (such as *hope, revise, is*). Some words can be used as both a noun and a verb:

> I *talked* (verb) to my friend Anna Lee twice yesterday. I always feel better after our *talks* (noun).

> The *trust* (noun) that I have in Anna Lee is rewarded by the extent to which she *trusts* (verb) me.

Some nouns can also be used as adjectives:

> Eric bought a *gold* (adjective) chain for Anna Lee because he knows how much she likes *gold* (noun).

> He bought it at the *jewelry* (adjective) store that sells all different kinds of *jewelry* (noun).

TYPES OF NOUNS

Nouns can be classified in different ways. For example, you can divide nouns into two groups based on the types of things that they name. A *common* noun names a class or a group of things (such as *university, president,* or *city*); a *proper* noun names a specific person, place, or thing (such as *Clark University, President Clinton,* or *Salt Lake City*). Remember to capitalize the first letter of each word in a proper noun. However, a common noun is not capitalized *unless* it begins a sentence, begins a quotation, or is part of a title. Here are some examples:

One of my favorite poets (common noun) is Gary Soto (proper noun), a teacher (common noun) at the University of California at Berkeley (proper noun). Childhood objects (common noun that begins a sentence) are the focus of many of Soto's poems. His first collection (common noun) of poetry, *The Elements of San Joaquin* (common noun that begins a title), won the U.S. Award (proper noun) at the International Poetry Forum (proper noun). Soto's poems also tell of his experiences (common noun) as a migrant worker (common noun) in the California fields (common noun).

WRITING ACTIVITY 1

For each of the common nouns below, think of a proper noun that is an example of it. Then write a sentence (on a separate sheet of paper) that includes the common noun and the proper noun. The first one has been done as an example.

1. teacher

   Prof. Harvey Wiener is the best teacher I have ever known.

2. river
3. car
4. movie
5. book

Another way of classifying nouns is by the number of things that they name. A *singular* noun names one person, place, or thing (*mother, state,* or *glass*); a *plural* noun names more than one (*mothers, states,* or *glasses*). You know how to form the plural of most nouns: Simply add *-s* to the end of the noun:

singer	singer*s*
video	video*s*
Soto	Soto*s*

To form the plural of a noun that ends in *-s, -x, -z, -ch,* or *-sh,* add an *-es* ending:

bush	bush*es*
ditch	ditch*es*
box	box*es*

To form the plural of a noun that ends in *y* preceded by a consonant, change the *y* to *i* and add *-es* (except for a proper noun that ends in a *y*):

story	stor*ies*
theory	theor*ies*
January	January*s*

To form the plural of a number, a letter, or a symbol, add an apostrophe and an *-s*. If you write out the number, letter, or symbol, add only the *-s*.

U	U*'s*
2	2*'s*
eleven	eleven*s*

The plural of a noun ending in *f* or in *fe* is formed in one of several ways: add an *-s* ending or change the *f* or the *fe* to a *v* and add *-es*:

roof	roof*s*
wolf	wolv*es*
knife	kniv*es*

To form the plural of compound nouns, add an *-s* ending to the main word.

runner-up	runner*s*-up
father-in-law	father*s*-in-law
baby-sitter	baby-sitter*s*

WRITING ACTIVITY 2

On a separate sheet of paper, write the plural form of each of these words:

1. bench
2. suffix
3. penny
4. thief
5. patio
6. roof
7. Abernathy
8. clue
9. belief
10. spy
11. two-year-old
12. church
13. Wednesday
14. mix
15. valley

GROUP WORK 1

Form a group with two or three classmates. Choose a person to record the group's responses on a separate sheet of paper. Together, read the following paragraph. Identify and correct errors in the capitalization of common and proper nouns. In addition, correct all the errors in noun plurals.

The *mountains of the moon* is the name given to the Mountain Range that runs between the Countrys of zaire and uganda in east africa. This Range is eighty mile long. It dips through River Vallies and ends below in lake albert, beneath massive cliffes. The name *mountains of the moon* is an old name. ancient Greek and Egyptian Philosopher (including aristotle and ptolemy) decided that the Source of the nile river in egypt was mountains that stretched all the way up to the Moon. These believes led them to name the peaks *mountains of the moon.* However, the real name of these peak is the ruwenzori mountain range. The range was discovered in 1888 by the American Explorer Henry morton Stanley. The Highest Peak in this Range, mount stanley, was named after him.

VERB FORMS

Remember that a sentence is a group of words that includes a subject and a verb and that expresses a complete thought:

> s v
> Right now, my sisters are repairing our computer.

The subject is the person, thing, place, or idea that the sentence is about. The verb states what the subject is doing or experiencing. In the sample sentence above, the subject is the plural noun *sisters* and the verb is *are repairing.*

In English, the time of the action or condition expressed by the verb is called its *tense.* Verb tense tells when the action or the experience in the sentence happens—in the past, in the present, or in the future:

> *Past:* My sisters *fixed* our computer.
> *Present:* They *fix* computers quite well.
> *Future:* They *will fix* our printer tomorrow.

The present tense describes what is happening or what is true right now *or* what happens regularly *or* what is generally true:

> My sisters *repair* (or *are repairing*) the disk drives now. Both of them *are* computer programmers, but they also *know* how to repair computers.

For most English verbs, the present tense is the form of the verb that follows the word *to* (as in "to *repair*" or "to *know*"). This form (called the *infinitive*) is the form you use to look up a verb in the dictionary. The *-ing* form of the present tense is usually used to indicate that the action or condition expressed by the verb is occurring at the moment that the writer is writing the sentence:

> My sister Renee *uses* MS-DOS 6 for her computer programs. (The verb "uses" indicates that she does this action on a regular basis.)

> My sister Renee *is using* MS-DOS 6 for her computer programs. (The verb "is using" indicates that she is doing this action at the moment the writer is writing about it—that the action is continuing.)

The future tense expresses an action or a condition that is yet to happen. You know how to form the future tense of a verb: Put the helping verb *will* or *shall* in front of the present-tense form:

> My sister Lauren *will create* a new computer program next week.

WRITING ACTIVITY 3

On separate paper, write five sentences using the present-tense forms of the following five verbs: *decide, plan, determine, succeed, learn.* (For fun, see if you can write these five sentences about the same topic, or if you can make them relate to one another.)

The past tense indicates that the action of a sentence has been completed or that the condition described in the sentence has ended. The past tense of most English verbs is formed by adding *-ed* to the end of the infinitive form (or just *-d,* if the verb already ends in an *e*):

> Lauren and Renee *developed* a new program this morning.

WRITING ACTIVITY 4

On separate paper, write five sentences using the past-tense forms of the following five verbs: *receive, decide, claim, produce, finish.* (Can you write these five sentences about the same topic? Can you make them relate to one another?)

WRITING ACTIVITY 5

Each of the sentences below has a verb error (an incorrect present- or past-tense verb form). Cross out the error and write in the correct form above it.

1. In 1967, some scientists receive two mysterious messages from outer space.

2. These scientists work in an astronomy laboratory in England.

3. Today, these astronomers no longer worked at this lab.

4. In 1967, the scientists' instruments pick up distant radio waves from space.

5. The signals come from an object that was light-years away.

6. The instruments indicate that the radio wave signals were pulsing.

7. They pulse regularly, like the pulsing of the blood in a person's wrist.

8. Thus, these scientists call the object that was producing the signals a *pulsar.*

9. Today, scientists knew that pulsars form when a massive star explodes.

10. The spinning pieces of the star gave off pulsing radiation.

English verbs also have two other past-tense forms. The *present-perfect* form indicates that the action or condition described in a sentence began in the past and is still occurring. (The name of the tense—*perfect*—has nothing to do with quality; it comes from the Latin word for ''completed'': *perfectus.*) To compose the present-perfect form of most English verbs, use *has* or *have* as a helping verb with the past-tense form of the verb. (For a reminder about how to use helping verbs, see pages 101–102 in Chapter 4.) Here are two examples of two verbs in the present-perfect tense.

> Renee *has used* the MS-DOS operating system for the past five years. Lauren and I *have switched* to DR-DOS to operate our computers.

The present-perfect verb tense is also used to describe an action or a condition that occurred some time in the indefinite past and is related to the present:

> Lauren *has programmed* with DR-DOS for about a year, but she still feels nervous about doing it. Most of her friends *have* never *used* DR-DOS, so she cannot ask their advice about this system.

If you want to refer to an action or a condition that has been occurring over a period of time and that is still occurring, you can combine the present-perfect form of the verb *to be* (*has been* or *have been*) and the *-ing* form of the verb:

> I *have been experimenting* with MS-DOS 6 during the past week, and I think that I may switch to that system.

WRITING ACTIVITY 6

On separate paper, write five sentences using the present-perfect-tense forms of the following five verbs: *need, rely, hope, achieve, triumph.* Try to write these five sentences about the same topic or to make them relate to one another.

The *past-perfect* verb-tense form is used to indicate that the action or condition described in the sentence occurred further back in time than another past action or condition that the sentence mentions. To compose the past-perfect form of most English verbs, use *had* as a helping verb with the past tense form of the verb:

> My sisters *had studied* several different computer systems for a few months before they chose DOS. They *had used* DOS before, but they *had* never *seen* the amazing things that DR-DOS and MS-DOS can do.

WRITING ACTIVITY 7

On separate paper, write five sentences using the past-perfect-tense forms of the following five verbs: *decide, try, realize, change, transform.* (Can you write these five sentences about the same topic? Can you make them relate to one another?)

WRITING ACTIVITY 8

The following paragraph is written in the present tense. Change the time of the paragraph to the past by doing the following:

1. Cross out each underlined present-tense verb.
2. Write its past-tense form or past participle form above it.

The first one has been done as an example.

The Opium War of 1839 between China and Great Britain happened ~~happen~~ because Chinese leaders refuse to establish regular trading with the British. People think that this war start because of opium, but it actually occur because the British want to increase their trade with the Chinese. The British East India Company import opium into China in return for Chinese tea and silk. Great Britain import opium into China for years before the Chinese leaders decide to do something about it. The leaders act because many Chinese people start to use opium and became addicted to it. Because of this addiction, they neglect their farms and their work. So Chinese officials seize a huge amount of British opium and destroy it. The British protest, but negotiations fail, and the two countries declare war against each other. The war end in 1842 with the signing of the Treaty of Nanking. According to this treaty, the Chinese agree to give their southern port, Hong Kong, to the British to pay for the opium they destroy. This treaty also specify that Great Britain must return Hong Kong to Chinese rule in 1997.

The *future-perfect* verb-tense form is used to express an action or a condition that will be completed before another future action or condition takes place. There are two ways to compose the future-perfect form. The first way is to use *will have* or *shall have* as helping verbs with the *-ed* or the *-en* tense form of the verb:

> By the time I learn MS-DOS 6, Microsoft (the company that makes it) probably *will have created* a brand new computer operating system. I *will have learned* a system that will no longer be used by most people.

The second way of forming the future-perfect tense is to use *will have been* or *shall have been* as helping verbs with the *-ing* form of the verb:

> By the time I learn the new system, I *will have been programming* computers for more than five years.

VERB FORM AND TENSE REVIEW

Infinitive	Present participle	Past	Past participle
study	studying	studied	studied

- Present tense: I *study* FORTRAN. I am *studying* FORTRAN.
- Past tense: Yesterday, I *studied* FORTRAN. Yesterday, I *was studying* FORTRAN.
- Present-perfect tense: I *have studied* FORTRAN almost every day for the past year.
- Past-perfect tense: I *had studied* COBOL before I decided to learn FORTRAN.
- Future tense: I *will study* COBOL again in the future.
- Future-perfect tense: By the time I study COBOL, I *will have learned* FORTRAN. I *will have been studying* computer languages for a long time.

Regular and Irregular Verbs. The technical name for the verb form that we use with the helping verbs *has, have,* and *had* to create the perfect tenses is the *past participle.* The past-tense form and the past participle form of most English verbs are the same:

> Today my sister *repaired* a disk drive that she *had repaired* before. I *learned* how to fix disk drives by watching her fix them. I *have learned* many valuable skills by watching my sister.

If the past-tense form and the past participle form of a verb are both produced by adding *-d* or *-ed* to the infinitive form, the verb is called a *regular* verb. Most English verbs are regular verbs. They have only two forms: the present (the infinitive) and the past (with an *-ed* ending). As the Verb Form and Tense Review chart on page 244 shows, the future tense of most verbs is composed of *will* plus the infinitive form, and the perfect-tense form is the same as the past-tense form. The present tense poses a problem for some writers because they forget to add an *-s* ending on present-tense verbs that they use with third-person singular subjects:

I *study* FORTRAN. You *study* FORTRAN. She *studies* FORTRAN.

Confused? Don't worry. We'll clear this up soon.

The problem that the past and perfect tenses often present for advancing writers is that they may forget to add the *-d* or *-ed* ending when they don't pronounce these endings. For example, look at the sentence below. It is clear that the writer is expressing a past-tense action:

Yesterday, my brother Jake try to repair a computer.

However, like most English speakers, the writer probably does not pronounce the *-d* ending of a word that is followed by a word beginning in a *t, d,* or *th.* Thus, she left off the past-tense *-d* ending of the verb ''try.'' Academic Written English requires this *-d* ending to indicate the past tense.

Yesterday, my brother Jake *tried* to repair a computer.

Some writers have a similar problem with the *-ed* ending on adjectives (words that describe nouns) that are created from the past participle. Here is an example:

I bought a *use* computer because I could not afford a new one.

The ''computer'' in this sentence was ''*used*'' by someone; thus, it is a ''*used*'' computer. The adjective *used* is actually the past participle form of the verb *to use.* Therefore, this adjective needs an *-ed* ending on it.

REMINDER

If you write a past-tense verb, a past participle, or a past participial adjective, check to make sure that you have written the correct ending (usually *-ed* or *-en*) even if you don't pronounce this ending.

If you look up a regular verb in the dictionary (under its ''to,'' or infinitive, form), you will see that many dictionaries do not list any other forms of the verb. Dictionary authors assume that you know how to create the future form (with *will*) and the past and participle forms (with *-ed*) of regular verbs.

However, a number of English verbs are *irregular.* Their past or past participle forms are *not* created by adding *-d* or *-ed* to the infinitive form.

Instead, the past-tense form and the past participle are produced by changing the spelling of the infinitive form. If you look up an irregular verb in the dictionary, it will list the past-tense form and the past participle directly after the pronunciation of the verb. Here is an example:

be-gin′ (bi-gin) [began, begun]

If you are ever unsure about the past-tense form or the past participle form of a verb, just look up the infinitive form in the dictionary. For example, what is the past participle of the verb *ride*? If you know the answer, write it now. If you don't, look it up in your dictionary. You will discover that the past participle is *ridden,* as in "We have ridden in this car before."

The most commonly used irregular verb is *to be,* which can be more confusing than other verbs because it is the only one that does *not* use its infinitive form for the present tense.

FORMS OF THE VERB *TO BE*

Present	**Past**	**Past participle**
I am	I was	I have been
You are	You were	You have been
He or she is	She was	He has been
We are	We were	We have been
They are	They were	They have been

The only way to master the forms of irregular verbs is to use them frequently and memorize them as you use them. Here is a list of the principal parts of common irregular verbs, grouped according to their spelling patterns.

COMMONLY USED IRREGULAR VERBS

Infinitive	**Past tense**	**Past participle**
	Begin, began, begun pattern	
begin	began	begun
drink	drank	drunk
ring	rang	rung
sing	sang	sung
sink	sank	sunk
spring	sprang	sprung
swim	swam	swum

Infinitive	**Past tense**	**Past participle**
	Break, broke, broken pattern	
break	broke	broken
choose	chose	chosen
freeze	froze	frozen
steal	stole	stolen
speak	spoke	spoken
	Blow, blew, blown pattern	
blow	blew	blown
draw	drew	drawn
fly	flew	flown
know	knew	known
throw	threw	thrown
	Drive, drove, driven pattern	
drive	drove	driven
ride	rode	ridden
rise	rose	risen
strive	strove	striven
write	wrote	written
	Bleed, bled, bled pattern	
bleed	blcd	bled
creep	crept	crept
feed	fed	fed
feel	felt	felt
lead	led	led
leave	left	left
mean	meant	meant
weep	wept	wept
	Bring, brought, brought pattern	
bring	brought	brought
buy	bought	bought
catch	caught	caught
fight	fought	fought
teach	taught	taught
think	thought	thought
	Verbs without a pattern	
be	was, were	been
do	did	done

(Continued)

Infinitive	Past tense	Past participle
eat	ate	eaten
find	found	found
forget	forgot	forgotten
go	went	gone
run	ran	run
see	saw	seen
take	took	taken
tear	tore	torn

GROUP WORK 2

Do this activity with one or two classmates. Here are eight sets of three sentences. The first sentence in each set uses the present-tense form of a verb. Do the following in each set:

1. Fill in the past-tense form of the verb (used in the first sentence) in the space in the second sentence.
2. Fill in the past participle form of the verb in the space in the third sentence.

The first one has been done as an example.

1. My brother Joey *is* a great tennis player. He

   ______was______ always a talented athlete. He has

   ______been______ playing tennis for about five years.

2. Most tennis players *need* to warm up for about fifteen minutes

   before they play. Last year, Joey ____________________

   only five minutes to warm up. He has never

   ____________________ more than ten minutes to get ready

   to play.

3. Joey *serves* the ball very quickly and accurately. Last week,

   he ____________________ a first serve at about forty miles

per hour. The fastest he has ever ______________________ a ball is fifty miles per hour.

4. Joey *breaks* the strings on his racket frequently. In fact, yesterday, Joey ______________________ two tennis rackets. He had never ______________________ the strings on two rackets before.
5. Usually Joey *brings* a few rackets to his games. Yesterday, he ______________________ only two rackets. In the past, he has ______________________ a third, but yesterday he forgot to, so he had to borrow someone else's racket to finish his game.
6. Joey *speaks* almost nothing during a game. This morning, he ______________________ only a few words to the other player. Many times, he has ______________________ nothing during the entire game.
7. Joey *gets* along well with most of the players we know. In the first three years that he played, he ______________________ into only three arguments. Other than these arguments, he had never ______________________ into fights with other players.
8. Now Joey *strives* to be good at everything. In the past, he ______________________ to be a great racquetball player. Before that, he had ______________________ to be the best paddleball player in our town.

Reread the list of Commonly Used Irregular Verbs. Notice that we form most of them by changing the spelling of the infinitive rather than by adding a *-d* or an *-ed* (which is the way to form the past tense and past participles of regular verbs). Some writers find this confusing, and they add *-ed* endings to the past tense or the past participle of irregular verbs. For example, they may write "I wish I had *chosened* my words more carefully before I *spoked* to him" (instead of "I wish I had *chosen* my words more carefully before I *spoke* to him.") Irregular verbs do *not* need *-d* or *-ed* endings in the past tense.

There are three other places where you do *not* have to add a *-d* or an *-ed* ending to a verb.

1. Don't add an ending to the infinitive form of a verb (the form that follows the word *to*).

   I wanted *to learn* [not "to learned"] about computers.

2. Don't add an ending to a verb that follows the helping verbs *do, does,* or *did.*

   I really *did fulfill* [not "did fulfilled"] my goal.

3. Don't add an ending to a verb that follows the helping verbs *can, could, should, would, may,* or *might.*

   I *could achieve* [not "could achieved"] other goals soon.

WRITING ACTIVITY 9

Write ten sentences that use the present perfect (*has* or *have* + past participle) *or* the past perfect (*had* + past participle) for the following ten verbs: *be, begin, become, do, know, build, say, see, shine,* and *strike.* Try to write these ten sentences about the same topic or make them relate to one another.

WRITING ACTIVITY 10

Edit the following paragraph so that all its verbs are in Academic Written English form. Cross out each incorrect past-tense form and each incorrect past participle. Then write in the correct version above it. The first one has been done as an example.

Last summer, my family ~~tooked~~ took a vacation together. We gone to visit my grandparents in San Jose. We brang many presents for our relatives, and they gived us gifts in return. They were surprised to seen how much we had growed. They had forgot that we are all adults now. We talk all day, and by the evening we felted as though we been living there for a week already. The vacation flown by. We were sorry when it was finally time to drived back home. The trip back taken two days. After we had rode in the car for such a long time, we getted very tired. We goed to bed as soon as we getted home. Thus, we didn't knowed that a hurricane was coming. If we had knowed, we could have tooken some precautions. The noise of the gusting wind waked us all up. We start yelling and we creeped into our parents' bedroom to seen what was going on. What a dreadful way to ended a vacation.

GROUP WORK 3

Here are five irregular verbs that were *not* included earlier in the list of Commonly Used Irregular Verbs. Form a group with one or two classmates, and look up each verb in the dictionary to find out its past-tense and past participle forms. Together, compose one sentence using the verb in the past tense and a second sentence using the verb in the present-perfect tense (*has* or *have* + past participle) or the past-perfect tense (*had* + past participle). Take turns writing these sentences on a separate sheet of paper. Here are the verbs:

grow, shake, show, shrink, thrive

(You should write ten sentences: two for each of the verbs.)

WRITING ACTIVITY 11

Here are ten sentences that follow the rules for forming the past and perfect tenses in other dialects. "Translate" each sentence into Academic Written English. Cross out the verb forms that are not Academic Written English. (Look up verb forms you are not sure of in the dictionary.) Then write in the Academic Written English form of the past tense or the past participle. The first one has been done as an example.

1. My father ~~play~~ plays basketball almost every evening.
2. He say that it help him to get rid of his stress.
3. He been playing basketball since he been five years old.
4. He good enough to play for semiprofessional team.
5. In fact, he was ask to try out for a local semipro team.
6. My father be too proud to tell anyone about this exciting opportunity.
7. He also feels that most people ain't care about it.
8. My family and I done tell everyone about my father's incredible basketball skills.
9. I was disappointed when my father didn't had a career in professional basketball.
10. However, I been very proud of his career in medical technology.

WRITING ACTIVITY 12

Write a paragraph about what your life would be like now if you had not decided to go to college. What would you have done? How would you have felt? Try to use as many past participles as you can to describe what your life might have been like if you had not gone to college. (Some examples of past participles include "would *have gone* to work" or "would *have learned* a trade at a vocational institute.") When you finish writing and revising your paragraph, underline all the past participles that you used. Make sure that you used the correct form of each one.

Verb-Tense Consistency. If you are writing about events that took place or that will take place at different times, you may need to switch verb tenses in the middle of a sentence or a paragraph. Here is an example:

> Talia *is* proud of herself for going to college because she *knows* that she *will become* the first college graduate in her family.

The time of the action in this sentence is the present (now), and two of the three verbs in this sentence are written in their present-tense forms: *is* and *knows*. However, the third action in this sentence (becoming a college graduate) has not yet occurred. It will take place in the future, so the correct verb-tense form to refer to it is the future form: *will become*.

Readers get confused when writers switch tenses for no obvious reason. Verb-tense shifts that communicate unintended time periods are very confusing. Here are some examples:

> When Luis *told* his family that he *had made* the dean's list in his junior year of college, they *congratulate* him and *encourage* him to do even better. He *was delighted* with their response and *decides* to make the dean's list every semester.

There isn't any logical reason for this writer to shift back and forth from the past tense to the present. The writer should have used the past tense for all the verbs:

> When Luis *told* his family that he *had made* the dean's list in his junior year of college, they *congratulated* him and *encouraged* him to do even better. He *was delighted* with their response and *decided* to make the dean's list every semester.

REMINDER

Edit your verbs to make sure they are consistent in tense. If the time that you are writing about does not change, then don't change verb tense.

WRITING ACTIVITY 13

The following student paragraph does not exhibit consistent verb tense. Cross out the verbs that are not written in the logical tense, and write the correct form above each verb that you cross out.

The population on our planet is increasing at a very rapid rate. The number of people on the earth has reached one billion in 1830.

That is more than one-and-a-half centuries ago. By 1930, the number increases to two billion. In one century, the earth's population doubles. Amazingly, only thirty years later, in 1960, there are an additional billion people on the planet. Today, the planet is home to almost four billion people. If the population continued to grow at this rate, we exhausted the earth's resources by the year 2020. The earth's population must be reduced soon or people began to experience severe shortages of food and space.

EXPLORING FURTHER: DIVISION AND CLASSIFICATION

This chapter asked you to think about different ways of dividing and classifying nouns and verbs. Division and classification are basic thought processes. We divide and classify in order to make sense of the people and the things in our lives. By placing objects in categories, we see interrelations among different things that share common features. For instance, consider the ways in which you classify food. People divide the clothes they wear in different ways (summer, fall, winter, spring clothes; play, school, ''dress-up'' clothes; machine-washable, hand-washable clothes; and so forth).

Division and classification are similar processes. When you divide, you break something down into its parts, types, or categories. With classification, you arrange several things or people into groups or categories based on features they share. This textbook itself illustrates the strategies of division and classification. It is divided into three parts, which are classified according to the skills that writers can practice in each part: ''The Principles of Effective Writing'' (paragraph and essay development), ''The Writer's Handbook'' (sentence structure and grammar), and ''Progress Logs'' (revision and editing).

DIVISION AND CLASSIFICATION

Effective division and classification paragraphs have the following characteristics:

- A clear focus and purpose that are appropriate for the intended audience
- A logical basis for dividing or classifying the subject
- Relevant examples and illustrations
- Appropriate transitional words and expressions to help readers understand the relations between ideas

WRITING ACTIVITY 14

Here is an activity that will illustrate how much you already know about dividing and classifying. Below are a student's brainstorming notes about "Teachers I Have Had." The writer has already divided the topic into many subtopics or details (characteristics of teachers). Imagine that this writer has asked you to help him classify these details into logical groups or categories. Think of the different ways in which he could sort these details into groups. Then take out a sheet of paper and write down a heading for each group. List the details that fit under each heading.

Teachers I Have Had

Men & women

friendly, caring teachers

unfriendly, self-centered teachers

Personalities—serious, funny, interesting, boring, challenging, witty, sarcastic

Some were incredibly brilliant. Others were merely smart, and a few seemed dumb.

Some were very strict, others were very lenient, and some were demanding.

Most were generous with their time and their office hours

Some were fair; others were unfair.

Make division and classification easier by narrowing your purpose before you begin. What exactly is your subject, and why are you dividing it into parts or classifying it? Here are some purposes for writing division or classification paragraphs:

- To gain a better understanding of a person, object, place, or concept by breaking it down into its parts and explaining how each part relates to the whole
- To clarify your understanding of people, objects, places, or concepts by sorting them into groups according to characteristics they share
- To increase your understanding of people, objects, places, or concepts by sorting them in different ways, according to differing characteristics or features

Once you have decided on your purpose for writing, you can begin selecting and organizing the details that you developed by brainstorming or clustering. Here is how the writer of the notes on page 255 classified his notes.

Types of Teachers I Have Had
(Organized by Classification)

1. Gender
   - Males
   - Females
2. Personality
   - Serious and boring
   - Serious and interesting
   - Funny and interesting
3. Intelligence
   - Brilliant
   - Smart
   - Not particularly knowledgeable
4. Discipline style
   - Very strict
   - Not strict but demanding
   - Lenient

Topic sentence: The types of teachers I had in elementary and secondary school fall into several categories.

Notice that each time the writer divided his details into different categories, he used a different *organizing principle* to classify his groupings. For example, the writer's first organizing principle was gender. Next he tried to divide his teachers according to his perceptions of their personalities. Then he focused on the teachers' intelligence. Finally, he classified his teachers by their discipline style.

REMINDER

The topic sentence of a division or classification paragraph should identify your topic and indicate the organizing principle you are using to classify your groups or types.

WRITING ACTIVITY 15

Go to a bookstore. Examine the ways in which the manager has divided and classified the products. Are certain products grouped together in areas or on shelves? What are the organizing principles of this classification? (For example, are products divided by type into hardcover books, softcover books, and magazines, or by the content of the books and magazines?) Write down the categories of products in the store. Then, under each category, write down the names of at least five things in this category. Finally, develop a topic sentence for a paragraph about how this store's classification system helps (or does not help) shoppers.

WRITING ACTIVITY 16

Think of at least four different organizing principles for dividing and classifying your friends. For example, one way to divide them is by "gender" (that is, male or female). On a separate sheet of paper, divide your friends into at least three different groupings, each classified according to a different organizing principle.

GROUP WORK 4

Form a group with one or two classmates and choose one person to write down the group's responses. Together, decide on an appropriate organizing principle for dividing and classifying each topic that follows. Then divide the topic into at least three categories according to the organizing principle that you have selected. The first one has been done as an example.

1. Schools
   Organizing principle: *grade level*
   Categories:
   elementary school, secondary school, college or university, graduate school

2. Children
   Organizing principle:
   Categories:

3. Holidays
   Organizing principle:
   Categories:

4. Television programs
   Organizing principle:
   Categories:

5. Cars
   Organizing principle:
   Categories:

Topic sentences for division or classification paragraphs often use language such as the following:

> [*This topic*] can be divided into three main types: . . .
>
> [*This topic*] can be classified according to how its members . . .
>
> [*This topic*] falls into three categories: . . . .
>
> Three kinds of [*categories*] make up [*this topic*]: . . .

REMINDER

Try out different words to describe the groups that you choose for your division or classification paragraphs. Instead of *groups,* use *types, categories, kinds,* or *classes.* (Look up these words in your dictionary or thesaurus to understand how they differ slightly in meaning.)

WRITING ACTIVITY 17

Select one topic from the five topics in Group Work 4 (on pages 257–258) and develop a topic sentence about it (on a separate sheet of paper). Then plan, write, and revise a paragraph about this topic.

As you revise your division or classification paragraphs, make sure you have included enough details so that readers will understand your points. Ask yourself the following questions:

1. Did I oversimplify when I divided my topic into two or three categories or groups? Did I overlook an important category?
2. Does each group or category that I have discussed include all parts or members of that group (or did I leave out any important parts or types)?
3. Did I describe or explain each part or type in approximately the same amount of detail (or did I write too little or too much about one of the groups or categories)?

GROUP WORK 5

Form a group with two or three classmates, and choose one person to write down the group's responses. Together, do some brainstorming about the topic "Types of Courses That Our College (or University) Offers." Then decide on an organizing principle to divide these types of courses. Use this organizing principle to develop at least three categories. Decide on a logical order for these categories. Develop a discovery draft of a paragraph or two about the kinds of courses that your school offers. (You can compose this paragraph individually or together in a group.)

WRITING ACTIVITY 18

Plan, write, and revise a paragraph or two about *one* of the topics below.

- Classify the books or magazines that you like to read.
- Classify the clubs you belong to.
- Classify the types of vacations you have taken.
- Classify pets with which you are familiar.
- Classify the sports you like to play or watch.

POINTS TO REMEMBER ABOUT NOUNS AND VERBS

1. Read each sentence, one at a time, to make sure that it has a subject and a verb.
2. Examine the nouns in your sentences to see if they are common or proper nouns. Capitalize the first letter of each word in a proper noun.

Do not capitalize common nouns unless they begin a sentence, begin a quotation, or are part of a title.

3. Examine each of your plural nouns. Make sure that you have added the correct ending.
4. Check your verb forms. Did you use the correct form of the verb in each sentence (its infinitive, present-tense, past-tense, future-tense, present participle, or past participle form)?
5. Look for every verb that follows a form of the verb *to be* or *to have.* Make sure that you follow these verbs with the correct form of the past participle.
6. If you used any past-tense verbs, past participles, or past participial adjectives, make sure that you have written the correct ending (*-ed* or *-en*) even if you don't pronounce this ending.
7. Check for verb-tense consistency. Don't switch verb tenses unless you have a logical reason for doing so.
8. Make sure that you have used Academic Written English for past-tense forms and past participles. If you are unsure of the correct spelling of any verb, look it up in a dictionary.

CHAPTER

10

GRAMMAR: SUBJECT-VERB AGREEMENT

One of the most troublesome aspects of Academic Written English grammar is subject-verb agreement. Here is a sentence that has an error in subject-verb agreement. Can you identify this error?

> My friend Amy like to go to concerts in the town park.

The form of the verb "like" in this sentence does not "agree" with the form of the subject "friend." Grammatical *agreement* means that the form of the verb matches the *person* and the *number* of the sentence's subject.

Person is a grammatical term that refers to the speaker's or the writer's relation to the subject of his or her sentence. If you speak or write about yourself, you know that you must use the *first-person* subject *I.* If you are discussing yourself as part of a group, then you use the *first-person* subject *we.*

> *I* wanted to go to a concert too, so *we* went to Crotona Park together.

If you are speaking or writing *to someone or to something,* you must use the *second-person* subject, *you. You* is used to address a single person or a group.

If you are talking or writing *about someone or about something,* you use a *third-person* subject: *he, she,* or *it* (for a single person, thing, or idea) or *they* (for a group). If the subject of a sentence can be replaced by the words *he, she, it,* or *they,* it is a third-person subject. For example, each underlined subject below is a third-person subject.

> My friend's <u>name</u> is Amy. <u>She</u> enjoys going to concerts in the town park. <u>It</u> has a band shell for the musicians. These <u>concerts</u> are usually free.

The subject of a sentence also has *number.* A subject can be *singular*—indicating one person or thing (*I, you, he, she, it,* or *one thing*)—or *plural*—indicating more than one (*we, you, they, several things*). As you learned in Chapter 9, all you have to do to make most singular nouns plural is to add an *-s* or an *-es* ending:

> The concert took place in the town park. We sat on a bench.
> The *concerts* took place in several *parks.* We sat on *benches.*

Some plurals are formed by a change in spelling:

> My child came to see the woman play the flute.
> My *children* came to see the *women* play the flute.

The problem that some writers have with subject-verb agreement concerns the *-s* ending on a present-tense verb that is used with a third-person singular subject. If you look at the following verb chart, you can see that the only verb that needs an *-s* ending is the one that is used with a third-person singular subject.

PRESENT-TENSE VERB CHART

	Singular	**Plural**
First person	I play	we play
Second person	you play	you play
Third person	she or he play*s*	they play
	it play*s*	

Now you know how to correct the subject-verb agreement error in the sample sentence on the first page of this chapter. The subject is a third-person singular noun, so the present-tense verb needs an *-s* ending:

> My friend Amy *likes* to go to concerts in the town park.

REMINDER

In Academic Written English, a third-person singular subject (anything that is a "he," a "she," or an "it") needs an *-s* ending on its verb in the present tense.

WRITING ACTIVITY 1

Circle the correct present-tense form of the verb in each set of parentheses in the following sentences. The first one has been done as an example.

1. The capital of the United States (are/is) Washington, D.C.
2. The letters *D.C.* (stands/stand) for the words *District of Columbia.*
3. This district (cover/covers) an area of about sixty-nine square miles.
4. The capital's name (comes/come) from the name of the first American president, George Washington.
5. Many important buildings (are/is) located in the capital.
6. These (includes/include) the White House, where the president and his family (lives/live).
7. The White House (contain/contains) the offices of many government officials.

The present-tense forms of the verbs *to be, to do,* and *to have* are different from those of other verbs. You have to change their spelling to indicate different types of subjects, as shown in the chart below.

PRESENT-TENSE FORMS OF *BE, DO,* AND *HAVE*

I *am*	I do	I have
you are	you do	you have
she *is*	he *does*	it *has*
we are	we do	we have
they are	they do	they have

PAST-TENSE FORMS OF *BE*

I *was*
you were
she *was*
we were
they were

WRITING ACTIVITY 2

Circle the correct form of the verb in each set of parentheses.

1. Football games (is/are) like war.
2. Players (is/are) often hurt during football games.
3. The most common injuries (is/are) tears in muscles of the players' legs, particularly their knees.
4. These kinds of injuries (is/are) common because opponents tackle the players to stop them from making touchdowns.
5. Fistfights also (occurs/occur) frequently in football, as the players push each other around.
6. The teammates of an injured player (is/are) like an army who try to avenge the wounded comrade.
7. Although football players wear padded uniforms, these uniforms (doesn't/don't) protect them from a fist in the stomach.
8. This warlike behavior (are/is) not in the spirit of the game.
9. Fighting (is/are) bad sportsmanship.
10. Football games, however, (is/are) becoming more violent each season.

GROUP WORK 1

Form a group with two classmates, and choose one person to record the group's answers. Choose the correct present-tense form of the verb in the parentheses in each of the following sentences.

1. Most people who like to go out in a boat __________ (to enjoy) the company of dolphins.
2. Dolphins actually __________ (to swim) in the wakes of boats.

3. In fact, a team of scientists ____________ (to have) proved that dolphins ____________ (to be) not just making friendly visits to people's boats.
4. According to the scientists the dolphins ____________ (to be) saving energy by riding the waves created by the moving boat.
5. In a sense, the dolphin ____________ (to appear) to be hitchhiking or catching a free ride behind boats.
6. Other research ____________ (to show) that by staying just below the surface in the wake of boats, a dolphin can swim twice as fast as it usually ____________ (to do).
7. Swimming after boats ____________ (to allow) dolphins to save energy.
8. Like the dolphin, fish also ____________ (to seem) to prefer swimming behind boats or larger fish.
9. Scientists ____________ (to think) that fish ____________ (to prefer) this because the movement of the waters ____________ (to make) swimming easier.
10. However, scientists ____________ (to do) not understand how dolphins ____________ (to use) the wake of moving boats to help them glide so easily through the water.

WRITING ACTIVITY 3

Fill in each blank space with the present-tense form of any verb that makes sense in the sentence.

(1) Did you know that your skin ____________ many different jobs? (2) One job ____________ to help you sense your environment. (3) The skin ____________ nerve endings that send signals to the brain. (4) When something ____________ any part of your skin, the skin's nerve endings ____________ this thing and tell your brain what it is. (5) In addition, skin also ____________ disease-carrying bacteria from entering your body. (6) If you ____________ your skin, you will bleed. (7) Then your skin ____________ scabs and skin cells to close the wound. (8) Thus, skin ____________ your body from germs. (9) Skin also ____________ your body from the harmful ultraviolet rays of the sun. (10) Skin ____________ a material called melanin that absorbs the sun's rays. (11) Sunlight ____________ skin to make additional amounts of melanin. (12) Too much sunlight ____________ skin cells and causes skin cancer. (13) Yet another function of skin ____________ to control your body's temperature. (14) Skin ____________ this job by sweating. (15) The evaporation of sweat ____________ the skin and the body cooler.
(16) If you ____________ of everything that your skin ____________ for you, maybe you will take better care of it.

SPECIAL PROBLEMS IN SUBJECT-VERB AGREEMENT

In order to make sure that each verb agrees with its subject, you have to determine whether the subject is singular or plural. Here are some tricky subjects that may confuse you.

I. When the Subject Is a Compound Subject. A compound subject is a subject that is made up of two or more nouns or pronouns. Most compound subjects are joined by *and* and name more than one thing. Thus they need a plural verb (a verb without an *-s* ending).

Julio ***tells*** the funniest jokes I have ever heard.
Julio and Henry ***tell*** jokes together sometimes.
Julio, Henry, and Jackie ***tell*** their jokes to anyone who will listen.

However, when two or more subjects in a sentence are joined with words like *or, either, neither,* or *nor,* the verb form is usually determined by the subject that is closer to the verb.

Julio or *his friends* ***are*** going to tell jokes at my party.
Julio's friends or *Julio* ***is*** going to tell jokes at my party.
Neither Julio nor his *friends* ***tell*** disgusting jokes.
Neither Julio's friends nor *Julio* ***tells*** disgusting jokes.

II. When Words Separate the Subject from Its Verb. Words or phrases that come between a subject and its verb do *not* affect the number of the subject. (They do not function like the word *and* in a compound subject.)

The *entertainer* at my party ***is*** going to be terrific.
The *entertainers* at my party ***are*** going to be terrific.

The word *party* is *not* the subject of either sentence above. The subject of the first sentence is "entertainer"; the subject of the second is "entertainers."

Be particularly careful about subject-verb agreement when the words that separate a singular subject from its verb sound as if they are making the subject plural. Expressions such as "in addition to," "as well as," "including," and "together with" do *not* make the subject plural *even though they sound as if they do.*

Julio and the other entertainers ***make*** any party come alive with excitement.
Julio, together with the other entertainers, ***makes*** any party come alive with excitement.

The first sentence above has a compound subject ("Julio and the other entertainers") and needs a plural form of the verb (without an *-s* ending). The subject of the second sentence is simply "Julio"; this subject needs a verb with an *-s* ending.

WRITING ACTIVITY 4

In each uncorrected sentence that follows, (1) underline the subject, (2) circle the main verb, (3) cross out every main verb that does not agree with its subject, and (4) write the correct form of the verb above it. The first one has been done as an example.

1. Riddles, jokes, and other forms of humor is used for many purposes.
2. One of these purposes are to have fun.
3. Many types of people tells jokes to make others laugh.
4. Adults and children knows how to use humor to amuse themselves and others.
5. However, sometimes funny stories or a riddle are used to make a person feel foolish.
6. This person, together with others who are listening, get embarrassed if he or she don't know the answer to the riddle.
7. The riddle teller and the other listeners laughs at the person who doesn't know the answer.
8. In this case, the riddle, as well as the lack of answers, become a cruel joke that hurt someone else.
9. Jokes or riddles of this type is not funny, especially if you are the person who are being laughed at.
10. Thus, I do not think that all forms of humor is always enjoyable.

WRITING ACTIVITY 5

In the uncorrected paragraph that follows, (1) underline the subject of each sentence, (2) circle the main verb, (3) cross out every verb that does not agree with its subject, and (4) write the correct form of the verb above it.

Not all the jokes of a comedian is always funny. A person in a room full of people laugh at a joke for several possible reasons. One of the obvious reasons are that the person finds the joke humorous. Another reason someone might laugh at jokes are to relieve tension. Sometimes a comedian's use of off-color ("dirty") words create tension in the listeners. People in the audience isn't sure how to handle this tension. Laughter, along with nodding one's head, are the easiest way to get rid of the tension. However, the laughs that result from tension is not related to the comedian's joke. Members of the audience is laughing from embarrassment rather than from amusement.

III. When the Subject Comes After Its Verb. A verb agrees with its subject, whether the verb comes after the subject or before it.

At the end of the joke ***is*** *a punch line.*
At the end of the joke ***are*** *two punch lines.*

If you begin a sentence with the "dummy" subjects *there* or *here,* the actual subject of the sentence *follows* the verb (and determines the form of the verb).

There ***is*** *a television program* that features new comedians every week.
There ***are*** *several television programs* that feature new comedians every week.

Note that the dummy subject *it* always requires a singular form of the verb, even if the subject that follows is plural.

It ***is*** the female comedians who make me laugh the most.

WRITING ACTIVITY 6

Write in the correct present-tense form of the verb in the parentheses in each of the following sentences.

1. There ____________ (to be) certain types of jokes that can be very hurtful.
2. Among the jokes that people ____________ (to use) to hurt others ____________ (to be) a type called the *fool joke.*
3. In this kind of joke, there ____________ (to be) stupid characters whose ignorance makes everyone laugh.

4. Sometimes, there ______________ listeners who identify with these
(to be)
characters and ______________ that the joke is making fun of them.
(to feel)

5. There ______________ more than one way to tell a fool joke.
(to be)

6. One of these ways ______________ to make fun of someone who
(to be)
is "different."

7. The targets of this kind of fool joke ______________ people who
(to include)
feel awkward or different from the other listeners.

8. Among the other victims of fool jokes ______________ people from
(to be)
different nationalities or ethnic backgrounds.

9. It ______________ these fool jokes that are often cruel and hostile
(to be)
instead of funny.

10. Underneath the seemingly funny jokes ______________ the mes-
(to be)
sage that the targets are less intelligent than the joke teller and the other listeners.

IV. When the Subject Is an Indefinite Pronoun. A *noun* is a word that names a person, a place, a thing, a quality, an action, or an idea. A *pronoun* is a word that can replace a specific noun or that can be used instead of a noun. (For additional information about nouns, see pages 236–238 in Chapter 9.) An *indefinite pronoun* is a pronoun that does not refer back to a specific, or "definite," noun.

Here is a brief list of indefinite pronouns that function as singular subjects:

each, either, neither
anyone, everyone, someone, one
anybody, everybody, somebody, nobody
anything, everything, everybody, nothing

Remember that when you use one of these indefinite pronouns as a subject, the pronoun is always singular, and it requires the singular form of the verb.

Everybody ***has*** at least one funny story to tell.
Each of these stories ***is*** funny in its own way.
Everything ***has*** the potential to be part of a joke.

However, five indefinite pronouns—*all, any, most, some,* and *none*—may take either a singular or a plural form of the verb, depending on their meaning in a particular sentence.

Some of Julio's comedy routine ***is*** not all that funny.
Some of Julio's jokes ***are*** not all that funny.

Most of his material ***is*** uproarious.
Most of his funny stories ***are*** uproarious.

All of Julio's humor at my party ***was*** playful.
All of Julio's humorous jokes at my party ***were*** playful.

WRITING ACTIVITY 7

In the paragraph below, fill in each blank space with the correct form of any verb that makes sense in the sentence.

Whenever I hear somebody ____________ a funny story, I find myself trying to figure out why the story is being told. Most humor ____________ several purposes. For example, if someone ________ a story about a mistake he or she made, the storyteller might want the listeners to know that everybody ____________ the same kinds of mistakes. This helps the storyteller feel as though he or she is a familiar person with whom all the audience ____________ comfortable. Because the speaker is the target of the joke, nothing in these kinds of stories ____________ anyone who is listening. When the speaker and the listeners laugh together at the speaker's mistakes, neither ____________ being hostile. Because everyone ____________ the joke, nobody ____________ ridiculed or humiliated. Thus, most listeners ____________ this kind of joke.

V. When the Subject Is a Collective Noun or a Quantity. A *collective noun* is the name of a group that usually functions as a single unit. Use a singular verb with a collective noun when you mean the group as a unit. Use a plural verb when you mean the individual members of the group. Here are some examples of collective nouns.

COLLECTIVE NOUNS

Collective nouns may be singular or plural.

assembly	club	group	series
audience	committee	herd	staff
band	faculty	majority	team
class	family	number	troop

Remember that if you are referring to all the individual members of the group, then the collective noun is a plural subject, and it requires a plural verb.

> This *group* of comedians ***has*** been telling jokes together.
> That *group* of comedians ***have*** been telling jokes about each other.

> My *family* ***has*** been telling jokes for years.
> My *family* ***have*** all been professional or informal comedians.

Like collective nouns, words stating a quantity or an amount (of time, money, height, length, width, space, or weight) usually function as singular subjects and need singular verbs. However, they can function as plural subjects when they refer to individual items.

> *Five seconds* ***is*** the average time it takes an audience to understand the punch line of a joke.

> *Three-quarters* of the audience ***are*** laughing at my jokes.

VI. When the Subject Looks Plural but Is Singular in Meaning. Some subjects look plural in form (in other words, they are nouns that end in *-s*), but they are singular in meaning, and they require a singular form of the verb. These include the names of some school courses, diseases, titles, and words like *politics, news,* and *mathematics.*

> *Politics* ***interests*** me because political *news* ***is*** often quite humorous.

> *The Los Angeles Times* ***is*** an important newspaper for anyone who is interested in politics.

GROUP WORK 2

Form a group with two other students to select verbs for the sentences below. Choose one person to fill in each blank space with the correct form of any verb that makes sense in the sentence.

Our family, the Clarkson-Smiths, ____________ a huge group of people. Each year, our family ____________ a reunion that most family members attend. Indeed, probably ninety percent of the living Clarkson-Smiths ____________ this family reunion every year. The entire group ____________ in a large campground near Missoula. By the time everyone arrives, about four-fifths of this campground ____________ filled with our family members. This large assembly of people ____________ very different backgrounds, so the family committee that ____________ each reunion must try to think of ways to get the family to meet new members. Probably one-third of the group at each reunion ____________ new family members coming to their first reunion. Thus, the committee ____________ strategies for introducing new Clarkson-Smiths to other members of our family. The whole family ____________ our annual reunions.

WRITING ACTIVITY 8

Identify and correct all the errors in subject-verb agreement in the following paragraph.

There is many wonderful traditions in my country, Ghana, West Africa. One of my favorite traditions are "Fofie." The name *Fofie* comes from the word *Efiada,* which means Friday in my language (Twi). My community celebrated Fofie every forty days. On Fofie, the chiefs of the town summons the drum players to beat the big drums. The beating of the drums remind everyone about the celebration. All the people goes to their farms to collect food. The food they bring to the Fofie celebrations are for the gods. Most people believes that the gods visit on Fofie. Thus, no one want to miss this important occasion. When the Fofie day ceremony start, the priests of the village goes into a kind of trance. The gods supposedly enters the bodies of the priests and talks to the village people. People asks the gods what will happen to their families and their farms. When the gods leaves the bodies of the priests, everyone offer a sacrifice and dance. Fofie remain a special tradition, one that I misses greatly.

WRITING ACTIVITY 9

Identify and correct all the errors in subject-verb agreement in the following paragraph.

Recently, employees of my company has been protesting the high salaries of our corporate executives. People who work in the company's factory is particularly angered by the high salaries that most of the executives receives. For example, each of the three people who manage the financial division receive a total compensation package of about $200,000 a year, despite the fact that their division are laying off dozens of workers each year. Why isn't companies like ours firing one or two executives and using their salaries to pay workers? Why do companies like my company pays the chairman hundreds of thousands of dollars when the company's earnings goes down and the price of its stocks decrease in value? This don't seem to make sense. The salaries of the chief executive officers in this company is not connected to people's performances. Also, it don't seem fair that it almost always are the workers who gets fired and the executives who gets salary raises.

EXPLORING FURTHER: CAUSE-AND-EFFECT ANALYSIS

In this chapter, you have been working on clarifying the connections between your subjects and verbs. In the section that follows, you will practice clarifying the connections between the ideas in your causes-and-effects paragraphs.

Cause-and-effect analysis answers the questions "Why?" "What made this happen?" "What will happen as a result of this?" The purpose of writing cause-and-effect analyses is to explain how events, conditions, or ideas are connected. All subject areas ask students to break down problems—to explain why and how a problem occurred, to explain or predict what its consequences were (or may be), and to consider ways of solving the problem.

The topic sentence of a cause or an effect analysis should state the event, condition, or problem you are analyzing and indicate whether you are emphasizing causes or effects. Here is a topic sentence for a paragraph focusing on *causes*:

> People begin smoking for a variety of reasons.

And here is a topic sentence that the writer wrote for a separate paragraph about the *effects* of smoking:

> If smokers really understood the damage they are doing to themselves and to those around them, they might try harder to quit smoking.

Developing Details for a Cause-and-Effect Analysis

Remember that your purpose in a cause-and-effect analysis is to provide evidence that will help readers understand the connections between the events, conditions, or problems that you are analyzing. Thus, you must think carefully about the amount of background information you will need to provide readers. Here are questions to help you think about this:

- Who are my readers, and what background information do they need about the topic I am analyzing?
- How familiar are these readers with some of the causes or effects that I am analyzing?
- Which causes or effects might readers feel strongly about? Will their feelings make them challenge my interpretation of certain causes or effects?

- What evidence do I need to provide to convince these readers that my analysis makes sense?

Depending on your purpose and your readers' expectations, you can use any of the strategies that you already have practiced in the ''Exploring Further'' sections of this book to develop a cause-and-effect paragraph: description, narration, process analysis, definition, comparison and contrast, or division and classification. For example, here is a student paragraph in which the writer used description to support her topic sentence about the effects of smoking.

If smokers really understood the damage they are doing to themselves and to those around them, they might try harder to quit smoking. My sister and brother both smoke, so I get a close-up view of how smoking affects health. Both of them constantly cough and clear their throats, trying to remove the smoke-filled mucous that coats their lungs. They get more colds and sore throats than anyone else in our family, probably because their throats are always raw from smoke. Smoking also lowers people's resistance to illnesses. This is another reason why my smoking siblings are sick so often. Even more upsetting, however, is the damage my brother and sister are inflicting on the rest of the family. We have to live with their filthy ashtrays that overflow with cigarette butts. We have to live with the constant stink of smoke that creeps into our clothes and our hair. Finally, we have to live with the fear that our siblings may get cancer. My brother and sister ought to wake up and realize the damage they are inflicting on themselves and their family.

This writer makes her point by describing details that support her point clearly and convincingly.

WRITING ACTIVITY 10

Think about a problem or a condition in your life that puzzles or confuses you. Do some freewriting, brainstorming, or clustering about this problem or condition. Use your notes to develop a draft of a paragraph explaining possible causes for this problem or condition. If you have difficulty thinking of a topic, here are some possibilities:

- Being rejected by a person whom you are interested in dating
- Having difficulty doing well in a particular course
- Dealing with a parent's attitudes or behavior
- Not feeling as confident as you might like to feel
- Not feeling as independent as you might like to feel
- Having difficulty saving money to buy something you really want to have
- Not having enough time to study

As you develop a cause-and-effect analysis, remember that most events, conditions, or problems have more than one cause. For instance, you might be having a problem with a parent, and you might assume that that person's behavior is causing this problem. However, if you think critically about the problem, you may realize that it has other causes, such as the person's reactions to your own attitudes or behavior. You might even determine that the current problem is part of an ongoing problem related to the ways in which all the members of your family treat each other.

As you gather information for an explanation of causes or effects, you need to think carefully about the relations between the events or conditions that you are describing. Avoid the two common errors in cause-and-effect analyses:

1. Do not *oversimplify* the causes of an event, a condition, or a problem by stating that it had only one cause. Here is an example of an oversimplified cause-and-effect statement: "My father won't let me borrow his car because he doesn't trust me." Maybe the writer's father is concerned that the car is having mechanical problems and is unsafe for an inexperienced driver to use. Remember that most effects have several causes.
2. Do not *make a false assumption* that something caused an event, a condition, or a problem just because it happened right before the event or the condition. Here is an example of this problem: "My father won't let me borrow his car this weekend because he doesn't want me to drive it late at night." Maybe the writer's father needs to use the car himself or maybe he has another reason for refusing to lend his car to his son. A cause and an effect that seem related may actually have occurred coincidentally (and may not be causally related at all).

Be a critical thinker: Consider all the possible causes of an effect and decide which ones are logically related.

GROUP WORK 3

Form a group with two or three classmates and choose one person to write down the group's responses (on a separate sheet of paper). Examine each topic sentence below. What is the problem (or problems) with the logic of the cause-and-effect analysis in each statement?

1. If students studied more, they would do better in school.
2. The American Civil War was caused by slavery.
3. Homelessness is increasing in our big cities because most people don't care about the homeless.
4. Teenagers drink alcohol to escape from their problems.
5. Information about contraception will lead to increased sexual activity among teenagers.

WRITING ACTIVITY 11

What is the most serious problem in your neighborhood or town? Write a "Letter to the Editor" of your local newspaper analyzing this problem. Describe the problem in detail. What are the obvious causes of this problem? What other conditions might be causing this problem? Can you recommend any solutions? When you finish drafting your letter, revise it. Then identify and correct any errors in Written Academic English sentence structure and subject-verb agreement.

WRITING ACTIVITY 12

Think about the best friend you ever had. How do you define "best"? (See Chapter 7 about defining terms.) Do some prewriting about the possible reasons you think this friend is or was so terrific. You might want to make a list of reasons why you like (or liked) this person or why you benefited from his or her friendship. Develop your ideas into an analysis that explains why you think this friend was special.

The organization of a cause-and-effect paragraph depends on whether you are emphasizing causes or effects and on the supporting details you have developed. If you are narrating events, you might want to develop your details chronologically. If you are explaining the reasons why a condition or a problem exists, you might use emphatic order (least important reason to most important). Below is an essay by Scott Lafee that uses emphatic order to present a cause-and-effect analysis of the problem of fathers who abandon their families. As you read this essay, underline each cause that the writer identifies and circle each effect.

Why Aren't Dads Held to Same Standards as Moms?

Compared to the male marsupial frog, human beings make lousy fathers.

The frog, which lives in Australia, permits his hatchlings to wiggle into various skin pockets on his flanks, where they complete their development. He does this instinctively, invariably, without a second thought.

A lot of human fathers, on the other hand, can't be trusted to even stick around. We've all seen the statistics. A million American children each year see their parents divorce or separate. One in three kids live apart from their biological father. Single-parent households run by women are a cliché, and in some demographic groups, having dad hanging around is cause for a news conference.

Why exactly this is so, I don't presume to know. But I do have some ideas.

First, there's a common cultural assumption that fatherhood is learned behavior. More often than not, we treat motherhood as if it is something innate, a maternal instinct passed genetically from generation to generation since the beginning of time.

Fathers, meanwhile, are presumed capable only of transmitting boorish behaviors and, perhaps, an intrinsic understanding of when to steal second base. To be sure, I've used this argument a few times myself, telling my wife that diapering is a profoundly unnatural behavior for fathers and thus should be avoided.

Of course, I'm wrong. Love comes not just from mom's hugs but also dad's good-natured half-nelsons. Fathers may not know best anymore, but they still know a few things. And most men (just like most, but not all, women) know what it takes to be a decent parent. The fact is, modern society doesn't generally require fathers to meet the standard.

A woman who abandons her children is the object of social outrage, and rightfully so. Mothers aren't supposed to do that. Those who do often become press witches or the subject of one of those made-for-TV movies shown on Lifetime or the [cable] family channel.

But a father who does the same is, well, often treated as just another statistic. A sad one, to be sure, but one a lot of people have come to expect. You know, guys will be guys.

We seem to expect more from women. The welfare rolls are full of single mothers, women whom society assumes will do OK without a man around as long as there's a steady income.

FACING THE MUSIC

The hard truth here is that a lot of what is wrong with American society can be traced to the fact that a lot of American fathers aren't hanging around to do the job. Fatherlessness breeds violence, abuse and irresponsibility.

A study by the National Center for Health Statistics in 1988 indicated children of single-parent homes (read: fatherless) are more likely to have emotional and behavioral problems than children in two-parent families.

Moreover, they're more likely to drop out of school, have children when they themselves are teenagers, abuse drugs and get into trouble with the law. Another study, for example, found more than 70 percent of juveniles in state reform institutions came from homes without fathers. And yet another said white, teenage daughters of single parents are 111 percent more likely to have children than other demographically similar groups.

Not every marriage can be saved, of course. Not every man turns out to be a good father. But fatherhood is an idea worth preserving—and not just as a hollow mockery of what it once was. We do ourselves no favors when we casually and institutionally allow wayward fathers to meet a lower standard of behavior and responsibility.

Fathers who bail out on their families because they feel they've lost control of their lives and need to find fulfillment elsewhere—an indulgence psychiatrists sometimes call "expressive individualism"—should be held accountable and in the lowest regard.

These men are not princes. They're not even frogs.

Discussion Questions

1. What was Mr. Lafee's purpose in this essay? What did he want to show readers or convince them of?
2. Did he accomplish this purpose? Why or why not?
3. Which details did you find most interesting or effective in this essay? Why?
4. Was Mr. Lafee's explanation of causes and effects logical? What evidence did he provide to support his analysis?
5. What other situations or information can you think of that support—or contradict—Mr. Lafee's analysis?

WRITING ASSIGNMENT

What is your response to Mr. Lafee's essay about the problem of fathers who abandon their families? Can you think of any reasons why divorced men might feel they can no longer continue interacting with their children? Should fathers (or mothers) remain in unhappy marriages "for the kids' sake"? Do you know any fatherless children who are doing well emotionally, socially, and academically despite the fact that they were reared by only one parent? Are there any positive effects of being reared by a single parent?

Plan, write, and revise a paragraph or two about this topic. Decide if you want to emphasize causes (reasons divorced fathers or mothers stop seeing their children) or effects (what happens to children who are reared by a single parent).

Develop your details and examples using one or more of the strategies that you practiced in this chapter. Decide on a logical order for your details, and end with a conclusion that leaves your reader thinking about the main point that you wanted to communicate in this piece of writing.

When you finish drafting your analysis, examine it for errors in sentence structure. Then use the "Points to Remember" checklist to edit your sentences for problems in subject-verb agreement.

POINTS TO REMEMBER ABOUT SUBJECT-VERB AGREEMENT

1. Read each sentence, one at a time, to make sure it has a subject and a verb.
2. Decide whether you have used the verb tense that indicates the time that you wanted to discuss. Edit your verbs so that they are all in the verb tense you have selected.
3. Check to make sure that the verb of each sentence agrees with its subject in person and number.
4. Use the chart on page 263 of this chapter to help you determine whether you have used the correct form of each *be, have,* and *do* verb.
5. Remember that words or phrases that come between a subject and its verb do *not* affect the number of the subject. (They do not function as the word *and* does in a compound subject.)

CHAPTER 11

GRAMMAR: PRONOUNS AND POSSESSIVES

In Chapter 10, you learned that a noun is a word that names a person, place, object, or idea. A pronoun is a word that stands for or is used in place of a noun that was mentioned previously in the sentence or paragraph. (This noun is called the pronoun's *antecedent noun.*) Choosing the correct pronoun can be tricky. For example, read the student sentence below and examine each underlined pronoun. Can you identify the word that it is referring to?

> During the past four years, the New York Yankees has had many problems with their managers. They have had to cope with several different managers in a rather short period of time.

The writer began the first sentence by referring to the Yankees as a singular collective noun. We can tell this because he used a singular form of the verb ("the Yankees *has*"). The writer should have also used a singular pronoun to refer back to the team (as in "the Yankees has had many problems with *its* [the team's] managers"). However, by the end of the sentence, the writer was thinking of the Yankees as a group of players, so he used a plural pronoun to refer back to them ("*their* managers"). This pronoun choice obviously influenced the writer's decision to use a plural pronoun and a plural form of the verb in the second sentence ("*They have*"). Although these pronoun shifts may seem clear to the writer, they are confusing to readers and they are incorrect. The writer should have examined these tricky pronoun choices more carefully when he edited his sentences.

FORMS OF PRONOUNS

It is important that you know the different forms of pronouns. Choosing the correct form depends on how you are using the pronoun in a sentence. These forms include the following:

- *Indefinite* pronouns (described on page 270 of Chapter 10) are used to refer to an indefinite person or thing (for example, *someone, everything, none*).
- *Demonstrative* pronouns (*this, that, these,* and *those*) are used to point out a specific person or thing.
- *Interrogative* pronouns (*who, what, which,* and *whose*) are usually used to begin questions.
- *Personal* pronouns (described below) refer to one or more people or things.
- *Relative* pronouns (described on page 288) are used to introduce adjectives and descriptive clauses.
- *Reflexive* pronouns (described on page 290) are used to refer back to or to intensify personal pronouns.

Personal Pronouns. Personal pronouns have different forms—called *cases*—which indicate their relationship to the verb in a sentence. English has three personal pronoun cases. *Nominative,* or *subjective,* pronouns act as the subject of a verb. *Objective* pronouns receive the action of the verb or show the results of the verb's action. *Possessive* pronouns indicate ownership or a relationship. The following chart illustrates these three cases.

FORMS OF PERSONAL PRONOUNS

	Nominative (subject)	Objective (receiver)	Possessive (owner)
First person:			
Singular	I	me	my, mine
Plural	we	us	our, ours
Second person:			
Singular and plural	you	you	your, yours
Third person:			
Singular	he	him	his
	she	her	her, hers
	it	it	its
Plural	they	them	their, theirs

A nominative, or subjective, personal pronoun is usually used as the subject of a verb. Here are two examples.

I went to class with Ariana. [''*I*'' is the subject of the verb ''went.''] *She* is my best friend. [''*She*'' is the subject of the verb ''is.'']

Objective personal pronouns are usually used after verbs and after prepositions. Here are some examples.

1. Objective pronoun after a verb:

   The teacher *gave* **me** the same questions as he gave Ariana. [''*Me*'' is the object of the verb ''gave.''] Then he *asked* **us** to work together. [''*Us*'' is the object of the verb ''asked.'']

2. Objective pronoun after a preposition:

   The questions were difficult, and we worked hard to find the answers *to* **them.** [''*Them*'' is the object of the preposition ''to.''] The work was a real challenge *for* **us.** [''*Us*'' is the object of the preposition ''for.'']

If you write a compound subject that includes a pronoun, you may be confused about which form of the pronoun to use. The easiest way to decide which form is correct is to try out the pronoun separately with the verb in the sentence. Here is an example of this process. Suppose you are not sure what form of the pronoun you should use in the space in the following sentence.

The teacher helped Ariana and ____________ find books.

First, try out the subjective pronoun:

The teacher helped ~~Ariana and~~ *I* find books.
The teacher helped *I* find books.

This pronoun does not sound right. A subjective form doesn't make sense in this sentence. Next try out the objective form:

The teacher helped ~~Ariana and~~ *me* find books.
The teacher helped *me* find books.

This pronoun sounds right and is correct.
You can also use this process to decide on the correct pronoun form when you write a compound subject that includes two or more pronouns:

The teacher asked ____________ and ____________ to find some books.

The teacher asked *she* to find some books. [Incorrect]
The teacher asked *her* to find some books. [Correct]

The teacher asked *I* to find some books. [Incorrect]
The teacher asked *me* to find some books. [Correct]

The teacher asked *her* and *me* to find some books.

WRITING ACTIVITY 1

Choose the correct form of the pronoun and write it in the blank space above it. The first one has been done as an example.

1. The teacher looked at Donald and ___me___ (I, me, my) suspiciously.
2. ____________ (Us, We, Our) are identical twins, and she could not tell ____________ (us, we, our) apart.
3. The teacher asked Donald and ____________ (I, me, my) to come up to ____________ (she, her, hers) desk and to show ____________ (she, her, hers) ____________ (us, our, our) homework.
4. She asked ____________ (we, us, our) ''Which of ____________ (your, yours, you) is Donald and which is Ronald?''
5. ____________ (Us, We, Our) told ____________ (she, her, hers) who ____________ (us, we, our) were and how to tell ____________ (us, we, our) apart.
6. ____________ (Him, He, His) and ____________ (me, I, my) also told the teacher that ____________ (us, we, our) had completed all ____________ (us, our, ours) work.
7. Our parents have always told ____________ (him, he, his) and ____________ (me, I, my) that doing ____________ (us, our, ours) work correctly and on time is important to ____________ (they, them, their).

8. We both appreciate ____________ parents' concern;
(us, our, ours)

____________ shows how much ____________ care for
(it, its, it's) (they, them, their)

Donald and ____________.
(me, I, my)

9. Our teacher was impressed by what ____________ said.
(us, we, our)

10. ____________ told ____________ that ____________ would
(She, Her, Hers) (us, we, our) (us, we, our)

probably do very well in ____________ course and in college.
(she, her, hers)

GROUP WORK 1

Form a group with two or three classmates, and choose one person to write the group's answers. Together, fill in each blank space with any pronoun that makes sense. The first one has been done as an example.

My twin sister and _____I_____ are allergic to many things. The two of ____________ are both allergic to grass, molds, and tree spores. Both of ____________ allergies are seasonal: ____________ get better or worse in different seasons. For example, my sister suffers more than ____________ do in the summer. ____________ nose and eyes water, and ____________ coughs constantly. Whenever someone in ____________ family hears someone sniffing and coughing in the summer, ____________ knows that it is ____________ who is having an allergy attack. On the other hand, I am much worse than ____________ is in the spring. When flowers and trees blossom in the spring, ____________ make me feel as though ____________ head is going to explode. I take antihistamines, but ____________ don't seem to help ____________ (or my sister). What the two of ____________ cannot figure out is why ____________ brother doesn't have any allergies. Trees, weeds, molds, and grasses do not bother ____________. ____________ doesn't experience any of the problems that ____________ do, so ____________ doesn't have much sympathy for ____________. My sister and ____________ feel that this is very unfair. We wish we could give some of ____________ allergies to ____________.

Possessive personal pronouns are used in two ways. The pronouns *my, your, her, its, our,* and *their* are used before a noun.

> I packed *my* lunch before I left for school this morning. Did you bring *your* lunch?

The pronouns *mine, yours, hers, ours,* and *theirs* are used as subjects or objects.

> The lunch on the desk is *mine.* Where is *yours*? *Hers* is still in *her* car.

The pronoun *his* is used both ways: before a noun or, standing alone, as the subject or object.

> Gerry left *his* lunch out. The bag by the window is *his.*

Here are additional examples of both uses of possessive personal pronouns:

> I am going to eat *my* lunch now. This lunch is *mine.* May I taste *your* lunch? *Yours* is probably better than *mine.* My father usually makes *our* lunches. Gerry's mother makes *his* lunch. *His* is the best lunch of all of *ours.*

The third-person singular possessive pronoun *its* is never spelled with an apostrophe. The word *it's* requires an apostrophe only when it is the contraction of "it is."

> *It's* time to eat lunch. I hope that the cafeteria does not have *its* usual disgusting odor of disinfectants.

REMINDER

Many languages do not use possessive pronouns to refer to things that are not actually *possessed.* For example, speakers of Spanish do not consider parts of the body as things that one possesses. Thus, they might say or write "I have hurt the leg" instead of "I have hurt *my* leg." If you are bilingual (or trilingual), remember that English uses possessive pronouns to refer to anything that is part of someone or something.

Relative Pronouns. In Chapter 7, you learned how to add information to a sentence by adding a word group that begins with a relative pronoun (*which, that, who, whom,* or *whose*):

> Superman, *who is a comic book character from the planet Krypton,* is probably the most famous alien in history.

You can also use relative pronouns to refer back to a word or a phrase that you have already mentioned in a sentence:

> The sentences *that* I am writing now need more adverbs.

Like personal pronouns, relative pronouns also have different case forms, as shown in the chart below.

FORMS OF RELATIVE PRONOUNS

	Subjective	Objective	Possessive
Human	who	whom	whose
Nonhuman	that which	that which	 whose

In spoken English, the use of the objective relative pronoun *whom* is dying out. However, it is still required in academic writing. Thus, the pronoun *who* is incorrect in the following sentence:

> The dean *who* I spoke to yesterday called me back today.

The relative pronoun in this sentence is the object of the verb and the preposition ''spoke to,'' so it must be in the objective form (*whom*):

> The dean *whom* I spoke to yesterday called me back today.

If you are still confused about *who* and *whom,* try substituting personal pronouns in the sentence to see whether the subjective pronoun or the objective pronoun sounds correct. First try the subjective pronoun.

> I spoke to the dean yesterday. I spoke to *she*?

She is a subjective pronoun—like *who.* It does not sound right, and it is not correct in this sentence. How about the objective personal pronoun?

> I spoke to the dean yesterday. I spoke to *her*?

Her (like *whom*) is an objective pronoun, and it is correct in this sentence. Thus, the original sentence needs the objective relative—*whom.*

The dean *whom* I spoke to yesterday called me back today.

WRITING ACTIVITY 2

Circle the correct relative pronoun in each of the following sentences. The first one has been done as an example.

1. My college's varsity basketball team is the team (which, who, whom) won the state championship this year.
2. This is the championship (which, who, whom) I have wanted to win since I have been on the team.
3. We won this year because the team, (which, who, whom) worked very hard all year, helped each other out during games.
4. We also selected a team captain (that, who, whom) cared about winning and about improving our skills.
5. The captain is the team member to (that, who, whom) I give the most credit for our tremendous success.
6. I called our captain, (that, who, whom) I admire greatly, to congratulate him on our winning season.
7. He told me that he gives the credit to the teammates (that, who, whom) had improved the most this year.
8. These teammates were men (that, who, whom) did not seem to have much talent at the beginning of the year.
9. Their basketball skills, (which, who, whom) they practiced every day, improved dramatically.
10. I am proud of these teammates (which, who, whose) work paid off in terms of their contribution to our success.

Reflexive Pronouns. Another type of pronoun is the *reflexive* pronoun, which is used to refer back to a personal pronoun. The following chart illustrates the forms of reflexive pronouns.

FORMS OF REFLEXIVE PRONOUNS

	Singular	Plural
First person	myself	ourselves
Second person	yourself	yourselves
Third person	himself herself itself	themselves

Here are some examples of reflexive pronouns.

The dean's secretary was busy, so she called the student *herself.* She told her secretary, "Don't bother, I will do it *myself.*" Then she told her, "Let's take *ourselves* out to lunch today."

Another reason for using a reflexive pronoun is to emphasize the noun to which it is referring:

The dean's secretary told the dean that she would have to make the call *herself.* Then she told the dean that the president *himself* had already invited her to lunch.

REMINDER
The plural form of each of the reflexive pronouns ends in *-ves.* Write *ourselves, yourselves,* and *themselves, not ourself, yourself,* and *themself.*

WRITING ACTIVITY 3

Write in the correct reflexive pronoun in the space in each of the following sentences. The first one has been done as an example.

1. My coworkers and I try to keep to ourselves most of the time.
2. When things need to be done, I prefer to do them ________.

3. My colleagues also prefer to do things by ________________.
4. However, our employer, Mr. Johnson, does not like to do things by ________________.
5. Once, when I was too busy to work on a project with Mr. Johnson, I told him, ''You will have to do it ________________.''
6. He was unhappy with this decision, but he did the work by ________________.
7. When he finished the project, we all agreed that we could not have done a better job ________________.
8. My colleagues made copies of Mr. Johnson's final report for ________________.

WRITING ACTIVITY 4

Choose the correct form of the pronoun and write it in the blank space above it.

1. My mother and father are first-generation Americans ____________ (that, who, whose) never went to college.
2. ____________ (Them, They, Their) want my sister and ____________ (I, me, my) to get college degrees.
3. ____________ (We, Us, Our) have worked hard to make ____________ (them, they, their) proud of ____________ (we, us, ours).
4. ____________ (We, Us, Our) parents think of ____________________ (themself, themselves, theirselves) as modern parents.
5. ____________ (Them, They, Their) want ____________ (them, they, their) children to learn American customs.

6. Sometimes ____________ (its, it's, its') difficult for ____________ (I, me, my) to see ____________ (I, me, my) father remembering how ____________ (he, him, his) ________________ (hisself, himself, himselve) was brought up in ____________ (he, him, his) old country.

7. My mother tries to comfort ____________ (he, him, his) by telling ____________ (he, him, his) that things are different today than ____________ (they, them, their) were when ____________ (he, him, his) was growing up.

8. ____________ (I, Me, My) sister and ____________ (I, me, my) are proud of ____________ (they, them, their) struggle to give ____________ (we, us, our) excellent educations.

GROUP WORK 2

Form a group with two or three classmates, and choose a recorder to write the group's answers. Together, fill in each blank space with any pronoun that makes sense. The first one has been done as an example.

When my two brothers and ______I______ were young, ____________ used to put on talent shows in ____________ backyard. ____________ planned the shows by ____________, so that ____________ could highlight ____________ individual talents. I played the piano, ____________ was located on the back porch. My older brother danced because ____________ could not sing or play an instrument. My younger brother could not sing or dance, so ____________ had to recite poems. Often, the audience for ____________ shows was composed of ____________ friends from the neighborhood. They laughed at ___________ because none of ___________ knew how to sing, dance, or perform well.

One time, my brothers and ___________ decided to add ___________ dog Spot to the show. ___________ tried to make Spot walk on ___________ hind legs across the "stage." ___________ was a big mistake. Spot got so annoyed at ___________ that ___________ ran all the way under the porch. Spot got ___________ stuck under the porch, and ___________ father had to crawl under ___________ to get ___________ out.

The incident with Spot really angered ___________ parents, ___________ yelled at us and told ___________ not to put Spot in the show ever again. They told ___________ that performing in a show was difficult and that Spot didn't have the patience for ___________. That was the end of ___________ animal shows. My brothers and ___________ decided that we would have to perform all of ___________ future shows by___________. And ___________ did.

PRONOUN REFERENCE

A pronoun should refer clearly to its antecedent noun (which should be stated earlier in the same sentence or in the preceding sentence). In the example below, each underlined pronoun clearly refers to the antecedent noun "dog."

> The dog wagged <u>his</u> tail because <u>he</u> was happy to see <u>his</u> owner return from work.

If a pronoun does not seem to refer to an antecedent, it will confuse readers. Here is an example of this problem in pronoun reference.

> I walk my neighbors' dogs, but *it* is just a way of making some spending money this summer.

What is the pronoun "it" referring to in the sentence above? Readers have to guess. One guess is that the pronoun probably refers to the unstated noun "dog walking." If this is the meaning that the writer intended, he or she should have made this meaning clear by including this noun in the sentence:

> I do some *dog walking* for my neighbors, but *it* is just a way of making some spending money this summer. [Include the noun to which the unclear "it" is referring.]
>
> I walk my neighbors' dogs, but dog walking is just a way of making some spending money this summer. [Delete the unclear "it," and substitute the noun.]

Another type of unclear pronoun reference results when you write two (or more) nouns in a sentence and then write a pronoun that can refer to either noun. Readers get confused about which noun the pronoun is supposed to be referring to:

> Ellen saw Roberta while *she* was walking *her* dog.

To whom are the pronouns *she* and *her* referring? Who was walking a dog? We cannot tell from this sentence. The writer must revise the sentence to clarify the pronoun reference:

> While *Ellen* was walking *her* dog, *she* saw Roberta.

If a pronoun doesn't have an obvious antecedent, or if you think that readers might be unsure about the pronoun's antecedent, replace the pronoun with a noun (even if this means that you have to repeat the noun a few times). Here is an example.

> *Draft with unclear pronoun reference:*
> In the animal hospital *we* used to go to, *they* made *you* wait a long time, even if *your* dog was violently ill. I hated *it.* I used to sit there and worry about *it.* [Who is "we"? Who is "they"? Who is "you"? What is the "it" referring to in the last two sentences?]
>
> *Revision:*
> In the animal hospital *my family and I* used to go to, *the receptionists* made *people* wait a long time, even if *their* dog was violently ill. I hated *having to wait when my dog was very sick.* I used to sit there and worry about *my dog.*

When you edit your drafts, look for pronouns that do not have antecedents.

WRITING ACTIVITY 5

The following sentences contain unclear pronoun references. Rewrite each sentence so that it is no longer confusing. You may have to add, omit, or change words. The first one has been done as an example, and the ambiguous pronouns are shown in italic throughout.

1. In a recent newspaper article, *it* said that thousands of Americans die each year from secondhand cigarette smoke.

   a recent newspaper article stated that thousands of americans die each year from secondhand smoke.

2. *This* means that people who don't even smoke can die from smoke-related diseases.

3. *They* say that simply by inhaling smoke from someone else's cigarette, *you* can get cancer.

4. In this newspaper, *it* also reported that nonsmoking spouses of heavy smokers have an 80 percent higher risk of lung cancer than spouses of people who do not smoke.

5. Secondhand smoke is linked to lung cancer, pneumonia, and asthma. Clearly, *that* indicates the health risks of doing *it*.

6. *This* should make *us* stop and think about the need to prohibit smoking in all public places.

____

____

7. All employers should provide smoke-free workplaces for employees, since *it* is the only way to protect *their* health.

____

____

8. Workers should insist that *they* provide *it.*

____

____

9. All companies should prohibit *it* in public places.

____

____

10. If *it* does not have smoke-free working areas, go to the president or the health manager and ask *her* to examine the evidence concerning secondhand smoke.

____

____

____

PRONOUN AGREEMENT

Just as verbs have to agree with their subjects, pronouns must agree with their antecedents (the nouns that they refer to or that they replace). Every pronoun should match its antecedent noun in three ways:

1. In *person:* first, second, or third
2. In *number:* singular or plural
3. In *gender:* masculine, feminine, or neuter (*it*)

Here is a chart that illustrates pronoun-antecedent agreement.

PRONOUN-ANTECEDENT AGREEMENT CHART

	Singular		**Plural**	
	Antecedent	**Pronoun**	**Antecedent**	**Pronoun**
First person:	Ms. Greenberg	I, me	my friends	we
Second person:	person being addressed	you	people being addressed	you
Third person:	man	he	men	they
	woman	she	women	they
	dog	it	cats	they

If you were writing about a ''hospital,'' and you wanted to refer back to this word with a pronoun, the pronoun you would choose to replace ''hospital'' is ''it.'' The noun *hospital* and the pronoun *it* are both singular third-person neuter word forms. If you were writing about a ''dog,'' and you wanted to refer back to this noun with a pronoun, you could use ''it'' or ''he'' or ''she'' (depending on the gender of the dog). The noun *dog* and the pronouns *it, he,* and *she* are singular and are in their third-person forms.

Often, people write nouns that do not indicate gender (such as the noun ''people'' in this sentence). What pronoun should you use to refer to or to replace a noun that can include males and females? What pronoun would you put in the space in the following sentence? Why?

> Each *student* should check ____________ revision for pronoun errors and make sure that ____________ has identified and corrected every error.

If you chose male pronouns (*his* and *he*) or female pronouns (*her* and *she*), your choice was incorrect. A ''student'' can be a male or a female. The correct pronouns must indicate this:

> Each *student* should check *his or her* revision for pronoun errors and make sure that *he or she* has identified and corrected every error.

When the antecedent noun is a singular human noun without the gender specified, the pronoun form that agrees with it is *he or she* (or *his or her, him or her,* or *his or hers*). Do not use a plural pronoun to refer back to or to replace a singular antecedent:

> Each *student* should check their revision for pronoun errors and make sure that they have identified and corrected every error.

If you don't want to use *he or she, his or her,* etc., then change the antecedent noun to a plural, and use forms such as *they* or *them* to refer back to it.

> All *students* should check *their* revisions for pronoun errors and make sure that *they* have identified and corrected every error.

SPECIAL PROBLEMS IN PRONOUN-ANTECEDENT AGREEMENT

I. When the Antecedent Is an Indefinite Pronoun. In Chapter 10, you learned that an *indefinite pronoun* is a pronoun that does not refer back to a specific or ''definite'' noun. People often use an indefinite pronoun when they do not know the name of the specific person or thing they are discussing or when they want to discuss people in general. In speech, most people use the plural form of a pronoun to refer back to an indefinite pronoun:

> *Everyone* in my class must do *their* revisions today if *they* want to work in groups tomorrow.

Academic Written English requires writers to use a singular pronoun to refer to the following indefinite pronouns:

> each, either, neither
> anyone, someone, no one
> anybody, somebody, nobody
> anything, something, nothing

The third-person singular pronoun that you should use to refer to an indefinite pronoun is *he or she* or *his or her.*

> *Everyone* in my class must do *his or her* revisions today if *he or she* wants to work in groups tomorrow.

Remember that you can avoid the awkwardness of using *his or her* and *he or she* by changing the indefinite pronoun to a plural noun. Then you can use a plural pronoun to refer back to this plural antecedent noun.

> All the *students* in my class must do *their* revisions today if *they* want to work in groups tomorrow.

Note that when you change the singular subject ''everyone'' to the plural subject ''students,'' you must change both the pronouns *and* the verbs to their plural forms (''his or her'' changes to ''their,'' and ''wants'' changes to ''want'').

REMINDER

Using the pronoun *his* to refer to a group that includes women is sexist. Instead, use *his or her,* or change the indefinite pronoun to a plural noun (as in ''the *people* in my class are working on *their* revisions today'').

Five indefinite pronouns—*all, any, most, some,* and *none*—require either the singular or the plural form of the pronoun, depending on their meaning in a particular sentence.

> I enjoyed *some* of my psychology professor's lecture because *it* was interesting.

> However, *some* of her remarks were confusing, and I didn't understand *them.*

II. When the Antecedent Is a Collective Noun. A collective noun (like *group, class, family, committee,* or *team*) requires a singular pronoun when the noun refers to the group as a single unit. If the collective noun refers to the individual members of the group, use a plural pronoun to refer to them.

> The *Chemistry Committee* has finished *its* project, but the *Physics Committee* are still working on *their* project's activities.

III. When Two or More Antecedents Are Joined by *Or* or *Nor*. When two or more nouns are joined by *or* or *nor,* the pronoun should agree with the noun that is closest to it.

> Neither the *doctor* nor the *nurses* are writing *their* reports today. [The verb ''are'' and the pronoun ''their'' are both plural because they match the closer noun, ''nurses,'' which is plural.]

> Neither the *nurses* nor the *doctor* is writing *her* reports today. [The verb ''is'' and the pronoun ''her'' are both singular because they match the closer noun, ''doctor,'' which is singular.]

WRITING ACTIVITY 6

Circle the correct pronoun in each of the following sentences. (Assume that the gender of the nurses is unknown.)

1. Only three nurses work at Ryder Nursing Home, so each of them must take care of ten patients on (their, his, her, his or her) shift.
2. All the nurses use (their, his, her, his or her) knowledge and skills to help (their, his, her, his or her) elderly patients.
3. However, only one of them has (their, his, her, its, his or her) certification in geriatric nursing (nursing the elderly).
4. Neither of the other two nurses has indicated that (they, he, she, it, he or she) is studying to obtain (their, his, her, its, his or her) certification in geriatric nursing.
5. The nursing home's Administrative Committee may decide that (they, he, she, it, he or she) want all the nurses to get (their, his, her, its, his or her) certification.
6. Either the Administrative Committee or the head nurse will decide when (they, he, she, it, he or she) will discuss this matter with the nurses.

WRITING ACTIVITY 7

Here is a student essay about burglary. On a separate sheet of paper, rewrite this composition, changing every *underlined* plural noun (such as "many homeowners" and "most burglars") to its singular form ("a homeowner" or "a burglar"). Changing each noun to its singular form will require you to change each main verb to its singular form. You will also have to make corresponding changes in the pronouns that refer to these nouns, and you may have to change the wording of some sentences. The first sentence has been changed as an example.

To make ~~their homes~~ *his or her home* safe from ~~burglars, homeowners have~~ *a burglar, a homeowner has* to be aware of several things. Most importantly, homeowners should know what burglars generally look for when they are choosing their targets. In general, burglars choose houses to watch for a week to see if anyone is home in the houses. They look to see if cars remain parked in the same place all week and if lights go on and off at the same time every day. Burglars also examine the bushes in front of each window to see how high they are. High bushes will hide burglars from people passing by in their cars. Houses that have all these features are perfect targets for burglars.

There are four ways that homeowners can try to prevent burglaries. First, homeowners should ask neighbors to collect their mail and newspapers and to move their cars each day. Second, homeowners should install chain-link fences around their houses. Another way for homeowners to protect their houses is to install alarm systems that makes loud noises when people open windows or doors without turning off the alarms first. Houses' alarm systems should be obvious to potential thieves, who usually avoid homes with alarm tapes in the windows or with signs stating that the homes are protected by alarms.

Homeowners should educate themselves about what burglars look for in potential targets. They should try to make their homes as safe as possible, so they do not have to worry about burglaries when they go away on vacations.

PRONOUN CONSISTENCY

When you edit a paragraph or an essay, check to make sure that your pronouns are consistent in person (first, second, or third) and in number (singular or plural). Don't shift from first-person pronouns (*I* or *we*) or from third-person pronouns (*he, she, it* or *they*) to the second-person pronoun (*you*). Illogical shifts in pronouns confuse readers. Here are examples of illogical pronoun shifts that the writer has identified and corrected:

The reason I decided to go to college is that it is the best place for ~~you~~ *a person* to learn new things and prepare for a good career. I know that if ~~people~~ *a person* want*s* to succeed in a profession, ~~you have~~ *he or she has* to get a college degree first. Also college provides ~~you~~ *a person* with knowledge about things ~~I~~ *he or she* never even knew existed before.

In the original version above, the writer began by talking about herself, but she switched to the second-person pronoun, "you," as she began to imagine herself talking directly to her readers. The shift from "I" to "you" is disorienting and incorrect. Moreover, if the writer intends this paragraph to be read by her teacher, then her shift to the pronoun "you" is potentially offensive to this reader. (Do college teachers need—or want—to be lectured about the importance of getting a college degree?)

Unless you are writing a set of instructions or an analysis of a process, do not address the reader directly with the pronoun *you* in your academic paragraphs and essays. (Notice that I just used "you" and "your" in the preceding sentence. I did that because I *am* addressing "you"—my reader. I am not talking about a person or people in general; I am giving advice to *you.*)

Instead of using *you,* use the noun that your paragraph or essay is about. For example, if you are writing a paragraph about "students," use that word (*students*) instead of using the pronoun *you.* Read the sentences below. What impression does the use of "you" give you about the writer and his tone?

College students who use computers have great advantages over those who don't. You can write and revise your papers on a computer, without ever having to retype a paper from scratch. You can also use a spreadsheet program to budget your money and your time. Also, if your computer has a modem, you can do research simply by phoning the college library. Best of all, using your computer will prepare you for computers in your future career.

By using "you" in this paragraph, the writer assumes that all his readers use computers. If they do, his use of "you" makes sense. However, if many of his readers do not have a computer, then the "you" is inaccurate and inappropriate. In this case, the writer should have changed each "you" to the appropriate noun or pronoun:

College students who use computers have great advantages over those who don't. *These students* can write and revise *their* papers on a computer, without ever having to retype a paper from scratch. *They* can also use a spreadsheet program to budget *their* money and *their* time. Also, if *a student's* computer has a modem, *he or she* can do research simply by phoning the college library. Best of all, using *a* computer will prepare *students* for computers in *their* future careers.

GROUP WORK 3

Form a group with two other students, and choose a recorder to write the group's answers. Together, examine the paragraph below, which *should* have been written in the third-person plural form throughout. Circle any pronoun that shifts to its singular form or to a different-person form, and write the correct third-person plural form above it. The first one has been done as an example.

New lifeguards at Laguna Beach learn quickly that (your) [their] job is not all fun in the sun. Being a lifeguard is a very demanding job: They are responsible for everyone's safety and your life. Effective lifeguards must keep a sharp eye on everything around you, because you never know when someone will have an accident or an emergency in the water. He or she must check the safety devices in the pool or at the beach where they work. You also have to familiarize yourself with the sights and sounds of a person who is having problems breathing or staying afloat in the water. Since lifeguards have to enforce water safety rules, he should wear a whistle and blow it to get the people's attention. They need to speak and act authoritatively so that swimmers will know that you are serious about water safety. And of course, lifeguards must know how to prevent drowning, and she should know lifesaving skills. People tend to underestimate the difficulty of a lifeguard's job. Listen to the lifeguard—it is your life that they are dedicated to protecting.

POSSESSIVES

The possessive form of a noun or a pronoun expresses ownership or a relationship:

Ownership: Edward's backpack is in the dining room.
Relationship: Edward's uncle is in the dining room.
Relationship: His uncle is in the dining room.

To form the possessive of most nouns, simply add an apostrophe and an *-s* ending to the noun.

student	student's
Jackson	Jackson's

To form the possessive of singular nouns that end in *-s,* also add an apostrophe and an *-s* to the end of the noun.

boss	boss's
Francis	Francis's

To form the possessive of plural nouns, add *only* the apostrophe.

students	students'
Jacksons	Jacksons'

To form the possessive of compound nouns, add the *-s* ending to the last word.

father-in-law	father-in-law's
editor in chief	editor in chief's

Do not add an apostrophe or an apostrophe and an *-s* to a possessive pronoun. (Write "hers," *not* "her's.") Also, remember that "it's" is the contraction of "it is," *not* the possessive form of "it" (which is "its").

REMINDER

Never use an apostrophe and an *-s* to form the plural of a word. For example, do not write "My classmate*'s* are revising their essays." The correct version of this sentence is "My classmate*s* are revising their essays."

WRITING ACTIVITY 8

On a separate sheet of paper, write the possessive form of each of these words.

1. video
2. wolf
3. spy
4. children
5. men
6. glass
7. Dr. James
8. city
9. hero
10. coaches
11. runner-up
12. citizens
13. nurse
14. brother
15. horse

REVIEWING *-S* ENDINGS

When editing your writing, look for the three types of words that need *-s* endings: present-tense verbs used with third-person singular subjects, plural nouns, and possessives. (You might want to review the guidelines for adding an *-s* ending to present-tense verbs, discussed on page 262 of Chapter 10.) Make sure you have used the correct *-s* endings:

1. Present-tense verbs need an *-s* ending when they are used with a third-person singular subject:

   Drinking alcohol ***causes*** hangovers for many people.

2. To make most singular nouns plural—more than one—add an *-s* ending:

   The ***causes*** of hangovers are compex.

3. To indicate that a noun "possesses" another noun, add an apostrophe and an *-s* ending to the first noun:

   My ***hangover's*** primary cause was the number of drinks I had last night.

REMINDER

The *-s* ending on a plural noun means that the noun expresses "more than one." An apostrophe and *-s* ending on a singular or a plural noun means that the noun "owns" or "is related to" the word or words that follow it in the sentence.

WRITING ACTIVITY 9

In the uncorrected student essay below, many verbs, plural nouns, possessives, and pronouns are missing *-s* endings, or have unnecessary or incorrect *-s* endings (according to Academic Written English conventions), or do not agree in number. Circle each word that needs an *-s* ending, or that has an incorrect one, or that does not agree in number. Write the correct form of the word above each error that you circled. The first one has been done as an example.

The dormitory room that my roommate's and I lives in is rather small, so we has to be considerate of one anothers' feeling. Because we has to lives together and gets along with one anothers, we has to respect each of our roommates feelings and property. We finds this easy to do because the threes of us are alike in many way. We has the same taste in clothes', and we often share one anothers' outfit's. None of us would wears an outfit that is very grungy or very sexy: We would all thinks its too tacky. All three of us works hard in school and study's every night. However, we do has some difference. One of my roommate is loud and boisterous, and the other are very quiet. My quiet roommate is a bit shy. My personality is similar to her's. I prefers to keeps to myself. Still, I really enjoy my roommate's friendship and concern. I wouldn't trades them for any other roommate's.

EXPLORING FURTHER: ARGUMENTATION

When you think of the word *argument,* what thoughts come to mind? Do you think of arguing as fighting or as debating? When you argue with someone, do you try to get him or her to understand you or to agree with you? When people argue face to face, they may get very emotional. In expressing a point of view and trying to convince others to agree with them, some people overwhelm their listeners with their feelings. Strong emotional appeals may—or may not—work in persuading people to agree with you. In academic writing, however, they rarely are appropriate. The aim of written argument is to influence others through logic and evidence rather than through emotional appeals; the goal is to persuade rather than to overpower.

When you write an academic argument, your goal is to convince readers that something you think or feel is valid, reasonable, or right. You can accomplish this goal by using one or more of the strategies you have learned (describing, narrating, analyzing a process, comparing, contrasting, dividing, classifying, defining, and analyzing causes or effects) to illustrate and explain your point or position. The key to writing strong arguments is to select effective examples or reasons that will encourage readers to share your viewpoint.

However, you cannot convince readers to accept or to adopt your position unless you know exactly what your point of view is. As you plan an argument, remember that your topic or opinion must be *arguable.* It must be open to debate, and other people may have different views about it. If you take a position that no one doubts or disagrees with, then why bother defending it in writing? For example, is either of the following assertions appropriate for an academic argument?

> Major league baseball players earn millions of dollars. [Statement of fact]
> Major league baseball games are often boring. [Personal opinion]

One way to test whether a position is arguable is to state it using the word *should* or *ought* (or *should not* or *must not*). If you cannot do this, then the position is probably a fact or a personal opinion, and thus not arguable. If you can state your position using *should* or *should not,* it still may not be suitable for debate; examine it to see if it is so general that no one would oppose it. Here is a student's first draft of an argumentative topic sentence.

> Major league baseball players *should not* earn the ridiculous amounts of money that they earn.

This topic sentence can be debated, but it is quite vague. What does the writer mean by ''ridiculous amounts''? Here is the writer's revision.

> Major league baseball players *should not* earn the multimillion-dollar annual salaries that many of them earn.

This statement is clear and specific. Most importantly, readers can agree with it or they can argue against it. Thus, it is an appropriate topic sentence for an argument paragraph.

Considering Readers' Knowledge and Opinions

If you don't have a specific audience in mind as you develop an argument, try to imagine one. Think about readers who either have no opinion about your topic or disagree with your position. In order to convince these readers of your position, you will have to consider their knowledge of and attitudes toward your topic. You might want to answer the following questions:

1. What is my purpose in writing about this topic? What do I want readers to think, believe, or do?
2. What do readers already know about the topic?
3. What values, beliefs, or concerns do readers share with me about this topic?
4. What objections might readers have to my position or my point of view?
5. What kinds of evidence might convince them to believe (or to consider) my point of view on this topic?

Building an Argument with Relevant Evidence

Most readers will not change their point of view about a topic simply because you tell them that they should change. In order to be convincing, your supporting details must be logical, relevant to the topic, and appropriate for your readers. Specific examples enable readers to see the writer's points.

Of course, good reasons vary from purpose to purpose and from audience to audience. For some arguments, you may be able to use reasons and evidence that come from your experiences or observations or that are common knowledge. For instance, here is an assertion that you could support with evidence from your personal experiences or from your observations of other students:

> Smoking should be prohibited in public places because it makes people sick.

You could support this assertion using information that you know from your reading or from experiences you have had with smoking, with smokers, or with people who have become ill from inhaling secondhand smoke. If you decide that your examples and reasons will not convince your intended readers, you need to do some reading to find facts to back up your assertion.

If you have difficulty thinking of reasons to support your position or point of view, try brainstorming about different categories of reasons (such as "emotional," "physical," "social," "financial," "environmental," and "political''). Here are a topic sentence and different types of supporting reasons, with an example of each.

Topic sentence: Smoking should be prohibited in public places because it makes people sick.

1. *Physical:* People who do not smoke can get a variety of illnesses simply from inhaling secondhand smoke (illnesses ranging in severity from nausea to lung cancer).
2. *Mental and emotional:* If smokers had fewer places in which they could smoke in public, they might be more motivated to fight their addiction to nicotine.
3. *Financial:* Cigarette smoking is an expensive habit. In addition, smoking-related illnesses and accidents cost hundreds of thousands of dollars a year (a cost that is passed on to all taxpayers).
4. *Social:* Smokers do not have the right to inflict their addiction on nonsmokers in public places.

WRITING ACTIVITY 10

What is your point of view about mothers who work? Here are some questions to assist in thinking through your position on this topic:

- Should mothers work? If so, should they work full time or part time? Why?
- If you think that mothers should not work, how else can they support themselves and their families?
- Does going to work benefit mothers (emotionally, socially, and financially)? If so, how? If not, why not?
- Does having a working mother benefit the children of mothers who work? If so, how? If not, why not?
- Do children suffer any negative consequences when their mothers work? If so, what? If not, why not?

Remember that you don't have to answer all the questions above in your paragraph or essay. You may want to use them to brainstorm ideas for your argument. When you finish brainstorming, plan, write, and revise a paragraph or two defending your position on this issue.

GROUP WORK 4

Form a group with three other classmates. Together, choose *three* of the following assertions to work on for this activity. Half the group should write down all the reasons they can think of to support the chosen assertions. The other group members should write down reasons why this assertion is wrong or will cause problems. As you do this activity, *ignore* your personal beliefs about each issue and try to imagine how a person who supports or opposes the assertion thinks and feels about it. When you and your classmates finish writing, take turns reading your reasons to each other.

1. Students should receive a grade of "pass" or "fail" rather than a letter grade in all college courses.
2. All colleges and universities should have free day care centers for the children of students.
3. People should not wear fur coats because killing animals for their fur is wrong.
4. Couples should live together before they get married to see if they are compatible.
5. Colleges and universities should require every student to learn how to use a computer for schoolwork.
6. A parent should never use physical force to discipline a child.
7. Handguns and assault weapons should be banned for sale to anyone except police officers.
8. In order to reduce the number of teenage pregnancies, high schools should provide contraceptives and information about how to use them.

WRITING ACTIVITY 11

Which of the eight assertions in the preceding Group Work do you feel most strongly about? What is your position or point of view about this assertion? Do some brainstorming or clustering, and develop a list of reasons supporting and opposing the assertion you have selected. Then plan, write, and revise a paragraph or two explaining your position and convincing readers to agree with your position.

GROUP WORK 5

Form a group with one or two other students. Take out the composition that you wrote for the preceding Writing Activity. Exchange papers, and on a separate sheet of paper write answers to the following questions about your classmate's paragraph or essay.

1. Does the argument have a clear topic sentence that is neither too narrow or too broad? If so, what is this idea? If not, what might it be?
2. Do you understand the writer's purpose in writing this paper? Did the writer accomplish this purpose? If so, how? If not, why not?
3. Are the writer's reasons logical? Are there any examples or reasons that confuse you or that are illogical?

Below are two opposing viewpoints about a controversial issue that is currently being debated in many secondary school districts. The writers of these viewpoints were asked to respond to the question "The state of Maryland and several school districts now require that students perform community service to graduate from high school. Should community service be a requirement?"

First Response

No—for four reasons. First, all schools have a duty to produce graduates who are strong on the essentials (like reading, writing, and mathematics). Maryland's schools and urban public schools around the country deserve failing grades now on the essentials. Students who aren't up to grade level in math shouldn't be spending time in a mandatory service program.

Second, community service programs are intertwined with current public controversies over environmental policies, governmental aid to the poor, policies on AIDS and Alzheimer's disease, and separation of church and state. A "service learning" program will give teachers and social workers a license to instill partisan doctrines, in a setting where students must profess agreement to graduate.

Third, this is a chintzy way for politicians to get cheap labor out of young people. Older people who resent young people's youth are using service requirements to try to humble young people by making them perform harsh and repugnant tasks. Instead of paying for social services directly or relying on private charities, busybody politicians are imposing additional petty and mean-spirited rules on young people.

Finally, coercion takes the spirit of generosity out of service. The idea of young people voluntarily helping others is an attractive one. But if a legislature or school board makes service mandatory, charities in which people once worked for the joy of helping others will be staffed by resentful young people fulfilling a requirement.

Williamson Evers, a political scientist and visiting fellow at Stanford University's Hoover Institution, is co-author of *National Service: Pro & Con.*

Second Response

I strongly support a service requirement for all students, starting in junior high school and extending at least through college. Community service is the best way possible to connect people to their communities. By getting involved, we learn why certain problems exist, how they affect us, and what we can do to eradicate them. Through service, people work toward solving a problem they care about. We often complain about what is wrong with society but rarely follow through by doing something about it. Experience shows that when we actually put time and effort into improving a situation, we feel satisfied because we addressed something we care about.

You may ask, "These are good reasons, but why do we need a requirement?" A requirement gives people the push they need to go out and actually start to do the service. Many will even go far beyond the basic requirement. I know this because at my high school there is a service requirement of 20 hours per year, and many students far exceed it.

When my class was presented with the requirement during our freshman year, we were apprehensive about taking risks and being in new situations. However, now as juniors, we are often frustrated because there isn't time to do all the service we would like to do. I believe a nationwide requirement would operate similarly. At first students would be apprehensive, but later service would become an important part of their lives.

Miriam Serxner recently finished her junior year at University High School in San Francisco, California.

WRITING ASSIGNMENT

What are your thoughts and feelings about a community service requirement in high school? Plan, write, and revise a paragraph or two that explains and supports your position on this issue. Then check to be sure you used pronouns, plurals, and possessives correctly.

✔ POINTS TO REMEMBER ABOUT PRONOUNS AND POSSESSIVES

1. Make sure that you have used the correct Academic Written English form of each pronoun.

2. Check to see that each pronoun agrees with its antecedent noun in number and person.
3. Take your reader's perspective, and check to make sure that he or she will understand all your pronoun references. Rewrite each sentence containing potentially confusing pronoun references.
4. Make sure that you have used the correct form of each possessive noun and pronoun.
5. Double-check to ensure that you added *-s* endings to present-tense third-person singular verbs, to plural nouns, and to possessives.

CHAPTER 12

VOCABULARY AND DICTION

The English language has a wealth of words for expressing thoughts and feelings. However, you cannot use words that you do not know. Thus, two important goals for you as advancing writers are to increase your vocabulary and to improve your diction (your choice of words and the way in which you use them). Vocabulary and diction are interrelated: You cannot choose words that you don't know or understand. This chapter will give you many opportunities to increase your academic vocabulary, and to select words that say precisely what you mean.

IMPROVING VOCABULARY AND DICTION

One excellent way to increase your vocabulary is to keep a *word bank.* This is a notebook in which you write each new word you read or hear, along with its definition. You should also write down the sentence in which you found the word, since a word's *context* (its surrounding words and the circumstances in which it is used) can help you understand and remember the word's meaning. Finally, you might want to use the word in a new sentence. Doing this will help you remember the meaning of the word. Here is a sample entry from a student's word bank:

cache ("She removed a candy from her cache.")
[pronounced "cash"] - a place in which food or

supplies are hidden; a place for hiding anything.

My sentence: I keep extra cans of soda in a cache in my bedroom.

WRITING ACTIVITY 1

Begin keeping a word bank today. Record words you see (or hear) that you do not know. Next to each word, write the sentence in which the word was used. Look up the word in a dictionary, and make sure that you have spelled the word correctly. Then copy the word's pronunciation and its definitions and write a sentence using the word. Add at least five words to your word bank *every day*.

USING THE RIGHT WORD

As you compose and revise paragraphs, choose your words carefully, since your diction reveals your thoughts and your attitudes as clearly as your behavior does. For instance, if you describe one friend as ''stingy'' and another as ''economical,'' your choice of words reveals a difference in your attitude toward these friends. These two adjectives are similar in meaning, but *stingy* suggests that one friend is a tightwad who dislikes spending money, whereas *economical* implies that the other friend is thrifty and spends money carefully.

Denotations and Connotations. Almost all words can have several meanings, or layers of meanings, depending on their context (who is using them and why and where they are being used). Words that share the same general meaning but have slightly different meanings are called *synonyms.* For example, the word *misfortune* and the word *disaster* have the same general meaning, but they differ in intensity. A ''disaster'' is a very serious or life-threatening form of ''misfortune.''

Dictionaries give a word's *denotations*—the objective, literal definitions of the word at the particular time the dictionary was written. Two words can have the same denotation, but suggest very different feelings. For example, the words *misfortune* and *disaster* have the same definition (''a serious problem, hardship, or calamity''), but they have different emotional associations. A word's emotional overtones are its *connotations.* Connotations convey the feelings people associate with a word. For example, the word *disaster* evokes more emotion than does its denotation (''a serious problem, hardship, or calamity'') or its synonym *misfortune.* Most people associate a ''disaster'' with images of a life-threatening problem or accident, whereas a ''misfortune'' implies a stroke of bad luck or a small problem.

A word's connotations vary, depending on who is using the word and how he or she is using it. For example, here are two descriptions of a group of people. The words in both sentences have the same denotations, but they paint very different pictures.

1. The *group* of *indignant* people outside the building were so *assertive* and *persistent* that the *police officers became alarmed.*
2. The *mob* of *angry* people outside the building were so *aggressive* and *stubborn* that the *cops panicked.*

Words with strong emotional connotations—like *mob, angry,* and *stubborn*—are *loaded words*—words intended to provoke strong feelings. Be careful when you use loaded words, since they can convey emotional messages that you did not intend. Choose words whose connotations express the meaning you intended.

WRITING ACTIVITY 2

Here is a list of words that may have positive, negative, or no emotional connotations for you. In the space next to each word, describe the feelings that the word elicits from you. The first one has been done as an example.

1. teacher positive – educator, coach, guide, mentor, someone who helps me
2. gang __________
3. home __________
4. cheap __________

5. slim ____

____

6. serious ____

____

GROUP WORK 1

Form a group with three or four classmates. Compare your responses to the words in the preceding Writing Activity with your classmates' connotations. Together answer the following questions.

1. Which words had similar connotations for everyone in the group?
2. Which words elicited different responses from the group members?
3. Why do you think these words elicited different responses?

WRITING ACTIVITY 3

For each set of words listed below, write an explanation of the meaning that the words have in common and an explanation of how their connotations differ. (Write your answers on a separate sheet of paper.)

1. fat, chubby, obese
2. ask, inquire, interrogate
3. inflexible, stubborn, obstinate
4. beautician, hairdresser, hair stylist

GROUP WORK 2

Form a group with two or three classmates. Choose one person to record the group's opinions as to how the connotations of the following underlined words differ.

What you wrote was incorrect.
What you wrote was wrong.
What you wrote was inaccurate.
What you wrote was inappropriate.
What you wrote was improper.
What you wrote was bad.

Dictionaries and Thesauruses. Did you know that there are different types of dictionaries? Go to a local bookstore and look in the "dictionaries" section. You will find abridged (shortened) dictionaries, unabridged dictionaries, bilingual dictionaries, synonym and antonym dictionaries, computer dictionaries, crossword puzzle dictionaries, idiom dictionaries, rhyming dictionaries, slang dictionaries, and gazetteers (geographical dictionaries).

Dictionaries are valuable learning tools. They provide the spelling, the meaning, and the pronunciation of words. In addition, a dictionary gives information about the history of each word, about its modern usage, and about its synonyms and their connotations. If you do not already own a dictionary, get a good one—an unabridged or college dictionary. These include *The American Heritage Dictionary of the English Language, The Random House College Dictionary,* and *Webster's New World Dictionary of the American Language, College Edition.*

Here is an entry for the word *necessitate* from a recent college edition of *Webster's*:

1 2 3 4 6

5 —— **ne·ces·si·tate** (nə-ses′ə-tat′), **v.t.** [NECESSITATED, NECESSITATING], [ML. *neccesitatus,* pp. of *neccesitare,* necessity], 1. to make (something) necessary or unavoidable; involve or imply as a logical outcome. 2. to compel; require; force: usually in passive, as I am *necessitated* to act alone.

7 9

The numbered key points out the following characteristics of the word.

1 Correct spelling of the word, with center dots indicating the separate syllables. (The dot indicates the place where you may hyphenate a word that has two or more syllables.)
2 Pronunciation with markers to indicate the syllable that gets the primary stress (′) and the one that gets the secondary stress (′).
3 Part of speech ("v.t." = *transitive verb,* or a verb that needs an object or that expresses an action directed toward a noun in the sentence).

4 Correct spelling of the past-tense form of the verb (which is the same as the past participle ending for this verb).
5 Correct spelling of the "-*ing*" ending for this verb.
6 History of the word's meaning ("ML" = "Medieval Latin").
7 First definition of the word's meaning.
8 Second definition of the word's meaning.
9 Example sentence indicating the use of one meaning of this word.

Note that the pronunciation of the word *necessitate* includes a symbol that looks like an upside-down letter *e*. This symbol is called a *schwa,* and it represents the sound *uh.* A schwa is used to indicate the sound of unaccented vowels in most English words:

alone [ə-lōn′]	item [ī′-təm]
melody [mel′-ə-di]	suppose [sə-pōz′],

Different dictionaries provide different information because each one represents the judgments of the group of people who wrote it, and these judgments mirror the constantly changing nature of language itself.

Most dictionaries arrange their words in alphabetical order. They begin with an introduction that explains what the book contains and how the entries for each word are arranged. Read the introductory material in your dictionary so that you will know how to use it and know what the abbreviations stand for. Carry it with you to every class and *use it.*

WRITING ACTIVITY 4

Get a college dictionary and follow the directions below on a separate sheet of paper.

Look up the word *harass.*

1. How do you spell each of the syllables that make up *harass*?
2. What are the different ways of pronouncing *harass*?
3. What language did the word *harass* come from, and what did it mean in that language?
4. What part of speech is *harass*?
5. List every definition of *harass* in your dictionary.
6. Write a sentence using *harass.*

GROUP WORK 3

Form a group with two or three classmates and choose one person to record the answers to the following questions (on a separate sheet of paper).

1. What two languages did the word *miscreant* come from, and what did it mean in these languages?
2. How is this word defined today? (What current definitions does your dictionary give for this word?)
3. What part of speech is *miscreant* today?
4. What did *miscreant* use to mean? (What "archaic" definitions does your dictionary give for it?)
5. What part of speech did *miscreant* use to be?
6. What is an "archaic" definition?
7. How has the meaning of the word *miscreant* changed over time?
8. Write a sentence using this word (with its current meaning).

A *thesaurus* is a dictionary of synonyms. You can use it to find synonyms for words that you repeat too often in your writing. You can also use a thesaurus to find more formal or more academic synonyms for informal or slang words and expressions. If you looked up the word *miscreant* in a thesaurus, you might find it listed under the word *unbelief.* Here is an excerpt from an entry for *unbelief* from a recent edition of *Roget's Thesaurus of English Words and Phrases.*

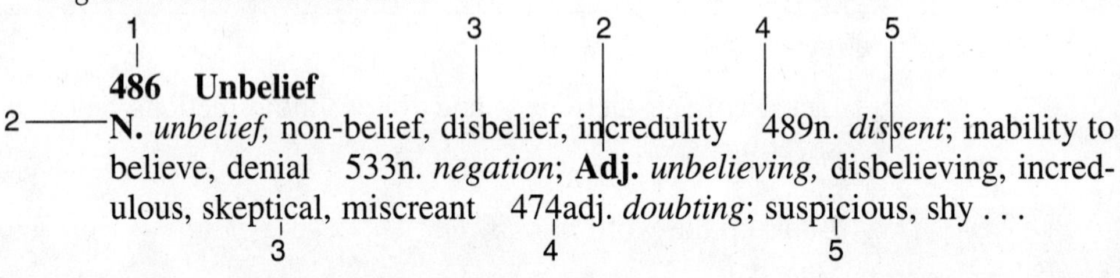

The numbered key identifies the following attributes of the thesaurus entry.

1 The number under which the "head" word ("unbelief") is indexed
2 Part of speech ("N." = "noun"; "Adj." = "adjective")
3 Synonyms for the head word
4 "Keyword" synonym (synonym that is described elsewhere in the thesaurus) and its part of speech ("n." = noun"; "adj." = "adjective")
5 Synonyms for each keyword

REMINDER

Many thesauruses do not list words alphabetically. Instead, they group synonyms according to subject categories (or head words), and you have to use the index to find the synonyms for the word that you are looking up. Buy a thesaurus that is alphabetically arranged, so that you can look up words easily.

WRITING ACTIVITY 5

Use a thesaurus to look up synonyms for each of the following words. Write down the first three synonyms for each word. Use a dictionary to look up the meaning of each synonym. Write a sentence using each synonym. The first one has been done as an example.

1. portly

First synonym stout

Definition strong; firm; fat; fleshy

Sentence Hitting the stout construction worker was like striking a brick wall.

Second synonym fleshy

Definition fat; plump; thickset; big

Sentence After deciding that I was too fleshy, I started exercising regularly.

Third synonym stately

Definition imposing; dignified; majestic

Sentence The king looked quite stately as he gave his speech.

2. mentor

First synonym ______________________

Definition ______________________

Sentence ______________________

____

Second synonym ______________________

Definition ______________________

Sentence ______________________

____

Third synonym ______________________

Definition ______________________

Sentence ______________________

____

3. brutal

First synonym ______________________

Definition ______________________

Sentence ______________________

____

Second synonym ______________________

Definition ______________________

Sentence ______________________

____

Third synonym ______________________________

Definition ______________________________

Sentence ______________________________

____

4. beleaguer

First synonym ______________________________

Definition ______________________________

Sentence ______________________________

____

Second synonym ______________________________

Definition ______________________________

Sentence ______________________________

____

Third synonym ______________________________

Definition ______________________________

Sentence ______________________________

____

5. elementary

First synonym ______________________________

Definition ______________________________

Sentence ______________________________

____

Second synonym ______________________________

Definition ______________________________

Sentence ______________________________

____

Third synonym ______________________________

Definition ______________________________

Sentence ______________________________

____

REVISING VAGUE WORDS AND EXPRESSIONS

"All-Purpose" Words. Read the sentence below. If someone said this sentence to you, how might you respond?

> *In the Line of Fire,* starring Clint Eastwood, was a great film, but Eastwood's greatest film was *Unforgiven.* That was a really great movie!

What is a "great" film? What makes one movie "greater" than another? "Great" is an *all-purpose* word that doesn't communicate much. Here are some other all-purpose words that can ruin the clarity of your writing.

"ALL-PURPOSE" WORDS TO AVOID

Circle these words in your drafts and substitute more specific words and expressions:

great, terrific, incredible, wonderful
good, fine, nice, okay, all right
terrible, awful, bad, strange, interesting
a lot, lots, many, plenty
thing, aspect, factor, stuff

WRITING ACTIVITY 6

Rewrite the following sentences by substituting more precise language for each vague word or expression. The first one has been done as an example.

The Fugitive was ~~an awesome movie.~~ a movie that kept me riveted. I had not seen the original version on television, but people tell me that the T.V. series was pretty good. My friends who saw reruns of the T.V. series said it was okay. A lot of them said that the movie version of *The Fugitive* was great—much better than the original. The best thing about the movie was the acting. Harrison Ford was really good as the fugitive, and Tommy Lee Jones was geat as the marshal who's trying to get him. Also, the special effects were incredible. The actors did amazing stuff, and the crash scenes were really terrific. Lots of exciting things happened in this movie as the marshal tried to catch the fugitive. It was so intense. The best part of the movie was the ending, which was wonderful.

Clichés. A cliché (pronounced "klee-shay") is an expression that has been used so often that it no longer communicates anything. Clichés are common in speech, but they do not belong in academic writing. Readers don't pay much attention to clichés because they don't carry any precise meaning. For example, what does each cliché in the following list communicate?

COMMON CLICHÉS TO AVOID

Circle these expressions in your drafts and delete them or substitute more specific language.

as quick as a wink
at a loss for words
busy as a bee
down and out
easier said than done
fair and square

(Continued)

hit the nail on the head	short but sweet
in the nick of time	slowly but surely
in the olden days	time and time again
in this day and age	to make a long story short
in this modern world	too close for comfort
in today's world	word to the wise
last but not least	work like a dog

Clichés give the impression that the writer is too lazy to think of an interesting way to say something. Clichés come to mind easily, so you will probably find them sprinkled among your discovery drafts. Cross them out, and substitute more precise language.

WRITING ACTIVITY 7

Rewrite the following sentences by substituting more precise language for each cliché. The first one has been done as example.

1. *Time and time again,* I get nervous when I have to make a sales pitch to a prospective client.

   I get nervous almost every time that I have to make a sales pitch to a prospective client.

2. I often *beat around the bush* because I don't want to seem too aggressive.

3. I wish that I could feel *calm, cool, and collected,* but instead I often feel *at a loss for words.*

4. I know *beyond a shadow of a doubt* that the product I am selling is exactly what the client needs.

____

____

5. However, explaining why a product is right for a client is *easier said than done.*

____

____

6. I think that I will have to *face the music* and take some lessons in public speaking.

____

____

7. If these lessons help me, they will be *worth their weight in gold.*

____

____

8. *Slowly but surely,* I will work at becoming a better salesperson, and I will *climb the ladder of success.*

____

____

9. I will *work like a dog.*

____

10. One day, I will be *on top of the world.*

____

Slang. *Slang* words and expressions are very informal usages that vary according to time and place. For example, when this book was written (1993), the slang term used by teenagers in New York City to describe an attractive female was *fly*. In Los Angeles, the slang term was *mink*. As you can tell from these examples, slang is a kind of code that people use with friends to communicate their shared unique meanings. Therefore, slang is almost always inappropriate for academic paragraphs and essays. Most slang words and expressions are unclear, and they go out of date or style quickly. Edit your paragraphs for slang, deleting any overly informal words or expressions that you have written. If you are not sure whether a word or a phrase is slang, look it up in an unabridged dictionary. The dictionary will indicate a slang expression (with the bracketed word ''[slang]'').

WRITING ACTIVITY 8

Rewrite the following sentences so that they are more ''academic'' and formal. Remember to replace all slang words with formal substitutes.

1. My classmates and I thought that our recent history test was a total bummer.

   ____

   ____

2. The test was a real drag because it included stuff that wasn't in our books or notes.

   ____

   ____

3. I had been busy most of the past week, so I had to pull an all-nighter to study, and I was nodding out when I got to class.

   ____

   ____

4. Then I got a stomachache because I had scarfed down my breakfast so quickly.

____

____

5. When I saw that the test had such difficult questions, I really flipped out.

____

____

6. Taking that test was a real downer.

____

____

GROUP WORK 4

Choose a revision that you wrote for one of the assignments in this book or for your teacher. Exchange papers with a classmate. After you read your partner's paper, write answers to the questions below on a separate sheet of paper (include your partner's name). Do *not* discuss each other's papers until you are both finished writing your comments.

1. What do you think the writer was trying to show or prove in this paper?
2. Which words don't seem to make much sense or don't communicate the writer's meaning clearly?
3. Which words suggest connotations that the writer might not have intended them to suggest?
4. Where is the writer's language too informal or inappropriate for his or her purpose and reader?

When you are finished answering the questions above, return the essay to your partner and discuss it. Suggest alternative words for any of the words that you noted in your comments.

AVOIDING SEXIST LANGUAGE

Sexist language consists of words and expressions that imply that women are inferior to men (or vice versa) or that imply gender-related roles or characteristics. Here are some examples:

office girl (implying that female office assistants are childlike)
man-sized (implying that a woman's portion is small)
lady doctor (implying that doctors are men)
male nurse (implying that nurses are women)

Many readers find sexist language offensive. Moreover, sexist language is often inaccurate. For example, can you figure out what is wrong with the following sentence?

Everyone in my class is proud of how hard he worked this past semester.

The pronoun "he" in the sentence above is inaccurate because rarely is a class composed of only male students. Traditionally, the pronouns people use to refer to "a person" or to an indefinite pronoun (like *anyone*) are masculine:

When a writer revises a draft, *he* has to look for problems in *his* diction. *He* must make sure that *he* has not used words that do not communicate *his* meaning clearly. The writer should also make sure that *his* choice of words will not antagonize *his* readers.

The use of masculine pronouns to refer to a person whose gender is not identified is a form of sexist language. This usage is as incorrect as are other types of errors. The pronouns in the following sentences also represent a kind of pronoun agreement error, as was the case for the masculine pronouns in the example above.

When a writer revises a draft, *they* have to look for problems in *their* diction. *They* must make sure that *they* have not used words that do not communicate *their* meaning clearly. The writer should also make sure that *their* choice of words will not antagonize *their* readers.

A "writer" is a single person so you cannot use a plural pronoun ("their," "they") to refer back to this person. You can use *his or her* (and *he or she*), or you can change all the nouns and pronouns to their plural forms.

When a writer revises a draft, *he or she* has to look for problems in *his or her* diction. *He or she* must make sure that *he or she* has not used words that do not communicate *his or her* meaning clearly. The writer should also make sure that *his or her* choice of words will not antagonize *his or her* readers.

or

When writers revise a draft, *they* have to look for problems in *their* diction. *They* must make sure that *they* have not used words that do not communicate *their* meaning clearly. Writers should also make sure that *their* choice of words will not antagonize *their* readers.

The preceding examples illustrate the fact that plural pronouns (''they'' and ''their'') are easier to read than is the repeated use of ''he or she'' and ''his or her.'' Change your nouns to plurals wherever possible so that you can avoid using the *he or she* construction repeatedly in a sentence or in a paragraph.

GUIDELINES FOR NONSEXIST DICTION

Here are some suggestions for avoiding sexist language:

1. Do not use the words *man* or *men* when you are writing about a person whose gender you have not identified:

   The *chairperson* [or the ''chair,'' but *not* the ''chairman''] joked that a *person's* [*not* a ''man's''] best friend is a computer.

2. Use *he or she, his or her,* and *him or her* to refer to indefinite pronouns:

   A student who revises every essay will probably improve *his or her* writing abilities.

3. Use plural nouns and pronouns instead of singular ones:

   Students who revise every essay will probably improve *their* writing abilities.

4. Omit unnecessary pronouns wherever you can:

   The writing abilities of a student who revises every essay will probably improve.

5. Use *Ms.* instead of *Mrs.* or *Miss,* unless you are writing to a woman who has a professional title (like *Dr.*) or who has asked you to use *Mrs.* or *Miss*:

   Dr. Eleanor Rojas is proud of her daughter, *Ms.* Joy Rojas-Smith.

(Continued)

6. Do not use sexist labels:

   Dr. Rojas is a doctor [*not* a "lady doctor"], who is proud that her daughter is a police officer [*not* a "policeman" or a "lady policeman"].

WRITING ACTIVITY 9

Reread an essay that you wrote for an assignment in this book or for your teacher. Circle every instance of sexist language, and write a nonsexist substitute for it. Revise the entire paragraph or essay so that it no longer has any sexist language in it.

UNDERSTANDING COMMONLY CONFUSED WORDS

English has many sets of words that writers frequently confuse because these words resemble each other. When you edit your revisions, find and correct every word that you have confused with another word. Here are some commonly confused words and their meanings.

an Used before a word that begins with a vowel sound (*a, e, i, o,* and *u*): Can I do *an* exercise?

a Used before words that start with a consonant sound: Can I do *a* writing activity?

accept (Verb) to receive willingly: We *accept* your invitation.

except (Preposition) excluding or leaving out: All of us *except* Larry will be attending your party.

affect (Verb) to influence or change: Larry's absence will not *affect* the party.

effect (Verb) to cause: Exercising can *effect* an improvement in a person's muscle tone.

effect (Noun) the result or consequence: Exercising also has a calming *effect* on my personality.

all ready All set or all prepared: The cast of the movie were *all ready* to rehearse their parts.

already Previously or by this time: They had *already* tuned their instruments twice.

all together Everyone in the same place: The cast of the movie were *all together* on the stage for this scene.

altogether Entirely: They were not *altogether* convinced that the play would be a success.

amount Refers to a quantity that is not thought of as being composed of individual units: The stage has a large *amount* of open space.
number Refers to a quantity that is thought of as consisting of individual units: The actors saw a *number* of familiar faces in the audience.

beside By the side of: We sat *beside* our friends.
besides In addition to: Did anyone *besides* you see where our friends went during intermission?

fewer Refers to things that can be counted as individual units: This theater has *fewer* seats than the other theater has.
less Refers to a quantity taken as a mass or to degree: We have *less* interest in seeing musicals than we used to have.

good Describes nouns and pronouns: The director of this play is a *good* organizer.
well Describes verbs: She works *well* with the cast and the crew.

lead (Verb, pronounced ''leed'') to go first: Will you please *lead* us out of this theater?
led (Verb) past-tense form of ''to lead'': The usher *led* us out of the theater at the end of the play.
lead (Noun, pronounced ''led'') a metal: The ancient pipes were made of *lead.*

moral (Adjective) good or having good values: I like plays with *moral* values.
moral (Noun) a lesson: The play implied an interesting *moral* about the need to care for others.
morale (Noun) spirit or mental condition: I enjoyed the play, for it lifted my *morale.*

passed (Verb) past-tense form of ''to pass'': The director *passed* out copies of the script to the actors.
past (Noun) a previous time or the history of a person or thing: The director described versions of the play that had been produced in the *past.*
past (Preposition) by or farther on than: The rehearsal went on *past* the time it was supposed to end.

principal The most important, or the head of a school: Dr. O'Reilly, the *principal* of our school, is the *principal* leader of the Curriculum Committee.
principle A law, fact, or rule of conduct: The committee is deciding the *principles* for curriculum development.

quiet Silence, silent, or still: The classroom was *quiet* because the students need *quiet* to compose their ideas on paper.
quite Rather, very, or exactly: The student was *quite* sure that her draft did not *quite* express her ideas.

than (Conjunction) used to compare people or things: That student is a better writer *than* I am.
then (Adverb) used to refer to a specific time: I asked the student where he was living *then. Then* I asked him if he planned to move.

there (Adverb) in that place: They had not gone *there* in a long time.
they're (Contraction of "they are"): *They're* going to go there every weekend this summer.
their (Pronoun) the possessive form of the pronoun *they*: My friends and *their* relatives went to Clancy Park yesterday.

weather (Noun) conditions outdoors: The *weather* today is perfect for a picnic in the park.
whether (Subordinator) indicates doubt or an alternative: My friends don't know *whether* they can join us.

GROUP WORK 5

Form a group with three or four classmates and work on this activity together. Circle the correct word in each set in the parentheses.

1. An increasing (amount, number) of people are learning how to use a raft to go down a river.
2. The (principal, principle) of my school recently told me about an exciting trip she took on the rapids of a river.
3. I asked her why she did not go on a trip with (fewer, less) people, and she said that she went rafting with friends because she enjoys (there, they're, their) company.
4. Everyone was (already, all ready) to begin the trip at 5 A.M. (accept, except) my friend.
5. She was convinced that the bad (whether, weather) would (affect, effect) the rafting trip, so she was not ready on time.

6. However, rain did not (affect, effect) the rafting trip. Indeed the only (affect, effect) that the rain had on the trip was that it depressed people's (moral, morale) for a while.
7. However, everyone became (quite, quiet) excited when they realized they were approaching the river's rapids.
8. They tied themselves to (their, there, they're) rafts so they would not fall off as they (past, passed) through the rapids.
9. The guides told the people that they had done a (good, well) job of navigating the rapids and that they had all worked (good, well) together.
10. The raft guides pride themselves on (their, there, they're) ability to (led, lead) new rafters through the river safely.
11. At the end of the trip, everyone became very (quite, quiet), reflecting on the fact that they had had (quite, quiet) a unique experience.
12. (Beside, Besides) being an exhilarating experience, white water rafting enables a person to test his or her endurance.

Comparatives and Superlatives. In Chapter 7, you practiced using modifiers—adjectives and adverbs—to describe people, places, things, ideas, and actions. Most English adjectives and adverbs require different forms when you use them to compare *two* people or things and when you use them to compare *three or more* people or things. For example, look at the different forms of the adjective *green* in the following sentences:

> The grass by the river is *green**er*** than the grass near my house. Indeed, the river bank has the *green**est*** grass I have ever seen.

The form of a modifier that you use to compare *two* people or things is called its *comparative* form. This form is usually created by adding *-er* to the modifier (green*er*) or by using the word *more* before it. The form that you use to compare *three or more* people or things is called the *superlative* form. It is usually created by adding *-est* to the modifier (''green*est*'') or by using the word *most* before it. Here are other examples.

Modifier	Comparative form	Superlative form
happy	happier	happiest
silly	sillier	silliest
quickly	more quickly	most quickly
slowly	more slowly	most slowly

Deciding whether to use *-er* or *more* for a comparative modifier (or *-est* or *most* for a superlative modifier) depends on the number of syllables in the modifier:

- With a modifier that is one syllable, use the *-er* or *-est* form: *large, larger, largest.*
- With an adjective that is two syllables and that ends in *-y,* use the *-er* or *-est* form: *happy, happier, happiest.*
- With an adverb that is two or more syllables, use *more* or *most*: *easily, more easily, most easily.*

Some modifiers do not follow the guidelines above; they have *irregular* comparative and superlative forms that you will have to memorize:

Modifier	Comparative form	Superlative form
bad	worse	worst
badly	worse	worst
good	better	best
little	less	least
many	more	most
much	more	most
some	more	most
well	better	best

Do not use a comparative or a superlative modifier if you are not comparing anything. For example, do not write ''*The Fugitive* is a better movie'' unless you explain what it is ''better'' than: ''*The Fugitive* is a better movie than *Jurassic Park.*'' Similarly, do not write ''*Aliens* is the scariest movie'' unless you explain what you mean by ''scariest'': ''*Aliens* is the scariest movie I've ever seen'' or ''*Aliens* is the scariest movie ever shown in our local movie theater.''

REMINDER

Do not add the word *more* or *most* to a modifier that already ends in *-er* or in *-est.* In other words, do not write ''*more* neat*er*'' or ''*most* neat*est.*''

WRITING ACTIVITY 10

Identify all the incorrect comparative and superlative forms in the following paragraph. Cross out each incorrect form and write the correct form above it. (Some of the forms may be correct.)

Yesterday, our town had the baddest storm that most of us can remember. The damage from this storm was more badder than the damage from any other weather event that I have ever experienced. What made this storm badder than previous ones was the fact that we had little time to prepare for it than we had for prior storms. It swept over our town quite suddenly, and it was more windier than a hurricane. The storm covered a much more bigger area than other storms have, and the torrential rain was the most bad that my neighbors had ever seen. The bestest place to stay was inside the living room because that room didn't flood. Also the living room was the most safest one in the house because people's attics protected their living rooms from falling trees. Fortunately, the town's emergency preparations were more gooder than they were during last year's hurricane. Town workers brought food and medical supplies to people much more quicklier than they did last year. Thanks to these people, there were less few deaths than there might have been.

WRITING ACTIVITY 11

Write a paragraph comparing three friends, teachers, or places that you know well. Which of the three people or places is better (or more interesting) than the other two? Why is this person or place the best of the three? Use the correct comparative and superlative forms of modifiers to describe these people or places.

EXPLORING FURTHER: USING THE STRATEGIES YOU HAVE LEARNED

Imagine that you have opened the "Personal Ads" section of your local newspaper or weekly magazine. Here are two ads that might appear in this section. They were both written by the same woman.

1. Single mother seeks friends. I'm new in town, and I'm looking for female friends to share babysitting and to have fun with. I like lots of things, and I know that happiness or pain feels better when it is shared with a friend. Please drop me a note (Box 142).
2. Single mother seeks an interesting man, aged 20–30, who is marriage-minded and likes children. I am tall, thin, and pretty. I like lots of things, and I would like to share them with a man who likes me as much as I like him. Please send me a note and a recent photo (Box 142).

Do you think this writer would receive any letters in response to these ads? Why or why not? Does either description give you a clear impression of the writer? Does either description let you know exactly what kind of person she hopes will answer her ad?

Composing an effective personal advertisement requires the writer to use several of the paragraph development strategies that you have been practicing in this book (including narration, description, classification, and definition). Here is an article about the difficulties involved in writing and revising this kind of ad. It was written by Susan Deitz, the author of a *Newsday* column about being single entitled "Single File."

DEAR READERS: When you know what you want, finding it is a lot easier.

And you know what I believe: While there is not only one Right Person for you, there is one Right Type of Person for you.

So, as you sit down to compose your symphony of words that will attract the RTP, think about the traits you admire and the sort of person who embodies them. As you're sifting through qualities, make a list of what you absolutely must have in a loved one and what you would like in her or him but what is not absolutely essential. Believe it or not, that one list holds the key to a successful personal ad.

But wait. One good list deserves another. Now write a list of your strong points, the things about you that set you apart from the crowd.

Now you're ready to write the first draft (yes, there will be more) of the ad you will place to find the person you deserve. Be specific, descriptive, daring. Avoid the usual: "sensitive," "attractive," "fun-loving." This is a picture portrait of you and no one else. Make it as individual as you are; use your imagination to dream up phrases and good copy.

Without baring your soul, expose things about yourself not readily known: private goals, lifelong dreams, fantasies. Your ad should catch the imagination of the readers, so be specific in descriptions and clear in your writing.

Write a first-draft ad, keeping in mind all of the above, and let it sit for at least a day. As it marinates, your subconscious will be at work on it, quietly probing for new words and new ideas for the ad. A day or two later, sit down and make the corrections, fine-tuning your ad.

Use words like ''curious,'' ''dynamic,'' ''soulful'' if they apply to you. I know a love story that began because the woman behind an ad had described herself as ''curious,'' and that word caught the eye of the right man. It turned out she was indeed curious, as well as bright and lively (don't the three qualities go together?), and the relationship lasted a long time. These two would never have connected had it not been for the personals. As the longest journey begins with a single step, the most torrid romance can start because of a single, well-chosen word.

The overall guideline to placing a personal ad is to make it *personal,* to write a description that would fit only you. That takes time—and soul-searching. Since there is no deadline in finding a love partner, time is on your side.

As for the soul-searching, well, it can bring only benefits—now and in the future. So go heavy on the marinade, all the while discussing with the people close to you what they would say about you. (You may not want to mention that the discussion is in preparation to place a personal ad, that's up to you. There is no shame in using the personals, but some single people are still squeamish about the roots of a personal-ad relationship. They feel it makes them appear desperate, although that is more in their perception than in reality.)

Use this waiting period to dig a little, to ''interview'' people in your inner circle and find out their views of you. If each ''interview'' yields just one good word, the time will have been worthwhile.

As you write your second draft, visualize the sort of person you hope will be drawn to your ad. Seeing the person in your mind's eye can bring your focus into sharper clarity and narrow down the thrust of the ad. Whether your RTP is blond or brunet, tall or short, 10 pounds overweight or balding is not the object of this visualization (those superficialities wound up on your not-crucial list, I hope). Seeing the goodness and the verve of the person is.

You want someone who will share your values, your priorities, some of your tastes (if they can introduce you to new sources of enjoyment, so much the better; the match is livelier if it is not a perfect meshing).

Get on the phone and read your second draft to a buddy, asking for feedback and not just an indulgent ''Good!'' Start thinking of appropriate newspapers that have a personal ad section.

Inquire about voice mail. With all that information in mind, sit down and write the third and final draft of your personal ad. Phone, fax or mail it in to your favorite newspaper.

But you're not through yet. Put a pad and pencil by your phone and write down words that will cue you in to the questions you want to ask respondents and what you want to say about yourself.

Don't tell your life story to the first caller, be friendly and warm and receptive—and compassionate. It's not easy for someone to call a stranger, even someone as nice as you. Don't grill the person—your job is to make the caller comfortable and at ease.

One more thing: Keep a sense of humor.

WRITING ASSIGNMENT

Compose a personal ad about yourself for your local newspaper or magazine. Your purpose is to make readers write to you (to get together for a possible friendship, romance, or marriage). Your ad should be 100 to 150 words long. The final version should be composed of complete, clear, correct sentences. As you revise your ad, look for words that may confuse or offend readers who do not know you. Make sure each word communicates the denotation and connotations that you intend it to express. Cross out any vague words or expressions, and substitute precise, specific language.

POINTS TO REMEMBER ABOUT VOCABULARY AND DICTION

1. If you are not sure of the denotation or the connotation of any of the words that you have used, look up the word in an unabridged dictionary.
2. Use a thesaurus that is alphabetically arranged to look up synonyms for words that you have used too often or words with inappropriate connotations.
3. Examine the words you have chosen and make sure they are appropriate for your purpose, your topic, and your readers.
4. Find more precise substitutes for overly informal words, for slang, for vague "all-purpose" words, and for clichés.
5. Reword any nouns and pronouns that readers might consider sexist.
6. Check words that you frequently confuse to make sure that you have used the word you meant to use.
7. Eliminate unnecessary words and phrases from overly wordy sentences.
8. Examine every comparative and superlative modifier and make sure you have used the correct form.

CHAPTER

13

SPELLING AND CAPITALIZATION

English words are generally not easy to spell. The spelling system of the English language is based on meaning rather than on sound. For example, the words *medical* and *medicine* are not pronounced similarly. The *c* in "medical" sounds like a *k*; in "medicine" it sounds like an *s*. However, these words are spelled similarly because they share a related meaning ("preventing or curing diseases") and the same history (both are derived from the Latin word for "healing"). Similarly, the word *sign* has a "silent *g*" but is related in meaning to words in which the *g* is pronounced: *signature* and *signal.* Thus, sometimes if you are not sure how to spell a word, you might think about the spelling of words that relate to it in meaning.

The easiest way to improve your spelling is to read more and to become aware of how words are spelled. In addition, always keep a paperback college dictionary with you and look up any word whose spelling you are unsure of. Each morning or evening, practice spelling new words (and words that you commonly misspell) in your word bank. Check for spelling errors *after* you have finished revising your draft. Identify possible spelling errors by reading each word slowly. If you see a word that you think might be misspelled, look it up in the dictionary. If you are writing on a computer, use a program with a spelling checker.

IDENTIFYING THE CAUSES OF YOUR SPELLING ERRORS

All writers have particular spelling errors that they repeat over and over again. As you edit your writing, look for the spelling errors that you usually make.

Try to figure out why you are making them. Here are five possible causes of many spelling errors.

FIVE CAUSES OF SPELLING ERRORS

1. Addition—you add a letter, usually because you pronounce the word with this letter:

   inte*r*grate (integrate)   ath*e*letes (athletes)

2. Deletion—you omit a letter, usually because you don't pronounce it:

   la*br*atory (laboratory)   Fe*bu*ary (February)

3. Transposition—you transpose (switch) a letter with the letter next to it:

   jew*le*ry (jewelry)   dec*ie*ve (deceive)

4. Substitution—you substitute a letter that has a similar sound:

   a*dd*itude (attitude)   excell*a*nt (excellent)

5. Homonym—you confuse a word with another word that it sounds like (see the list of "Commonly Confused Words" on pages 332–334 of Chapter 12):

   past/passed   sight/cite/site

Each writer has a personal set of troublesome words to look for and correct every time he or she edits a paragraph or an essay. Experienced writers make spelling errors, but they remember to proofread for their typical errors. They examine tricky words to see if they "look right." Good spellers use a dictionary to check the spelling of words that are difficult for them to spell or words whose spelling they are unsure about.

WRITING ACTIVITY 1

Here is a student paragraph. Find every spelling error and circle it. Then write the correct spelling of the word above it. The first misspelled word has been corrected as an example.

Council

The Student Counsel is an important organization for students at any college or university. Basicaly, the buisiness of the Student

Counsel is to represent students' interests and conserns. The oficers of the Student Counsel are elected each year. They're job is to go to student goverment meetings and to meet with the school's administraters. They must illicit students' viewpoints about academic, socail, and finantial matters and reprasent these veiwpoints at college meetings. They also have input into the day-to-day managment of the school. Most Student Counsel oficers work hard to reduse the problems caused by beurocracy and to increase students' oportunities to take part in meetings where importent dicisions are made. Attendence at these meetings is important. Students who cannot manege to attend these meetings should make sure that there Student Counsel oficers represent there positions acurately.

GROUP WORK 1

Work with a partner or two on this activity. Together identify and circle every misspelled word in the following paragraph. List the misspelled words on a separate sheet of paper and write the correct spelling—in capital letters—next to each word. Examine the list and decide why this writer is making spelling errors. Which *two* of the five causes (listed earlier in this chapter) seem to be causing most of his errors?

Being a champion athelete is not easy. A champion needs excellant physical strength and endurance. A week person can become a good athelete, but he or she probly won't become a champion. In addition to having strong mussels and good eye-hand coordination, a champion must have an even temperment. He or she must have the patients to work out and to practice every day, even when he or she is very tired or board. Furthermore, a champion needs a good coach, someone who'se advise he or she can except and trust. Most importanly, an athelete cannot acheive greatness unless he or she is willing to work hard for it. Hundereds of people make it to the semifinals in they're sport, only to loose in the finals because they give up physically or mentally.

WRITING ACTIVITY 2

What words do you misspell frequently? What words have you misspelled in your recent writing assignments? Can you identify the causes of your common spelling errors? Can you find particular patterns of errors: Do you often add, delete, transpose, or substitute letters? Do you misspell homonyms or commonly confused words? Write down the causes of your spelling errors so that you can look for your typical spelling errors whenever you edit your writing.

STRATEGIES FOR IMPROVING SPELLING

Often, you may not be able to spell a word by ''sounding it out'' because a particular sound may be represented by several different combinations of letters. For instance, the ''long e'' sound can be spelled *eleven* different ways in English: *e* (he), *ee* (sheet), *ea* (beat), *ie* (relieve), *ei* (receive), *eo* (people), *ae* (Caesar), *y* (silly), *ey* (donkey), *i* (machine), and *oe* (amoeba)! If you are not sure how to spell a particular sound in a word, use your dictionary to look up the word.

Here are other strategies to help you become a better speller.

1. *Do not worry about spelling while you are writing or revising a piece of writing.* Concentrate on developing your ideas and on crafting precise sentences. Wait until you are finished revising your writing before you check your spelling. If you start checking your spelling before you get all your ideas on paper (or on screen), you may forget what you wanted to write.
2. *Write every word that you misspell in your word bank.* If you write down every misspelled word (and its correct spelling), you will begin to understand your typical patterns of spelling errors and you will become a better speller.
3. *Write your assignments and your entries in your word bank neatly.*

Sloppy handwriting often produces a confused image of words and uncertainty about how they are spelled.

4. *Use a dictionary to look up the spelling and the pronunciation of words when you are editing.* If you don't know the first few letters of a word (which you must know in order to look it up), ask a classmate, a teacher, or a friend for help.

SPELLING RULES

Most spelling rules are overly complicated or have so many exceptions that they are useless. There are only three rules that you might want to memorize.

Rule 1: Doubling a Final Consonant. If you want to add a suffix (an ending) to a word that ends in a single consonant, double this final consonant if it meets *both* of these conditions:

1. The suffix begins with a vowel.
2. The word consists of only one syllable *or* is accented on the final syllable.

Doubled	**Not doubled**
drop—dropped	forget—forgetful
hop—hopping	hope—hoping
hid—hidden	happen—happened

The exception to this rule is any word that ends in an *x*: wax—waxed, tax—taxed.

Rule 2: Silent e. If you want to add a suffix to a word that ends in a silent *e* (i.e., an *e* that you don't pronounce), drop the *e* if the suffix begins with a vowel, but keep the *e* if the suffix begins with a consonant.

care—caring	care—careful
rare—rarity	rare—rarely

Some exceptions to this rule include the following words:

true—truly	mile—mileage
argue—argument	agree—agreeable

Rule 3: Changing *y* to *i*. If you want to add a suffix to a word that ends in a *y*, change this *y* to an *i* if the suffix begins with any letter except *i*. (Keep the final *y* if the suffix begins with *i*.)

marry—marriage	marry—marrying
fry—fried	fry—frying

Three exceptions to this rule are *pay, lay,* and *say*:

pay + ed = paid
lay + ed = laid
say + ed = said

WRITING ACTIVITY 3

Check your understanding of these spelling rules by combining the following words and suffixes. The first one has been done as an example.

1. ready + ness = readiness
2. leave + ing = ____________
3. guide + ance = ____________
4. confer + ed = ____________
5. admit + ing = ____________
6. true + ly = ____________
7. benefit + ed = ____________
8. forty + eth = ____________
9. logic + ally = ____________
10. plenty + ful = ____________
11. advise + able = ____________
12. try + ed = ____________
13. employ + ing = ____________
14. argue + ment = ____________
15. tax + ed = ____________
16. win + er = ____________

17. forget + able = ______________________

18. write + ing = ______________________

19. require + ment = ______________________

20. desire + ing = ______________________

21. change + able = ______________________

22. please + ure = ______________________

Problems with *ei* and *ie*. Do you confuse *ei* and *ie* when you spell words containing these pairs? The general rule for spelling words with these letters is stated in the elementary school rhyme:

> Write *i* before *e* except after *c* or when sounded like *ay* as in *neighbor* and *weigh.*

Remembering this rhyme may be helpful. It works for many words (including *grief, friend, believe, field, mischief, deceit, ceiling, eight,* and *vein*). There are exceptions to this rule. For example, some words are spelled with an *i* before an *e* even when the *ie* combination follows a *c,* for example, *financier, science,* and *conscience.* Exceptions that are spelled with an *e* before an *i* include *seize, weird, foreign,* and *height.* If *ei* or *ie* transpositions are a spelling problem for you, you should look up the correct spelling of every word that includes these letters.

WRITING ACTIVITY 4

Circle every spelling error in the following paragraph and write the correct spelling above each error. The first misspelling has been corrected as an example.

Several nights ago, I thought I heard a (their) [thief] trying to break into my house. At first, I could not beleive what I was hearing. I thought that the noise I heard was the result of a nieghbor's child making some kind of misheif. The noise was breif, but just as I was starting to feel releived, it began again, louder than before. I realized that someone was trying to break the window below my bedroom cieling. The hieght of the window made it impossible for me to see exactly what was happening. (The window is about eieght feet up from the floor.) I started to shake, since I beleived that I was in great danger. I siezed the big stone paperwieght that I keep on my desk and threw it at the window. My cheif concern was stopping the theif, so I didn't care about the glass that fell on me. I felt wierd and scared, but I finally got the nerve to stand on a chair and look out the broken window. To my great releif, I saw a large cat. What I thought was a theif was actually a hungry animal.

Numbers. The rules for spelling out numbers vary, depending on how you are using the numbers and on how often you use them in a paragraph or an essay. Some of the guidelines for whether to spell out numbers or use numerals are included in the chart that follows.

WHEN TO SPELL OUT NUMBERS OR USE NUMERALS

1. Use numerals for addresses, dates, time, and money:

   I made an appointment with my neurologist, Dr. Chung, at her office at *142 East 89th Street* on *May 2* at *9:30 A.M.*

2. When you begin a sentence with a number, always spell out the number:

   One hundred fifty dollars is the amount that Dr. Chung charges for an office visit.

3. Within a sentence, spell out numbers (that are *not* addresses, dates, time, or money) *if* they can be written as one or two words (numbers ''one'' through ''one hundred''). Numbers from twenty-one through ninety-nine require a hyphen when they are spelled out:

Dr. Chung has been practicing medicine for *twenty-one* years.

4. When you use more than one number in a sentence, if any of the numbers are more than two words, use numerals for all the numbers:

   Of the *122* female neurologists in this city, *96* work at major teaching hospitals.

WRITING ACTIVITY 5

Circle every incorrect number in the following paragraph and write in the correction above the mistake. The first one has been done as an example.

three

My favorite job is the one I currently have as one of the 3 part-time managers at Smithtown Food Mart in the Smithtown Mall. The store employs thirty-nine workers—12 full-time employees and 27 part-time employees. The full-time people work 8 hours a day (with a one-hour lunch break from 12:00 to one o'clock). The part-time employees work 5 hours a day (with two fifteen-minute breaks). I am an exception to this rule. I punch in at two-thirty p.m. (after school), and I work until 8:30 p.m. (a total of 6 hours). I get a 1/2 hour dinner break at six o'clock. The store has 2 cafeterias, one for managers and 1 for workers. I eat with the workers because I enjoy their company (even though this means walking up 3 flights of stairs because the employee cafeteria is on the 4th floor). I am friends with about 20 of the other employees at the Food Mart. In addition to enjoying these friendships, I also receive an excellent salary. Last year, ! was paid nine dollars an hour. This year, I received an increase of seventy-five cents, so I am making $9.75 an hour. I enjoy my work so much that I am considering a career in food market management.

GROUP WORK 2

Form a group with two or three classmates and, together, proofread the following paragraph. Identify every spelling error and incorrect treatment of numbers. Then choose one person to rewrite the paragraph with all the words corrected.

The student workers in the office of the Department of English have had to acomodate to cutbacks in the department's payrole. Five of the 7 students who currently work part-time in the office will have to raduce their hours, espeshally in the afternoon, when everyone wants to work. Since all seven of us agreed that fireing any of us was unaceptable, we agreed to redezign our work scheduals. Each of us now has a choice of 5 morning hours (from eieight o'clock until 1) or five afternoon hours (1 o'clock until six p.m.). Some of us who were acustomed to working 8 hours were very disapointed with this reduction. (Reduceing our hours had a disasterous effect on our finances.) However, after we discussed and debatted alternitives, we reelized that this was the most sensable plan. We were also pleezed that the department considered our arguements and our conserns.

EDITING CAPITALIZATION

Just as readers expect to see correct spelling in academic and professional writing, they also expect to find correct capitalization. Errors in capitalization distract readers, so memorize the rules governing the conventions of capitalization in Academic Written English. Here are the five most important rules.

1. Capitalize the first word of every sentence and of every sentence within a sentence or a quotation:

   My teacher said, ''Please revise your essay again.''

   Do *not* capitalize the first word of a quote that is not a complete sentence:

   My teacher described a revision technique called ''branching.''

2. Capitalize the names of specific people, places, groups, businesses, and events:

   On May 12, Professor Wiener, of Adelphi University (in Garden City), will discuss literature written during the Renaissance. This seminar will take place in Kaye Auditorium from 9:30 to 11:30 A.M.

3. Capitalize people's titles and their abbreviations:

   My editor's name is Prof. Harvey S. Wiener, Ph.D.

4. Capitalize the names of specific courses, religions, languages, and organizations:

   This semester, I registered for Political Science 101 and History 210 but could not get into the religion course that I wanted, because it was closed. [Note that ''religion course'' is not capitalized, because the writer has not identified the number or the name of this course.]

5. Always capitalize the first word in a title and the first word after a colon in a title. Capitalize all the other words except for *a, an, the,* coordinators (like *and* and *for*), and prepositions (like *of* and *to*):

   Jason Goes to Hell: The Final Friday [movie title]
   PC Computing [magazine title]
   ''My Favorite Place'' [essay title]
   ''Ebony and Ivory'' [song title]
   The Spirit of St. Louis [name of airplane]
   Valentine's Day [holiday]

REMINDER

Do *not* capitalize titles used without names (such as ''the president'' or ''the professor''), institutions or organizations without names (such as ''college'' or ''political party''), and school courses that are not languages or that are used without a number (such as ''algebra'' or ''chemistry'').

WRITING ACTIVITY 6

For each noun listed below, think of an example that is a person's name or a title. Use the noun and the name or title together in a sentence. The first one has been done as an example.

1. baseball player My favorite baseball player is Frank Thomas.
2. movie ______________________
3. state ______________________
4. album or compact disc ______________________
5. park ______________________
6. musical group ______________________
7. college course ______________________
8. holiday ______________________
9. team ______________________

10. religion ______________________________

____

WRITING ACTIVITY 7

Compose a sentence that uses each of the following words exactly the way that they are capitalized. The first two have been done as an example. (Note that plural forms of the word are acceptable.)

1. monument Washington, D.C., has many magnificent monuments and memorials.
2. Monument The building that I want to visit first is the Washington Monument.
3. professor ______________________________
4. Professor ______________________________
5. department ______________________________
6. Department ______________________________
7. communication ______________________________
8. Communication ______________________________

9. island ______________________________

____

10. Island ______________________________

____

11. doctor ______________________________

____

12. Doctor ______________________________

____

13. north ______________________________

____

14. North ______________________________

____

GROUP WORK 3

Work on this activity with a classmate. Together, identify every word with an error in capitalization and write in the correction above the error.

Last christmas, when I heard that my Parents were taking my sisters and brothers on a weekend vacation to new orleans, i told them, "take me too." I had always wanted to see this City. I have read several books about it, and i wanted to see jackson square, the cabildo, and the superdome, where the saints play Football. I explained to my parents that i had finished studying for my final exams (in Calculus, History, and French), and i really wanted to be with the family during the Vacation.

We left on december 20 and arrived in new orleans on december 21. When we got to our Hotel, my father said, "leave the suitcases on the bed. let's go see bourbon street before it gets dark." So we went to the french quarter and did some shopping. We looked up each store in our Guide Book, *new orleans: the good times guide.* Next we strolled down famous old Streets that I had read about: St. philip street, dumain street, and the esplanade. Then we visited the beauregard-keyes house, built in 1826 by general pierre g. t. beauregard. It was Magnificent. We ate dinner at the jackson brewery, a Brewhouse that was built in 1891. All of us ate Creole-style fish.

The next day, we went to see the aquarium of the americas in the Morning and the destrehan Plantation in the Afternoon. The destrehan is the oldest remaining home in the mississippi valley. At the end of the day we headed for brennan's for a Seafood dinner. We had to return Home the following day. When we got back, we all agreed to return to new orleans again, probably during mardi gras (so that we could participate in this Famous Festival).

REMINDER

If you use a computerized word-processing program to write, make sure that the program has a ''spell-checker'' to edit your spelling and capitalization, and use it!

WRITING ACTIVITY 8

Circle every error in spelling and capitalization in the following paragraph. Write in the correction above each error. The first sentence has been corrected as an example.

At this point in my life, I beleive that the best profesion for me is Physical Therapy. I am a 3rd-year student at louisiana state university, and I am a health sceinces major. After my 1st year, I decidded that I should persue a degree in Physical Therapy. A phusical therapist has many jobs, the most important of witch is to help patience get there bodys back into shape after an acident or a disableing injury.

Currently, I am learning how to help pateints recover. I now no how to give varyous treetments for back injuries including Ultra-Sound, Moist Heat, and Masage Therapies. I have also learned how to teach pateints diferent Range of Motion Excercises. These exercises help pateints stretch their tendens and ligiments and regain full use of they're mussels.

In my career as a physical therapist, I will have to do much writting. I will have to write notes on pateints' Charts, record all Treatments and Excercises, and write memoes and letters to doctors and lawers. Writting well is an important part of this profession. Thus, I am hopeing to improve my writting skills as well as my knowlege of Physical Therapy.

EXPLORING FURTHER

The assignment that follows will enable you to practice everything you have learned in this book:

- The processes of prewriting, drafting, revising, and editing
- The strategies of description, narration, process analysis, comparison and contrast, definition, division and classification, cause-and-effect analysis, and argumentation
- The skills of identifying and correcting errors in Academic Written English

The topic for this assignment is *discrimination.* Here are some questions for you to think about. (Do not write answers. Use these questions to get your ideas about this topic flowing.)

- What is discrimination?
- Why do people discriminate?
- How do they discriminate?
- How do people feel when someone discriminates against them?
- What can people do about discrimination?

Here is an argumentative essay about a type of discrimination, entitled ''Discrimination at Large.'' It was written by Jennifer A. Coleman and published in the ''My Turn'' section of *Newsweek.*

Fat is the last preserve for unexamined bigotry. Fat people are lampooned without remorse or apology on television, by newspaper columnists, in cartoons, you name it. The overweight are viewed as suffering from moral turpitude and villainy, and since we are at fault for our condition, no tolerance is due. All fat people are ''outed'' by their appearance.

Weight-motivated assaults occur daily and are committed by people who would die before uttering anti-gay slogans or racial epithets. Yet these same people don't hesitate to scream ''move your fat ass'' when we cross in front of them.

Since the time I first ventured out to play with the neighborhood kids, I was told over and over that I was lazy and disgusting. Strangers, adults, classmates offered gratuitous comments with such frequency and urgency that I started to believe them. Much later I needed to prove it wasn't so. I began a regimen of swimming, cycling and jogging that put all but the most compulsive to shame. I ate only cottage cheese, brown rice, fake butter and steamed everything. I really believed I could infiltrate the ranks of the nonfat and thereby establish my worth.

I would prove that I was not just a slob, a blimp, a pig. I would finally escape the unsolicited remarks of strangers ranging from the ''polite''—''You would really be pretty if you lost weight''—to the hostile (''Lose weight, you fat slob''). Of course, sometimes more subtle commentary sufficed: oinking, mooing, staring, laughing and pointing. Simulating a foghorn was also popular.

My acute exercise phase had many positive points. I was mingling with my obsessively athletic peers. My pulse was as low as anyone's, my cholesterol levels in the basement, my respiration barely detectable. I could swap stats from my last physical with anyone. Except for weight. No matter how hard I tried to run, swim or cycle away from it, my weight found me. Oh sure, I lost weight (never enough) and it inevitably tracked me down and adhered to me more tenaciously than ever. I lived and breathed ''Eat to win,'' ''Feel the burn.'' But in the end I was fit and still fat.

I learned that by societal, moral, ethical, soap-operatical, vegetable, political definition, it was impossible to be both fit and fat. Along the way to that knowledge, what I got for my trouble was to be hit with objects from moving cars because I dared to ride my bike in public, and to be mocked by diners at outdoor cafés who trumpeted like a herd of elephants as I jogged by. Incredibly, it was not uncommon for one of them to shout: ''Lose some weight, you pig.'' Go figure.

It was confusing for a while. How was it I was still lazy, weak, despised, a slug and a cow if I exercised every waking minute? This confusion persisted until I finally realized: it didn't matter what I did. I was and always would be the object of sport, derision, antipathy and hostility so long as I stayed in my body. I immediately signed up for a body transplant. I am still waiting for a donor.

Until then, I am more settled because I have learned the hard way what thin people have known for years. There simply are some things that fat people must never do. Like: riding a bike (''Hey lady, where's the seat?''), eating in a public place (''No dessert for me, I don't want to look like her''). And the most unforgivable crime: wearing a bathing suit in public (''Whale on the beach!'').

Things are less confusing now that I know that the nonfat are superior to me, regardless of their personal habits, health, personalities, cholesterol levels or the time they log on the couch. And, as obviously superior to me as they are, it is their destiny to remark on my inferiority regardless of who I'm with, whether they know me, whether it hurts my feelings. I finally understand that the thin have a divine mandate to steal self-esteem from fat people, who have no right to it in the first place.

Fat people aren't really jolly. Sometimes we act that way so you will leave us alone. We pay a price for this. But at least we get to hang on to what self-respect we smuggled out of grade school and adolescence.

Hating fat people is not inborn; it has to be nurtured and developed. Fortunately, it's taught from the moment most of us are able to walk and speak. We learn it through Saturday-morning cartoons, prime-time TV and movies. Have you ever seen a fat person in a movie who wasn't evil, disgusting, pathetic or lampooned? Santa Claus doesn't count.

Kids catch on early to be sensitive to the feelings of gay, black, disabled, elderly and speech-impaired people. At the same time, they learn that fat people are fair game. That we are always available for their personal amusement.

Never thin enough: The media, legal system, parents, teachers and peers respond to most types of intolerance with outrage and protest. Kids hear that employers can be sued for discriminating, that political careers can be destroyed and baseball owners can lose their teams as a consequence of racism, sexism or almost any other ''ism.''

But the fat kid is taught that she deserves to be mocked. She is not OK. Only if she loses weight will she be OK. Other kids see the response and incorporate the message. Small wonder some (usually girls) get it into their heads that they can never be thin enough.

I know a lot about prejudice, even though I am a white, middle-class, professional woman. The worst discrimination I have suffered because of my gender is nothing compared to what I experience daily because of my weight. I am sick of it. The jokes and attitudes are as wrong and damaging as any racial or ethnic slur. The passive acceptance of this inexcusable behavior is sometimes worse than the initial assault. Some offensive remarks can be excused as the shortcomings of jackasses. But the tacit acceptance of their conduct by mainstream America tells the fat person that the intolerance is understandable and acceptable. Well it isn't.

Discussion Questions

1. What does Coleman mean when she states, ''The overweight are viewed as suffering from moral turpitude and villainy''?
2. Do you view overweight people this way? Why or why not?
3. Do you agree with Coleman's assertion that ''by societal, moral, ethical, soap-operatical, vegetable, political definition, it [is] impossible to be both fit and fat''? Why or why not?
4. What is your response to Coleman's assertion that children learn that they should not make fun of minorities or disabled people but that ''fat people are fair game''?
5. What does Coleman want? Why did she write this essay?

WRITING ASSIGNMENT

The broad topic for this assignment is *discrimination.* Your job is to narrow down this topic to a more focused topic that you can write about in an essay of four or five paragraphs. Do you want to write about an experience that you had with discrimination? Do you want to describe the way in which discrimination has affected someone you know? Do you want to compare or contrast two different types of discrimination? Do you want to analyze some of the reasons why people discriminate against others?

Another way of responding to this writing assignment is to write an essay that responds to Coleman's essay. Do you agree or disagree with Coleman's assertions and conclusions? Why?

When you finish writing and revising your essay, edit it for errors in sentence structure and grammar. Then reread your essay, one word at a time, looking for errors in spelling and capitalization. Use a dictionary to correct these errors.

✔ POINTS TO REMEMBER ABOUT SPELLING AND CAPITALIZATION

1. Do not worry about spelling or capitalization while you are writing or revising a piece of writing.
2. Keep a word bank and in this book list every word that you misspell.
3. Try to identify the cause or causes of your common spelling errors. (Do you often add, delete, transpose, or substitute letters? Do you misspell homonyms or commonly confused words?)
4. Use a college dictionary to look up the spelling and the pronunciation of words when you are editing.
5. Proofread for *ie/ei* transpositions.
6. Proofread for numbers and make sure that you have spelled each correctly or written the numeral form of each if it's required.
7. Proofread for correct capitalization.

CHAPTER

14

PUNCTUATION AND PAPER FORMAT

Punctuation marks are tools that writers use to communicate their ideas clearly and correctly. Punctuation tells readers where to stop, to pause, or to notice the writer's emphasis. Punctuation also signals the relations between ideas and between parts of sentences. Thus, your final job in preparing a paper for a teacher, another student, or an employer is to make sure you have used the appropriate punctuation. Reread each sentence aloud slowly to see if your punctuation communicates your meaning and emphasizes the ideas that matter to you. You must also check to see that your use of punctuation follows the conventions of Academic Written English.

When you speak, you have many vocal and visual options for "punctuating" your meaning, including your tone of voice, pitch, pauses, and facial expressions. When you write, you have only punctuation marks to communicate your emphasis and your pausing. If you leave out punctuation or insert unnecessary punctuation, you can change the meaning of a sentence and confuse readers. Here are two sentences that illustrate this problem. How does the punctuation in the second sentence affect the meaning of the sentence?

A. My coworker quit breaking her promise to me.

B. My coworker quit, breaking her promise to me.

Sentence A states that the writer's coworker stopped breaking her promise to the writer. Sentence B says that the coworker resigned, and—by resigning—broke a promise to the writer. Do you see how a single comma can change the meaning of a sentence?

Here is a chart of the ways in which punctuation helps writers shape meaning.

THE FUNCTIONS OF PUNCTUATION

Punctuation serves six basic functions in writing:

1. Punctuation ends sentences.
2. Punctuation combines sentences.
3. Punctuation separates items in a series within a sentence.
4. Punctuation separates words or phrases that modify a sentence.
5. Punctuation separates quoted words or phrases from the rest of a sentence.
6. Punctuation indicates the possessive case of nouns.

I. PUNCTUATION USED TO END SENTENCES

The period, the question mark, and the exclamation mark are called *end punctuation* because they are used at the end of sentences:

> I will never forget the first essay I got back from a teacher in college. The paper had a big red *F* on it. I thought I was going to faint. Why did my paper fail? I examined the paper more carefully, and then I almost did faint from relief. The grade was an *A*, not an *F*!

Here are some guidelines for using end punctuation.

The Period. Use a period to end a sentence that makes a statement or a command:

> My professor asked me to revise my narrative essay. ''Please add more specific examples,'' he told me.

Also use a period for most abbreviations:

> Now that Ms. Stone has gotten her Ph.D., we should call her Dr. Stone.

REMINDER

When the period of an abbreviation comes at the end of a sentence, that period also serves as the sentence's final punctuation mark: ''I left work at 6:30 P.M.''

WRITING ACTIVITY 1

Use a caret (^) placed over a period to indicate the appropriate places for periods in the sentences that follow. Capitalize the letter that follows each period that you insert if it ends a sentence. The first one has been done as an example.

Our whole community is planning to attend a wedding this weekend on Saturday, Mr David R Simpson and Dr Gloria L Hancock are getting married the groom's father, Dr Henry Simpson, is the town doctor practically everyone in town knows him or has been his patient the bride's father is the principal of our high school his name is Prof Allan Hancock, PhD these two men have been friends for years they are well known and well liked by everyone in town therefore they invited almost the whole town to the wedding the wedding will take place at 2:00 pm at Town Hall (on Cooper St) everyone is invited back to the Hancock's house for a reception following the wedding

---

The Question Mark. Use a question mark to end a sentence that asks a question:

> What title do you think Wendy Stone would prefer? Wendy overheard my question, and she asked, ''Wouldn't you feel funny calling me Dr. Stone?''

Some sentences, called *indirect questions,* report a question but do not directly ask it. Indirect questions generally include the word *whether* or *if.* They end in a period *not* a question mark.

> *Direct question:* Wendy asked us, ''Wouldn't you feel funny calling me Dr. Stone?''

> *Indirect question:* Wendy asked us if we would feel funny calling her Dr. Stone.

Note that you put the question mark inside the final quotation mark when the quotation is a question. The question mark goes outside the quotation mark when the quoted material is not a question, but the rest of the sentence is a question:

> *When the quotation is a question:*
> The secretary asked Wendy, ''Would you prefer to use *Ms.* or *Dr.* in your formal letters?''

> *When the sentence is a question but the quotation is not:*
> Did Wendy tell him, ''I think I would prefer to use *Dr.* in my formal letters''?

WRITING ACTIVITY 2

Use a caret to insert question marks or periods in the appropriate places in the sentences below. Capitalize the letter that follows each mark of end punctuation that you insert. The first one has been done as an example.

Did you ever wonder about wedding customs and traditions?The modern custom of exchanging wedding rings originated in Roman times what kinds of rings did people exchange then the first wedding bands were probably iron circles did you know that people in different countries wear wedding bands on different hands people in English-speaking countries wear the wedding ring on the third finger of the left hand why the answer is probably an old belief that a nerve from that finger ran directly to the heart people in Europe usually wear their wedding bands on the third finger of the right hand what is the reason for this difference the answer is that in Europe, the right hand was traditionally used for making vows

GROUP WORK 1

Form a group with two classmates and choose one person to record the group's answers. Rewrite the following paragraph (on a separate sheet of paper), inserting question marks or periods wherever the group thinks they are needed. Capitalize the letter that follows each end mark of punctuation.

Another interesting wedding custom is the exchange of wedding vows did you ever listen to a bride and groom exchange their vows the person who is performing the ceremony asks each, "Do you take this person to be your lawfully wedded husband (or wife)" many people question whether the verb "take" is still appropriate today does a man actually "take" a wife or does a woman "take" a husband recently many people who perform wedding ceremonies have started asking the couple if they want to write their own wedding vows did you ever hear a couple exchange wedding vows that they have written for each other I have, and I was deeply touched by them they did not include the traditional wedding question, "Do you promise to love, honor, and obey your spouse" instead the couple asked each other if they promised to love, cherish, and respect each other everyone enjoyed hearing these vows however, wouldn't you agree that the things that matter most in wedding vows are not the words but the feelings behind the words

---

The Exclamation Point. Use an exclamation mark to end a sentence that expresses strong emotion, surprise, or emphasis:

> We couldn't believe what Wendy just said!

WRITING ACTIVITY 3

Here is an uncorrected student paragraph that is missing all end punctuation. Use a caret to insert the appropriate end punctuation mark, and capitalize the letter that follows each.

We recently got married, and many people have been asking us what our honeymoon was like we don't answer we simply smile my wife and I are outdoors people, so when we got married last month we went on a honeymoon hike you may wonder why anyone would go hiking on his or her honeymoon we went hiking because we are as much in love with nature as we are with each other however our hike turned into a honeymoon horror we were following a trail when suddenly we heard a loud rumbling noise "is it supposed to rain today" my wife asked me, thinking that she was hearing thunder before I could answer I saw a cloud of rocks hurtling down the hill toward us "look out" I screamed at my wife she dashed into a small cave the rockslide missed her by only about a foot when she stood, she was shaking I asked her if she was okay she said she was then she pointed to a sign that we had not seen before it said, "Caution: Avalanche Area"

II. PUNCTUATION USED TO COMBINE SENTENCES

You can combine sentences with a semicolon, a colon, or a comma with a coordinator. (See pages 154–155 in Chapter 6 for additional information on coordination.)

The Semicolon. Use a semicolon to join two sentences when (1) the idea in the second sentence is a continuation of the one in the first *and* (2) a period could be used to separate the two sentences. A semicolon expresses a pause that is greater than a comma's but not as great as the pause indicated by a period:

All my friends are married; I am the only one who is still single.

You can use a semicolon to join two sentences with a transition:

My friends are happily married; *however,* I don't feel any desire to get married.

Transitions (also known as *conjunctive adverbs*) are words and phrases that signal the relationship between ideas or details. Here is a chart of some common transitions, arranged according to the type of signal they provide readers.

TRANSITIONAL WORDS AND PHRASES

Here are some transitions (that you can use with semicolons to combine ideas):

To signal the time relationship of the next detail: first, second, third, next, then, after, before, during, as, now, meanwhile, at last, immediately, finally

To signal that the next detail is similar or is an additional example or reason: also, in addition, furthermore, moreover, similarly, first, next, finally

To signal that the next detail is an example: for example, for instance, thus, in particular

To signal that the next detail is different: on the other hand, however, nevertheless, although, even though

To signal that the next detail is a consequence: thus, therefore, consequently, as a result

To signal that the next detail is a conclusion: in summary, in conclusion, thus, therefore

Do *not* use a coordinator if you are using a semicolon:

All my friends are happily married; ~~*and*~~ I am happily single.

The Colon. Use a colon to connect a sentence with a phrase or another sentence if the phrase or the second sentence contains an illustration of the first:

> There are several keys to success in college: the ability to set priorities and manage time effectively, the willingness to do work carefully and study adequately, and the ability to use learning resources. College and high school are different: In college, students must be willing to learn independently.

Phrases such as "the following" or "are as follows," together with a colon, often introduce lists of people or items:

> Most colleges have goals such as the following: to help students develop more sophisticated ways of thinking, to increase their understanding of academic language and concepts, and to help them use learning to free themselves of biases and prejudices.

A colon is also used after the opening in a formal letter and between the hour and the minute when you write time in its numeral form:

> Dear Prof. Greenberg:
> I would like to make an appointment for a conference with you this Wednesday, after class (at 3:00 P.M.). Thank you.
>
> Sincerely,
> Antonio Sabella

THE COLON: A REVIEW

1. Use a colon to connect a sentence to a phrase or another sentence if the phrase or second sentence contains an illustration of the first sentence.
2. Use a colon to introduce a list of items.
3. Use a colon after the opening in a formal letter.

The Comma Followed by a Coordinator. Use a comma and a coordinator to link two related sentences:

> Prof. Greenberg received Mr. Sabella's letter, and she told him that the time was fine.

GROUP WORK 2

Form a group with two or three classmates, and edit the following letter. This uncorrected student letter has many run-ons. (If you are not sure how to identify and correct run-ons, see pages 151–168 in Chapter 6.) Together, decide where each sentence ends and the next one begins. Use a caret to insert a *period,* a *colon,* a *semicolon,* or a *comma and a coordinator* at each sentence boundary. Where necessary, capitalize the first letter of the next sentence.

Professor Allan Brick

Department of English

Hunter College

New York, NY 10021

Dear Prof. Brick:

I am planning to major in English at Hunter College I am completing my third semester and I have enjoyed my English courses immensely I have received *A*'s in almost all my courses I love school I realize that I am missing something that thing is a mentor

Thus I am writing to you to ask you to consider serving as my official mentor for the remainder of my undergraduate career the reason I am asking you to be my mentor is that, in many respects, you define the person I hope to be someday in the future you are incredibly smart and thoughtful you are also very knowledgeable about English literature and composition in addition you are the most caring, compassionate teacher I have ever known you help students solve problems (in and out of the classroom) and you value each student's thoughts and feelings thus I would be honored and delighted if you would agree to be my mentor

Sincerely,

Karen Klein

III. PUNCTUATION USED TO SEPARATE ITEMS IN A SERIES

Commas. Use a comma to separate items in a series of three or more words, phrases, or sentences:

Words in a series:
A mentor is a teacher who is *knowledgeable,* *understanding,* and *caring.*

Phrases in a series:
Students can choose an appropriate mentor by *asking other students about teachers,* *talking with teachers,* and *asking the dean about possible mentors.*

Sentences in a series:
The best mentors have similar qualities: *They love teaching,* *they know their students well,* and *they encourage students to express their personal viewpoints.*

REMINDER

Use a comma after each item in the series except the last one. The second-to-the-last item should be followed by a comma (unless your teacher tells you that this comma is not necessary).

Semicolons. A semicolon—rather than a comma—should be used to separate items in a series if any of the items contains a comma:

> Jaime Alfonso Escalante Gutierrez is a teacher who cares about students; who is tough, but fair; and who knows each of his students personally. He taught at Garfield High School, a Hispanic barrio school in Los Angeles; he was named "The Best Teacher in America"; and he was the subject of the 1988 film *Stand and Deliver.*

WRITING ACTIVITY 4

Decide which sentences below need commas, semicolons, or commas and semicolons. Use a caret to insert each comma and semicolon. The first one has been done as an example.

1. Jaime Alfonso Escalante Gutierrez was born in Bolivia in 1930; he was educated in a small school in La Paz, Bolivia.
2. He wanted to be an engineer because he loved science math and technology.
3. His family did not have enough money to send him to the university to engineering college or to vocational college.
4. Escalante went to a teacher training college because it was cheaper it was nearby and it had courses in engineering.
5. After he graduated, he became a high school math teacher in La Paz discovered that he loved teaching and gained a reputation as an excellent teacher.
6. In 1963 Escalante and his family emigrated to America but he could not get a teaching job because he did not speak English well he did not have a degree from a U.S. college and he had no experience teaching in the United States.
7. Escalante went to school at night worked as a cook and a waiter in the day and earned his B.A. and his M.A. degrees.
8. He was hired by Garfield High School in 1974 to teach basic mathematics to tutor remedial math students and to coach students especially those who were failing their math courses.
9. In 1978 he began teaching an Advanced Placement (AP) calculus course to his basic mathematics students almost all of whom worked hard studied daily and passed the AP test for credit for college calculus.
10. The Education Testing Service (which administers the AP tests) didn't believe that the students had passed accused the students of cheating and made twelve students retake the test. All twelve passed the test a second time.

THE SEMICOLON: A REVIEW

1. Use a semicolon to combine two sentences whose ideas are closely related.
2. Use a semicolon instead of a comma to separate items in a series if any of the items contains a comma.

IV. PUNCTUATION USED TO SEPARATE MODIFIERS FROM THE REST OF THE SENTENCE

In Chapter 7, you practiced adding and moving descriptive words and phrases in sentences to make the sentences more interesting and informative. These descriptive modifiers include adjectives, adverbs, prepositional phrases, appositive phrases, and participial phrases (phrases that begin with an *-ing, -ed,* or *-en* verb). Descriptive modifiers can be placed at the beginning, the middle, or the end of a sentence:

Beginning:
In most cases, having a mentor helps students adjust to college and achieve their goals.
By choosing an effective mentor, students can get the support and encouragement they need.

Middle:
Having a mentor, *in most cases,* helps students adjust to college and achieve their goals.
Students, *by choosing an effective mentor,* can get the support and encouragement they need.

End:
Having a mentor helps students adjust to college and achieve their goals *in most cases.*
Students can get the support and encouragement they need *by choosing an effective mentor.*

As the examples above illustrate, writers have options for using commas to punctuate modifiers at the beginning or in the middle of a sentence. Here are some guidelines for punctuating modifiers that introduce or interrupt a sentence.

Descriptive Words and Phrases That Introduce a Sentence. Use a comma to separate an introductory word or phrase from the main sentence:

Adverb: Interestingly, most students remain friendly with their college mentors long after they graduate.

Transitional expression: As a result, these students have a role model to consult as they pursue their professional goals.

Prepositional phrase: For this reason, students should choose a mentor who personifies their career goals.

Appositive phrase: A trusted adviser, the college mentor helps motivate students to do their best.

Participial phrase: Working closely with each person he or she is advising, the mentor maps out academic and personal objectives for the student.

As will be discussed in more detail in the next section, if you move an introductory word or phrase to the middle of a sentence, you have to surround it with commas:

Most students, *interestingly,* remain friendly with their college mentors long after they graduate.

The college mentor, *a trusted adviser,* helps motivate students to do their best.

WRITING ACTIVITY 5

Decide which of the following sentences need a comma to separate the modifying words or phrases from the rest of the sentence, and use a caret to insert each comma. The first one has been done as an example.

1. To protect yourself and your family, you should make sure that your home has equipment to put out or to escape a fire.
2. Surprisingly most homes do not have this equipment.
3. In fact a recent survey conducted by our state's health department revealed that only 15 percent of the surveyed homes had working fire extinguishers.
4. To put out a fire you must have at least one working fire extinguisher in your home.
5. All family members including the children should know where the fire extinguisher is located.
6. Moreover everyone should know how to operate the extinguisher beforehand rather than learning how to use it when a fire occurs.
7. In addition to fire extinguishers a folding ladder is a must for everyone who lives in a home with upstairs rooms.
8. A folding ladder a chain ladder that folds up into a small pile can be hung over a windowsill in an upstairs bedroom or bathroom.

9. Using this ladder people trapped upstairs by a fire can climb out the window to safety.
10. With the right equipment people can survive even the worst fire in their homes.

Descriptive Word Groups That Interrupt a Sentence. Use a comma before and after descriptive words or word groups that interrupt the flow of a sentence *if* these word groups do not provide *distinguishing* information about the subject of the sentence.

> Many people, *amazingly,* are unaware of the need for fire safety equipment. Unprepared homeowners or apartment dwellers, *who lack fire extinguishers,* may get severely burned in fires. [The pair of commas in each of these sentences indicates that the information they enclose could be left out without confusing readers about the subject of the sentence.]

Words or word groups that begin with a relative pronoun (like *who* or *which*) can be inserted between a sentence's subject and verb to add information about the subject. In the example above, the word group "who lack fire extinguishers" provides *additional* information about the subject ("unprepared homeowners or apartment dwellers"). However, this word group is *not* necessary for the reader to understand who or what the sentence is about (its subject). The writer could leave out this phrase, and readers would still know that the subject of the sentence is "unprepared homeowners or apartment dwellers." Thus, this phrase is called a *nonrestrictive* or a *nonessential* phrase.

Nonrestrictive word groups add information that is not necessary for identifying the subject. Put a comma before and after nonrestrictive word groups because the information in them is not essential for the reader to understand the main idea of the sentence. However, do *not* use commas to surround interrupting word groups that *are* essential to the meaning of the sentence:

> People *who care about safety* often make sure that their homes have fire prevention equipment that everyone knows how to use. [In this sentence, the word group that starts with the relative pronoun *who* is necessary to let readers know exactly which people the writer is referring to.]

In the example above, if the writer had left out the word group "who care about safety," readers would not know which people the writer was discussing. This word group is called a *restrictive* or an *essential* phrase. (It "restricts" the subject's meaning, and it is "essential" for the readers to understand the sentence.) Do *not* use commas to surround a restrictive word group.

GROUP WORK 3

Work with one or two classmates on this activity. Together, decide which sentences below need commas to set off modifying words or word groups from the rest of the sentence. Use a caret to insert each comma wherever the group thinks it is needed.

1. Research on effective teachers in both public and private schools suggests that there are three teaching styles.
2. One common type of high school and college teacher is the "teacher-centered" instructor.
3. This kind of teacher values his or her ability to help students master information and skills.
4. An instructor who is "teacher-centered" often engages students with his or her personality, so they pay attention and learn.
5. Another type of teacher is the "content-centered" teacher who unlike the teacher-centered instructor is most concerned with the material that he or she is teaching.
6. Content-centered teachers who can be found in almost any school believe that their main job is to "cover" the material in their course outline.
7. The third and most popular type of teacher is the "student-centered" instructor.
8. Student-centered teachers also known as "student-focused" teachers think that student participation is the most important aspect of teaching and learning.
9. This kind of teacher who is usually well liked by most students feels that students must take active responsibility for their own learning.
10. Few teachers of course always teach the same way in every class every day. Most teachers at every level of education combine elements of all three teaching styles.

USING THE COMMA TO SEPARATE A WORD OR WORD GROUP FROM THE REST OF THE SENTENCE: A REVIEW

1. Use a comma to set off an introductory word, word group, or transitional expression from the rest of the sentence.
2. Use a comma before and after descriptive words that interrupt

a sentence *if* these words do not provide restrictive information about the subject of the sentence.

3. Use a comma before and after a nonrestrictive (nonessential) word group that interrupts a sentence.

Enclosing or Emphasizing Interrupting Material. You can use two other punctuation marks to add information in the middle of a sentence or at the end of a sentence: *dashes* and *parentheses.* Use dashes when you want to make the interrupting words stand out; use parentheses to deemphasize the interrupting material. Here is an example of each.

Dashes:
Writing a doctoral dissertation—the equivalent of a book—is a requirement for a Ph.D. degree.

Parentheses:
Writing a doctoral dissertation (the equivalent of a book) is a requirement for a Ph.D. degree.

The dashes make the information that they surround sound more important than do the parentheses, by stressing the sudden break in the main idea of the sentence.

WRITING ACTIVITY 6

Each of the following sentences has "interrupting" information between the subject and the verb. Decide whether to enclose the underlined words in each sentence in a pair of commas, a pair of parentheses, or a pair of dashes. Use a caret to write in the punctuation marks that you think are most appropriate for each sentence. The first one has been done as an example.

1. When I came to the United States last year, I thought that I—a sophisticated international student—would have no problem adjusting to American customs.
2. I soon discovered much to my surprise that many things are different in the U.S. than they are in other countries.
3. The biggest difference one which I had not expected was in the way Americans spend time.

4. The people I met in the U.S. unlike the people in Europe and Asia do everything very quickly.
5. I had difficulty getting used to the brief amount of time less than an hour that most people allow for lunch and for dinner.
6. I knew that the U.S. was the home of fast-food places such as McDonalds, Burger King, Pizza Hut, and Taco Bell but I didn't realize what ''fast'' meant until I ate in one of these places.
7. In Spain where I lived for the past four years most people took an hour for lunch and two hours for dinner.
8. In fact, Spanish dinners which often consisted of three or four courses were usually followed by at least a fifteen-minute rest.
9. Getting used to American dinners one or two courses that my friends eat in thirty minutes has not been easy for me.
10. I miss Spanish food especially paella but most of all I miss the tradition of eating and enjoying one's meal slowly and leisurely.

DASHES OR PARENTHESES: A REVIEW

1. Use dashes before and after information that interrupts a sentence if you want to emphasize this information and make it stand out from the rest of the sentence.
2. Use parentheses before and after information that interrupts a sentence if you want to deemphasize this information.

V. PUNCTUATION USED TO SEPARATE QUOTED MATERIAL FROM THE REST OF THE SENTENCE

Use two pairs of quotation marks to set off the exact words that someone has spoken or written. Quotations of three or more words are usually preceded by a comma:

> My friend remarked, ''Americans seem to eat their meals more quickly than Europeans do.'' [The friend's exact words are enclosed within a pair of quotation marks.]

When you begin a sentence with a quotation, put the comma *inside* the closing quotation marks.

> ''Americans seem to eat their meals more quickly than Europeans do,'' my friend remarked.

DIRECT AND INDIRECT QUOTATIONS

Use quotation marks to set off a *direct* quotation—a quotation consisting of the exact words that someone has spoken or written.

> My friend remarked, ''Americans seem to eat their meals more quickly than Europeans do.''

Do *not* use quotation marks to set off an *indirect* quotation—a quotation that summarizes what was spoken or written (and is usually preceded by the word *that*):

> My friend remarked *that* Americans seem to eat their meals more quickly than Europeans do.

Use pairs of quotation marks to set off the titles of stories, poems, magazine articles, and chapters in books:

> My friend read an essay entitled ''Cultural Eating Habits'' in a sociology journal.

Always put commas and periods *inside* the closing quotation marks:

> The author of the essay stated, ''There are cultural differences in the average length of time allotted for each meal.''

However, put colons and semicolons *outside* the quotation marks:

> The author of the essay stated, ''There are cultural differences in the average length of time allotted for each meal''; however, he also noted, ''The time allowed for each meal depends on a variety of noncultural factors.''

Put question marks, exclamation points, and dashes *inside* the closing quotation marks when they are part of the quoted material:

> My friend asked me, ''What are noncultural factors?'' [The question mark is part of the direct question being quoted.]

However, question marks, exclamation points, and dashes go *outside* the closing quotation marks when they are part of the larger sentence in which the quotation is enclosed:

> What did the writer mean by ''cultural differences''? [The question mark ends the question in which the quoted words ''cultural differences'' are enclosed.]

WRITING ACTIVITY 7

Decide which sentences are composed of (or include) direct quotations. Insert quotation marks (using carets) wherever they are needed. Wherever you insert quotation marks, check to see if you also have to capitalize the first letter of the quote. Also check to see if you have to insert punctuation before or after any quotation marks you add. The first one has been done as an example.

According to a recent article entitled "What Speed Is a Safe Speed?" most American drivers drive faster than the posted speed limits. The researchers who wrote the article wanted to answer the following questions: How often do you exceed the legal speed limit when you drive By how many miles an hour do you exceed the posted speed limit? The researchers discovered that speeding has become a regular part of American driving, especially for young males. They wrote that more than one-third of American males exceed the speed limit by at least five miles an hour every time they drive a car. The inability to observe the legal speed limits is the number 1 cause of car accidents noted Charles Butler, one of the researchers. The author of the essay, Wink Dulles, added that exceeding the speed limit on local streets is a prime cause of fatal car crashes. He wrote highways and parkways are wider and smoother than local roads; in other words, according to my understanding of Dulles's writing highways and parkways are safer than other local streets. The author concluded if American drivers could swear never to exceed speed limits by more than five miles an hour, they would dramatically reduce the number of fatal car accidents each year.

QUOTATION MARKS: A REVIEW

1. Use quotation marks before and after a direct quotation—the actual words that someone spoke or wrote.
2. Use quotation marks before and after the titles of stories, poems, magazine articles, newspaper articles, and chapters in books.

VI. PUNCTUATION USED TO INDICATE THE POSSESSIVE CASE

Add an apostrophe and an *s* to form the possessive of nouns that do not end in *s*:

> I have noticed that my *teacher*'s role changes when he leaves the classroom.

Add only the apostrophe to form the possessive of nouns that already end in *s*:

> I have noticed that *teachers*' roles change when they leave the classroom.

REMINDER

Do *not* add an apostrophe to a possessive *pronoun* (e.g., his, hers, yours, ours, and its).

WRITING ACTIVITY 8

Edit the following sentences for missing or incorrect apostrophes. (Some of the apostrophes are correct.) Circle every word that has an incorrect apostrophe or that is missing an apostrophe. Write in the correction above each error that you circle. The first one has been done as an example.

1. Alzheimers disease is a progressive, degenerative disease that attacks some peoples' brains.
2. It's primary targets in a persons' brain are the cell's responsible for critical thinking and memory.

3. In the early stage's of Alzheimer's disease, people may have trouble finding words or following direction's.
4. The afflicted persons' family doesn't always notice the persons' problems remembering names, places, and other basic' information.
5. Alzheimers slowly robs a person of his' or her' personality.
6. Even worse, this disease usually leaves' its victims totally unable to care for themselve's.
7. Families' of people afflicted with this disease are usually devastated by their loved one's slow decline into senility.
8. Alzheimer's victims and their families need their friend's and relatives' help and support to battle this dreadful disease.

OTHER USES OF COMMAS

Three other conventional uses of commas are as follows:

1. Use a comma to separate items in dates, numbers, and addresses:

   My family moved to Austin, Texas, on December 10, 1981. I attended a community college that had more than 1,500 students enrolled in it.

2. Use a comma before and after a title or an abbreviation if it comes after a person's name:

   My favorite teacher was Sonia Mercato, Ph.D., who used to write each student a letter every day. I also liked my mentor, Robert Mendez, Jr., who helped me maintain a 4.0 grade point average.

3. Use a comma after the salutation of a friendly letter and after the words before the signature. [If you are writing a formal letter, use a colon after the salutation ("Dear Dr. Greenberg:").]

THE COMMA: A REVIEW

1. Use a comma and a coordinator to link two related sentences.
2. Use commas to separate items in a series (three or more words,

phrases, or sentences), unless one of the items includes a comma. If it does, use a semicolon to separate the items in the series.

3. Use a comma to separate an introductory word or phrase from the main sentence.
4. Use commas before and after descriptive words, phrases, or clauses that interrupt the flow of a sentence *if* these words, phrases, or clauses do not provide *restrictive* information about the subject of the sentence.
5. Use a comma before quotations of three or more words.
6. When you begin a sentence with a quotation, put the comma inside the closing quotation marks.
7. Use a comma to separate items in dates, numbers, and addresses.
8. Use a comma before and after a title or an abbreviation if it comes after a person's name.
9. Use a comma after the salutation of a friendly letter and after the words before the signature.

PROBLEMS WITH COMMAS

Commas are important tools for signaling meaning in written sentences and paragraphs. However, unnecessary commas confuse and distract readers. Indeed, adding unnecessary commas usually confuses readers more than leaving out commas where they are needed. Here is an example of how unnecessary commas can distort meaning and confuse readers.

> Every person performs, different roles each day. According to sociologists a role is a set, of behaviors appropriate for a particular social, context or interaction. ''Performing different roles,'' does not mean acting nor does it mean, pretending. It means, behaving in ways that we perceive, as appropriate for each situation and, for the people in the situation. For example a woman, may behave very differently, in her roles as, ''wife'' ''mother'' ''student'' and ''professional.''

Did you understand the writer's meaning in the paragraph above? It is difficult to grasp the meaning of a piece of writing that is missing commas, but sentences with unnecessary commas are even more difficult to read. The commas keep forcing the reader to stop in the middle of a chunk of meaning, and this is extremely annoying. Some writers can read their writing aloud and hear the pauses where the various punctuation marks belong. For example, read aloud the correctly punctuated version of the preceding sample paragraph, and consider whether you pause very briefly at the commas.

> Every person performs different roles each day. According to sociologists, a role is a set of behaviors appropriate for a particular social context or interaction. ''Performing different roles'' does not mean acting, nor does it mean pretending. It means behaving in ways that we perceive as appropriate for each situation and for the people in the situation. For example, a woman may behave very differently in her roles as ''wife,'' ''mother,'' ''student,'' and ''professional.''

If you did not hear the pauses at the commas, you will have to rely more on the rules in this chapter in order to use commas correctly.

PLACES WHERE YOU SHOULD *NOT* USE COMMAS

There are two places where commas are not needed:

1. Do *not* use a comma to separate a subject and its verb. For example, the comma in the following sentence is *not* needed.

Every person, performs different roles each day.

2. Do *not* use a comma before a coordinator if the words that follow the coordinator do not include a subject. For example, the comma in this sentence is wrong:

''Performing different roles'' does not mean acting, or pretending. [The phrase ''or pretending'' does not have a subject, so the ''or'' that precedes this phrase does not need a comma before it.]

WRITING ACTIVITY 9

Proofread the following paragraphs for comma errors. Insert commas (with carets) where they have been omitted, and cross out commas that are not necessary. The first one has been done as an example.

When a person's car breaks down, what should he or she do? Most mechanics, whom I have spoken with, agree that people should have a broken car, towed to an auto specialty shop. In this kind of shop mechanics can provide quick service, because the shop stocks parts for all cars except, rare or antique cars. Auto specialty shops which can be found in almost every city usually employ mechanics, who are familiar with many different, cars and trucks. In addition, to fixing cars the mechanics, at auto specialty shops can perform other services, that most cars need such as tune-ups, and oil changes.

Many people think, that they should return to their dealer, when their car breaks down. Dealership service departments, are usually excellent but they often charge more, than do auto specialty shops. Moreover if a person owns, more than one type of car he or she would have to take them, to several different dealers, when they break. Another disadvantage, of dealership service departments, is that they are often not conveniently located. Therefore the cost of towing one's broken car, to the dealership, is usually more than, the cost of towing it to the closest auto specialty shop. Finally many auto specialty shops, own their own tow trucks so they can respond, to emergency breakdowns quickly and, relatively inexpensively.

GROUP WORK 4

Form a group with two classmates and work together on this activity. Here is a paragraph from the autobiography of Lech Walesa, the founder of the Polish union Solidarity and the first freely elected president of Poland. All of Walesa's punctuation marks have been deleted. Use a caret to insert punctuation marks (periods, semicolons, dashes, commas, parentheses, and apostrophes) wherever they seem appropriate. Some will be necessary to signal pauses or emphases. If you put in a period, capitalize the first letter of the following word. The first one has been done as an example.

The greatest experience of my boyhood was my first communion the evening before the whole family had gone to confession and all the kids me especially asked the adults to forgive us for misbehaving we also had to kiss our stepfathers hand and settle old quarrels with each other the day of the ceremony without having eaten because of course one must take communion on an empty stomach we headed to church in our finest clothes inside the church I remember it was stiflingly hot some children fainted that always happened at times like this after all the buildup and preparation during the whole year before first communion a nun and the priest had taught us the catechism and the articles of faith at the end of the year we were grilled on what we d learned in those days the church ceremony wasnt followed by a noisy celebration as it is today nor did people try to outdo each other with presents we were very poor and our festivities consisted of a formal dinner it was a spiritual and communal occasion.

When you finish this activity, turn to page 388 to see the author's punctuation marks.

PLANNING THE PAPER'S FORMAT

A paper's appearance sends an important message to readers. A messy final draft, filled with scratch-outs or "typos," tells readers that the writer did not value what he or she wrote. If your writing matters to you, make sure that the final version of every paper is neat and that it follows the conventions of academic manuscript format. Each subject area in college may have different requirements for the format of paragraphs, essays, and reports. If teachers don't specify the format for papers in their disciplines, ask them about their format requirements. Here are general guidelines for the format of college writing assignments.

Typed or Computer-Printed Papers. Unless your instructor accepts handwritten reports, type your paragraphs and essays on a typewriter or a computer. Use $8\frac{1}{2}$- by 11-inch, unruled, white standard typing paper (*not* onionskin or erasable paper, both of which smudge). Leave $1\frac{1}{4}$-inch margins on all *four* edges of the paper. Type or print on only one side of each sheet of paper, and use only a black typewriter or printer ribbon. *Double-space each line.* Leave two spaces after a period (before the next word); leave one space after all other punctuation marks.

If you are using a word-processing program, make sure that your computer and printer are working correctly and that your software is operating correctly. Check to see that your disk is formatted correctly. Proofread your writing on the monitor screen and use your spelling checker (and grammar checker, if you have one) before you print the essay or report. Save your work; do not print until you have created a backup file of your essay or report. Never use coated or erasable bond paper in a computer printer because the ink characters smudge on these kinds of paper. Also, don't use printer paper that is thinner than "20-weight"; it will tear too easily. Finally, if you are using computer paper with hole-punched edges, carefully tear off these edges after you print.

Handwritten Papers. Use 8½- by 11-inch, ruled, white paper. Leave 1-inch margins on all *four* edges. Write on only one side of each sheet of paper and skip lines. Use dark-blue or black ink (*not* a pencil). Make sure that your capital letters are distinct from your lowercase letters. Write all punctuation marks clearly.

Corrections. Use correction paper or fluid to correct small errors. If your teacher permits it, add missing letters, words, or punctuation marks with a caret. Don't make more than three corrections on a page; instead retype or reprint the entire page.

First Page. Ask your teacher where to put your name, the course name and number, and the date. Some teachers prefer this information on a cover page; others want it typed at the top of the first page. In addition, some teachers prefer the title of the paper to appear only on the cover, whereas others tell students to put it on the cover *and* on the top of the first page.

Center the title of the composition on the first line of the first page. Do *not* underline this title; do *not* put quotation marks around it. Capitalize the major words in the title. Skip two lines between the title and the first line of the text. Indent the first line of every paragraph about half an inch (five spaces) from the left margin.

General Layout. Number all pages except the cover page and the first page. Although you should not number the first page, think of it as page 1, so the second page should be numbered as page 2. Use numerals ("2") to number the pages, but do *not* precede these numerals with any words or letters. (Do not write "page 2" or "p. 2.") Write or type the number in the upper-right-hand corner or center it on the top of each page.

EXPLORING FURTHER

Several examples in this chapter discussed the "roles" that people play in their lives. The illustration below depicts nine roles that a typical young man or woman performs each day.

WRITING ASSIGNMENT

Write a paragraph or two about the roles you perform on a regular basis. Begin by freewriting, brainstorming, and clustering about this topic. Here are some questions you might want to think—and write—about: How do you perceive yourself? How does your behavior change in different situations? How does your behavior change in response to different people? What roles do you play at home, in your neighborhood, in school, and at work? How are you different in each of these roles?

Narrow down this topic and compose a discovery draft about your roles or about one (or more) roles that you perform each day. When you finish drafting, revise your composition. Then edit each sentence for errors in sentence structure, grammar and usage, diction, spelling, capitalization, and punctuation. Finally, retype your paper so that it follows the conventions of the academic paper format, described in this chapter.

✔ POINTS TO REMEMBER ABOUT PUNCTUATION AND PAPER FORMAT

1. Do not worry about punctuation or paper format while you are composing or revising a piece of writing. However, remember to check both when you are finished revising.
2. Try to identify the punctuation errors that you make frequently. Proofread for these errors in all your papers.
3. Remember the six functions of punctuation marks:
   a. Use a period, a question mark, or an exclamation point to end each sentence.
   b. Use a semicolon, a colon, or a comma followed by a coordinator to combine sentences.
   c. Use a comma or a semicolon to separate items in a series within a sentence.
   d. Use a comma, a dash, or parentheses to separate words or phrases that modify a sentence.
   e. Use quotation marks to set off quoted words or phrases from the rest of a sentence.
   f. Use an apostrophe to indicate a possessive noun.
4. Proofread for correct paper format.
5. If you have typed your paper, proofread it for typos.
6. If you have word-processed your paper, use the Search command to search for troublesome punctuation marks, and make sure that you have used each one correctly.

Here is the punctuation that Lech Walesa used in his autobiography, *Lech Walesa: The Struggle and the Triumph.* Compare these punctuation marks with the ones you inserted on pages 383 and 384:

The greatest experience of my boyhood was my first communion. The evening before, the whole family had gone to confession, and all the kids, me especially, asked the adults to forgive us for misbehaving; we also had to kiss our stepfather's hand, and settle old quarrels with each other. The day of the ceremony, without having eaten, because, of course, one must take communion on an empty stomach, we headed to church in our finest clothes. Inside the church, I remember, it was stiflingly hot. Some children fainted—that always happened at times like this, after all the buildup and preparation. During the whole year before first communion, a nun and the priest had taught us the catechism and the articles of faith; at the end of the year we were grilled on what we'd learned. In those days the church ceremony wasn't followed by a noisy celebration, as it is today, nor did people try to outdo each other with presents. We were very poor, and our festivities consisted of a formal dinner; it was a spiritual and communal occasion.

APPENDIX
Progress Logs

I. Writing-Editing Log

II. Teacher Conference Log

Use these logs to keep track of your writing progress and problems.

WRITING-EDITING LOG

Each time an instructor returns a piece of your writing, make notes about the piece in this log. You will be able to chart progress and improve your ability to identify areas that need further improvement.

Date ______________ Course ______________________________

Title of Paper ____

Strengths:

Problems and Errors:

If you need more Writing Progress Log pages, make copies of this page.

Date ______________ Course ______________________________

Title of Paper ____

Strengths:

Problems and Errors:

TEACHER CONFERENCE LOG

After each conference with your writing teacher, summarize his or her comments in the space below. These notes will help you remember your teacher's comments and suggestions for future papers.

Date of Conference ______________

Material Discussed ____

Teacher's Comments, Suggestions, and Assignments:

If you need more Conference Log pages, make copies of this page.

Date of Conference ______________

Material Discussed ____

Teacher's Comments, Suggestions, and Assignments:

Dear Reader:

Please let me know your opinion of this textbook and of its strengths and weaknesses. When you finish the book, please write me a letter about what you liked and disliked about it. (Send the letter to the address below.) If you don't have the time to write a letter, please fill out the form that follows and return it to the address below.

Karen L. Greenberg
c/o Basic Skills Editor
HarperCollins College Publishers
10 East 53rd Street
New York, NY 10022-5299

Please be honest and be very specific so that I can make the next edition of the book better. If you include your name and address, I will write you a letter back. Thank you.

If you are writing a letter to me, please use a separate sheet of paper. If you are filling out the following form, please do so in the spaces provided below.

1. How does this textbook compare with other writing texts or English texts

you have used? ____

____

____

____

____

2. Which chapters were most helpful to you? Why? ____________

____

____

____

____

____

____

3. Which chapters were least helpful? Why? ______

______

______

______

______

______

4. What materials or exercises in this book did you *dis*like? Why? ______

______

______

______

______

______

5. What materials, exercises, readings, or writing tasks would you like to see in the next edition of this textbook?

______

______

______

______

______

CREDITS

TEXT CREDITS

Chapter 1

Peter Elbow, WRITING WITH POWER, Oxford University Press, 1981.

Chapter 2

From ''Living the Cambodian Nightmare'' by Joel Brinkley, *Courier-Journal*, Louisville, Kentucky, December 2, 1979. Reprinted by permission.

Chapter 3

Joseph A. Fernandez, TALES OUT OF SCHOOL: *Joseph Fernandez's Crusade to Rescue American Education.* Boston, Massachusetts: Little, Brown and Company, 1993.

''Barbie'' from ESSAYS THAT WORKED, edited by Boykin Curry and Brian Kasbar. Reprinted by permission of Mustang Publishing.

Chapter 4

Maya Angelou, THE HEART OF A WOMAN. New York: Random House, 1981, pp. 4 and 5.

Chapter 5

''Sustenance of My Life'' by Marcy Donahue. Appeared in THE RETURNING WOMAN, Spring 1992. Reprinted by permission of the author.

Chapter 6

''Twenty-one Ways to Succeed in College'' from YOUR COLLEGE EXPERIENCE edited by A. Jerome Jewler and John N. Gardner with Mary-Jane McCarthy. Copyright © 1993 by Wadsworth. Inc. Reprinted by permission of Wadsworth, Inc.

Chapter 7

''Detasseling'' by Celia Rothenberg from ONE HUNDRED SUCCESSFUL COLLEGE APPLICATION ESSAYS.

Chapter 8

Untitled essay by Heather L. Nadelman from ONE HUNDRED SUCCESSFUL COLLEGE APPLICATION ESSAYS. Originally published in the *Harvard Independent.*

Chapter 10

''Why aren't dads held to the same standards as moms?'' by Scott Lafee, *The San Diego Union-Tribune.* April 3, 1993. Reprinted by permission of The San Diego Union-Tribune.

Chapter 11

Article by Williamson Evers used with permission from ASCD Update, August 1993. Copyright by ASCD.

Article by Miriam Sexner used with permission from ASCD Update, August 1993. Copyright by ASCD.

Chapter 12

''Your Ad Should Intrigue But Not Bare All'' by Susan Deitz. Reprinted by permission of The Los Angeles Time Syndicate.

Chapter 13

''Discrimination at Large'' by Jennifer A. Coleman. From NEWSWEEK, August 2, 1993. Copyright © 1993, Newsweek, Inc. All rights reserved. Reprinted by permission.

Chapter 14

Lech Walesa, THE STRUGGLE AND THE TRIUMPH: AN AUTOBIOGRAPHY. New York: Arcade Publishing, Inc. (Translation), 1992, p. 302.

INDEX